T0230759

Computer Security Literacy
Staying Safe in a Digital World

Computer Security Literacy
Staying Safe in a Digital World

Douglas Jacobson and Joseph Idziorek

CRC Press
Taylor & Francis Group
Boca Raton   London   New York

CRC Press is an imprint of the
Taylor & Francis Group, an **informa** business
A CHAPMAN & HALL BOOK

CRC Press
Taylor & Francis Group
6000 Broken Sound Parkway NW, Suite 300
Boca Raton, FL 33487-2742

First issued in hardback 2017

© 2013 by Taylor & Francis Group, LLC
CRC Press is an imprint of Taylor & Francis Group, an Informa business

No claim to original U.S. Government works

ISBN 13: 978-1-138-43687-9 (hbk)
ISBN 13: 978-1-4398-5618-5 (pbk)

This book contains information obtained from authentic and highly regarded sources. Reasonable efforts have been made to publish reliable data and information, but the author and publisher cannot assume responsibility for the validity of all materials or the consequences of their use. The authors and publishers have attempted to trace the copyright holders of all material reproduced in this publication and apologize to copyright holders if permission to publish in this form has not been obtained. If any copyright material has not been acknowledged please write and let us know so we may rectify in any future reprint.

Except as permitted under U.S. Copyright Law, no part of this book may be reprinted, reproduced, transmitted, or utilized in any form by any electronic, mechanical, or other means, now known or hereafter invented, including photocopying, microfilming, and recording, or in any information storage or retrieval system, without written permission from the publishers.

For permission to photocopy or use material electronically from this work, please access www.copyright.com (http://www.copyright.com/) or contact the Copyright Clearance Center, Inc. (CCC), 222 Rosewood Drive, Danvers, MA 01923, 978-750-8400. CCC is a not-for-profit organization that provides licenses and registration for a variety of users. For organizations that have been granted a photocopy license by the CCC, a separate system of payment has been arranged.

Trademark Notice: Product or corporate names may be trademarks or registered trademarks, and are used only for identification and explanation without intent to infringe.

Library of Congress Cataloging-in-Publication Data

Jacobson, Douglas.
  Computer security literacy : staying safe in a digital world / Douglas Jacobson, Joseph Idziorek.
    pages cm
    Includes bibliographical references.
    ISBN 978-1-4398-5618-5 (pbk.)
    1. Computer security. I. Idziorek, Joseph. II. Title.

QA76.9.A25J224 2013
005.8--dc23   2012028121

Visit the Taylor & Francis Web site at
http://www.taylorandfrancis.com

and the CRC Press Web site at
http://www.crcpress.com

Contents

Preface

APPROACH

Traditional computer security books educate readers about a multitude of topics, ranging from secure programming practices, protocols, and algorithm designs to cryptography and ethics. These books typically focus on the implementation or theory of security controls and mechanisms at the application, operating system, network, and physical layers. Breaking this traditional model, *Computer Security Literacy: Staying Safe in a Digital World* instead seeks to educate the reader at the user layer and focuses on practical topics that one is likely to encounter on a regular basis. It has long been recognized that the user is in fact the weakest link in the security chain. So, why not effect change by providing practical and relevant education for the normal user of information technology? As it turns out, we, the users, often have the greatest impact on the security of our computer and information as a result of the actions that we do or do not perform. This text provides practical security education to give the context to make sound security decisions. The outcomes of this book will enable readers to

- Define computer security terms and mechanisms

- Describe fundamental security concepts

- State computer security best practices

- Describe the strengths, weaknesses, and limitations of security mechanisms and concepts

- Give examples of common security threats, threat sources, and threat motivations

- Explain their role in protecting their own computing environment and personal and confidential information

- Discuss current event topics and read security articles in the popular press

- Assess computing actions in the context of security

The approach of this book is to provide context to everyday computing tasks to better understand how security relates to these actions. One of the most common ways that security professionals attempt to bestow knowledge is through awareness campaigns and the creation of websites that contain security tips and advice. If you have discovered this book, then you are likely aware computer security is a real and ever-present problem. Whether seen or unseen, everyday users of information technology encounter a number of security threats whether it be in the form of suspect emails, social networking posts, hyperlinks, or the downloading of files or programs from the Internet. While awareness is key, it does not provide the context for one actually to go forth and make sound security decisions. Security tip and advice websites, on the other hand, attempt to supplement learning by the offering of a handful of security best practices. A popular tip found on such a website is "make passwords long and strong." While this statement makes logical sense, it does nothing to inform the user of the threats that this security tip protects against. Furthermore, and more important, it does not discuss the limitations of this suggestion and if simply creating a long-and-strong password is sufficient to protect against all the threats that seek to learn, steal, or observe passwords. As discussed in Chapter 3, creating a long-and-strong password is important, but it is only a small part of the equation necessary to create and maintain secure passwords.

Because there is a common perception that computer security is a topic of concern only for the technological elite, there exists a significant gap between the types of books currently offered in computer security and the demographic of people who stand to benefit from learning more about the practical aspects of computer security. Many of the previously written texts on computer security are too technical for a broad audience and furthermore do not contain practical computer knowledge about common security threats, best practices, and useful content on how security mechanisms such as antivirus software and firewalls protect against hackers and malware. One of the unique qualities that differentiates this book from past security texts is that it was written specifically for a diverse and nontechnical audience. To do this, the key concepts of the book are balanced by commonly held analogies. In addition, relevant and recent current events are used to provide tangible evidence regarding the function and impact of security in everyday life.

Computer security education need not be made exclusive to technical audiences. If abstracted correctly, it is our belief that practical security education can be made accessible to readers of all technological backgrounds. As it turns out, we all perform the same basic routines on our computers and the Internet each day. During an average day, people use passwords, connect to the Internet on an unsecure wireless connection, share media via external devices, receive suspicious emails, surf the web, share information via social networking, and much, much more. Each of these actions involves a potential risk and can result in consequences with malicious intent. However, the understanding of these risks and corresponding defensive strategies is not as complicated as you would think and does not require an engineering degree as a prerequisite to gain working knowledge. While defensive security measures like antivirus software, firewalls, and software patches have been around for quite sometime, we truly believe that practical security education—the content found in this book—is the future of innovation in computer security.

ORGANIZATION

The content of this text is presented in a logical progression of topics that allows for a foundation to be constructed and context to be built on as the reader progresses through the chapters. The organization of the book is as follows:

- **Chapter 1** presents an introduction to the topic of computer security, defines key terms and security truisms, as well as discusses commonly held, but inaccurate, conceptions about the topic of computer security.

- **Chapter 2** provides the technological foundation for the remainder of the book by developing a working model for how a computer operates and how the Internet moves data from one computer to another.

- **Chapter 3** discusses the many threats that seek to steal, observe, and learn passwords. Once the threats are understood, this chapter provides password security best practices and defines a secure password as not only a strong password but also a unique and secret password.

- **Chapter 4** focuses on the topic of email and broadly presents how email is sent and received on the Internet. With this context in hand, the many threats that plague the common uses of email are discussed, and mitigation strategies are presented.

- **Chapter 5** focuses on all the different ways that malware infects a computer and what malware does once it infects a computer.

- **Chapter 6** supplements Chapter 5 by providing a defense-in-depth strategy to mitigate against the many malware threats that one is likely to encounter. The defense-in-depth strategy consists of data backup, software patches, firewalls, antivirus software, and last but not least, user education.

- **Chapter 7** deals primarily with the operation of the web browser and how functions that afford convenience also are at odds with security and privacy. This chapter also discusses the popular and applicable topics of HTTPS and cookies, among other types of information stored by web browsers.

- **Chapter 8** presents the topic of online shopping by discussing common security threats and online shopping best practices, such as the motivation why using a credit card is more secure than a debit card when making online purchases.

- **Chapter 9** explains the security vulnerabilities that wireless networks present. Included in this discussion is an explanation of the differences between a secure and unsecure wireless network and the security threats and best practices for both a user of a wireless network (as typically found in a coffee shop) and as an administrator of a home wireless network.

- **Chapter 10** takes a different approach to social networking security and privacy by focusing on the higher-level concepts as they relate to public information sharing. A key discussion includes how information that is found on social networking sites affects one's job or career prospects.

- **Chapter 11** unravels the many different ways that cyber criminals use social engineering tactics to trick their victims into revealing personal information or installing malware on their computers. Included in this chapter are the steps one can take to dissect a URL (Uniform Reference Locator) and how to consider each part of the

URL in the context of security—a key skill to detect phishing emails and messages.

- **Chapter 12** examines the human threat of practical security by discussing a number of concepts and scenarios of how actions in the virtual world can have negative repercussions in the physical world.

- **Chapter 13** provides context to many of the security best practices discussed throughout the chapters by way of case studies or scenarios that one will typically encounter in the everyday use of information technology.

- **Chapter 14** summarizes the text and presents the steps to continue learning about computer security as well as daily, weekly, and monthly tasks individuals should perform to keep their defense-in-depth strategy current.

- **Appendix A** suggests a number of books and websites for readers to continue their exploration of computer security and to stay current on the latest security trends.

- **Appendix B** delivers supplemental context and a brief background into the topic of cryptography. Included are the terms and concepts that form the basic building blocks of cryptography as well as the function of cryptography in everyday computing.

- **Appendix C** introduces a number of web and Internet-based technologies that can be used to further increase one's defense-in-depth strategy when surfing the web. Technologies such as link scanners, virtual private networks (VPNs), and private browsing are presented to help prevent against common Internet-based threats or privacy concerns.

- A **Glossary** is provided as a quick-access resource for common security terminology.

TARGET AUDIENCE

This book is truly meant for anyone interested in information technology who wants to understand better the practical aspects of computer security. The only prerequisites that a reader needs are prior use of a computer, web browser, and the Internet. Depending on your motivation for wanting to learn more about practical computer security knowledge, this book serves many different audiences. Although originally written to provide a much-needed textbook for a course on introduction to computer security literacy at the university, college, community college, or high school levels, by no means is this an exclusive audience. The content presented in this book would also be a great resource for corporate training as many of the same activities that one performs when using a computer and the Internet for personal reasons overlap with many common business functions (i.e., email, surfing the web, social networking). Furthermore, the layout and presentation of the content of this book are tailored toward a normal user of information technology and would serve as an excellent read for anyone desiring a self-guided introduction to practical computer security.

Perhaps you have had your identity stolen, had your email account hacked, or have experienced a number of malware infections in the past. On the other hand, maybe you are interested in learning how antivirus software works, the weaknesses of firewalls, or how malware spreads and its function once it infects a computer. Or, maybe you want to acquire a working knowledge of computer security terminology, security mechanisms, and threats to give you an edge at work. Each of these reasons, and many more, are the exact motivations that the content found in this book seeks to address. Information technology has become ingrained into almost every aspect of our daily lives, from browsing the web and social networking to email and surfing the Internet at a coffee shop. However, it has been our experience that as technically savvy as our society has become, the same savviness has not extended into the realm of practical computer security knowledge. Whatever your motivation, this text serves as a practical guide to navigating the many dangers that unfortunately accompany the numerous conveniences that technology affords.

SCREENSHOT DISCLAIMER

It should be noted that technology is constantly evolving, and as this evolution takes place, the provided screen shots will likely become outdated. Despite this challenge, we have strived to provide underlying context so that even if the appearance of a particular screenshot changes, the explanation of the core technology will remain relevant.

Website: www.dougj.net/literacy

ACKNOWLEDGMENTS

Doug Jacobson: I want to thank my wife, Gwenna, and our children, Sarah, Jordan, and Jessica, for their support, patience, and love. And a special thank you to Sarah for designing the art for the book cover.

Joseph Idziorek: Thank you to my fiancé, Arlowyn, the love of my life, to my parents and my sister Katie for all their support, and to my amazing friends.

Both authors would like to thank Dr. Terry Smay for his input and editing help.

About the Authors

Douglas Jacobson is a university professor in the Department of Electrical and Computer Engineering at Iowa State University. He is currently the director the Iowa State University Information Assurance Center, which has been recognized by the National Security Agency as a charter Center of Academic Excellence for Information Assurance Education. Dr. Jacobson teaches network security and information warfare and has written a textbook on network security. Dr. Jacobson's current funded research is targeted at developing robust countermeasures for network-based security exploits and large-scale attack simulation environments; he is the director of the Internet-Scale Event and Attack Generation Environment (ISEAGE) test bed project. Dr. Jacobson has received two R&D 100 awards for his security technology, has two patents in the area of computer security, and is an IEEE Fellow.

Joseph Idziorek received his PhD in computer engineering from the Department of Electrical and Computer Engineering at Iowa State University. As a graduate student, he developed an introductory course, Introduction to Computer Security Literacy, and taught the course 10 times to over 250 students. Dr. Jacobson and Dr. Idziorek have also authored two publications regarding this course. Apart from practical security education, Dr. Idziorek's research interests include cloud computing security and the detection and attribution of fraudulent resource consumption attacks on the cloud utility pricing model. He has authored a number of conference and journal publications on this research topic. Dr. Idziorek now works as program manager at Microsoft.

What Is Information Security?

1.1 INTRODUCTION

Information security has become a common term used by many, often in reference to a conflict between "hackers" and security professionals, or what many see as a war of the geeks. The term *information security* can have many definitions; some use it as an overarching term defining all security-related issues with technology, while others use it as a subclassification of a broader category, such as information assurance. Simply put, information security is the **process of protecting information from threats.** In the context of this book, the terms *computer security*, *cyber security*, and *information security* are synonymous and can be used interchangeably. Information security is a broad field of study and employs a large number of people to implement and maintain computer and data security controls at a cost of billions of dollars per year. At first glance, information security may seem to be too complex a topic for average people to understand, let alone play an active role in protecting themselves from threats. It is the goal of this book to change that perception because, in fact, everyone who uses a computer and the Internet has a role to play in protecting themselves and their information. Often, you, the user, play the most significant role in protecting your own security by the decisions you do or do not make.

This chapter introduces you to the practical side of information security since, after all, practical security is the need that this book seeks to fulfill. Understanding basic security terminology and commonly held security truisms is important for understanding the material in subsequent chapters. This chapter not only covers introductory material but also brings forth topics such as cyber ethics and explores common security myths. The chapter further develops a simple threat model in which users are able to determine who and what they are protecting their information and computing resources from as well as the value of these resources.

1.2 HOW MUCH OF OUR DAILY LIVES RELIES ON COMPUTERS?

Before the topic of information security is explored, it is important first to understand the impact computers have on our daily lives and what information computers store that is personally important to us. As we all know, computers are everywhere and are responsible for making virtually every aspect of our lives better. Computers control everything from how you receive electricity, water, and other utilities to services ranging from air traffic control to online banking and everything in between. Because the protection of these computer systems is primarily the concern of their owners (e.g., corporations), the typical user of the system or service has little if any role to play in protecting them. Since this book focuses on the user and what typical users can do to protect themselves, the focus is not on the impact of computers in general, but rather on the computers and information that you have control over and how you can protect your information from the many threats that lurk in the Internet.

One way to view how people rely on computers is to examine how the average person perceives the privacy of information stored on computers. People often use two different standards of privacy, one for computer data and one for noncomputer data. While most people would never walk up to a stranger on the street and hand the stranger their business card containing a wealth of their personal information (noncomputer data), people seem more than willing to disclose such information when it is in its digital form (computer data) on the Internet. Two questions you should always ask yourself when disclosing digital information in the cyber world are, Would I give this information to someone I do not know in the real world? and What will this person do with my personal information? The answer to these questions should help guide you in classifying information as private or nonprivate.

When considering private information stored on computers, there are two different classifications of computers: personal and nonpersonal. The owner of a "personal" computer owns both the computer hardware and the information stored on that hardware, as exemplified by the typical home computer situation. A "nonpersonal" computer is one that is owned by a third party but contains information that relates to a person. A bank computer, for example, may be bank property, but it contains personal information about both you and the bank's other clients. As will be discussed, the personal or nonpersonal categorization of a computer does not change with respect to whether the information stored or processed is private or not, but it does change how we, as individuals, handle information privacy and possibly what information we choose to store on such computers.

Computers are often regarded as powerful tools that can help people manage their daily lives; for this reason, many own personal computers. It is estimated that 90% of individuals in the United States own a computing device, and that worldwide personal computer sales exceeded more than 364 million units in 2011. People use computers to play games, to access the Internet, to manage finances, to keep in touch with friends and family, and to retain information about their lives. Everything you do on a computer either uses or generates information or both. While a great deal of the information stored on your personal computer is nonprivate, there is usually some information that would be considered private. Stop and think about the information stored on your computer to which you would answer "no" to the question posed previously: Would I give this information to someone I do not know? Such information is private and therefore should be protected. Since private information is stored on a computer owned by you (a personal computer), it is your responsibility to protect that information. Several of the chapters in this book focus on methods to help you keep such information private.

Nonpersonal computers, on the other hand, are not owned by individuals but instead by third-party entities that store private information on behalf of their clients or users. Overall, there exists an enormous volume of private information stored on commercial, government, or third-party nonpersonal computers, and these entities handle the safeguarding of the information stored on these systems. While a typical user has little or no control over many aspects of the security of the information stored on nonpersonal computers, in certain cases the user has control over what information is stored and, just as important, how that information can be accessed (i.e., passwords). For example, a client of an e-commerce website freely chooses to disclose his or her name, address, and credit card number in exchange for the convenience of buying an item online. While the client cannot directly control the security of the system that processes and stores this private information, the client does have the ability to choose which e-commerce website he or she prefers to shop at or whether to shop online at all. Furthermore, if the client chooses to create an account on an e-commerce website for future use, the security of the password chosen is also a factor controlled by the client that can contribute to the overall security of the client's information. This book discusses the types of private information you should entrust to nonpersonal computers and how to safeguard access to this information.

1.3 SECURITY TRUISMS

As discussed previously in this chapter, information security is a large and complex subject. There are, however, several overarching statements—security truisms—that can be made about information security. These security truisms apply to both personal and nonpersonal computers and should be used as guiding principles when considering information security.

Security Is a Matter of Economics: When deciding what information to protect and how to protect it, the first question that should be asked is, Is it worth it? In other words, security costs time and money, and if the information or object that is being protected has little value, it does not make much sense to spend resources to protect it. A difficult task in this type of assessment is determining the value of what you are trying to protect on your computer. It is easy, for example, to decide how much insurance you need for your home or any other such tangible item. It is much more difficult to place an exact dollar value on the loss of information like pictures, videos, and documents containing personal and private information, especially because many people regard this type of information as invaluable. Even defining loss in the context of information security is difficult since you may still possess the information after someone else has gained access to it. Likewise, it is difficult to estimate the cost of security implementation, in time, money, or both, and to measure the effectiveness of security controls. What is certain, however, is that the effort you put forth in time, money, education, or effort should be at least equal to the perceived value of the information you are trying to safeguard.

Security Should Be Composed of Layers of Defenses: There is no one single security mechanism that can protect all information from potential attacks. A layered approach will make it more difficult for someone to gain access to your information since an intruder must bypass multiple security methods to gain access. For example, a deadbolt lock can be used to safeguard a home. In addition, a motion detection alarm system can be used to detect whether the lock did its job or whether the intruder circumvented the lock by breaking in through a window. You might also take your most valuable items and place them in a safe within the locked and alarm-equipped house. If one layer fails, there are additional layers in place to compensate and prevent a breach of security.

Absolute Security Does Not Exist: We cannot protect against every possible event, especially when we cannot predict every potential security threat. No security system can be perfect in dealing with either the physical or the computer world. In the physical world, the goal of security is to make a potential attacker's cost greater than the value of the asset you are trying to protect. While the same is true in the cyber world, the task of information security is generally regarded as a more challenging task due to cyber thieves' inherently low cost of entry to perform attacks. An attacker may need only very modest resources to carry out a globally impactful attack that could victimize millions of people, and often there is little or no chance of the cyber attacker being caught. Obviously, this gives cyber attackers an advantage over their physical world counterpart.

From the perspective of a practical computer user, no matter how much time and effort one places in protecting a computer, it will always be vulnerable to a certain number of attacks. Therefore, the objective of practical computer security is to raise the bar high enough to greatly reduce the number of threats able to mount a successful attack. By employing the defense-in-depth strategy discussed throughout this book, one can greatly improve the overall security of computing devices and the protection of personal information.

Security Is at Odds with Convenience: In the physical world, security often involves extra steps or procedures to protect a valued object. For example, houses are often protected with a locked door, and a key is then needed to gain access to the house. Information security is similar; passwords are used to gain access to information, requiring the user to remember and use the password every time the desired information is accessed. The more security mechanisms added to a computer system, the more intrusive security measures might be, often causing user frustration. This frustration may cause individuals to take shortcuts, like leaving a door unlocked or using a simple and easy-to-remember password that weakens the security safeguard. While added measures provide enhanced security, they are also at odds with convenience and over time convenience tends to trump security.

1.4 BASIC SECURITY TERMINOLOGY

Security professionals use a number of terms to describe various aspects of information security. This section provides definitions for several such commonly used terms. The first three terms dealing with the protection of information are often referred to as the **C-I-A model**.

Confidentiality: Preventing unauthorized users from reading or accessing information. Confidentiality is what most people think of when they refer to information security. A loss of confidentiality would include an attacker learning your password or credit card number.

Integrity: Ensuring that an unauthorized user has not altered information. A bank account balance is a sound example of information that requires a high degree of integrity. A loss of integrity in this case would be detrimental to the bank or its customers.

Availability: Making sure that information can be accessed when needed by authorized users. If a hard drive were erased as a result of a malware infection, this type of action would be considered a loss of availability.

The next five terms are used to describe methods attackers may use to gain access to your information or to your computer system.

Vulnerability: A weakness in some aspect of a computer system that can be used to compromise a system during an attack. Vulnerabilities can exist in the *design*, the *implementation*, or the *configuration* of computers and software. Design vulnerabilities occur when flaws in the design of the computer or software can be used to bypass security. As illustrated in Figure 1.1, a physical example would be if a house plan used by a developer does not specify locks on any of the outside doors. If a thief discovered such a flaw, the thief would then be able to break into any of the houses sold by that developer (i.e., houses denoted with yellow x's).

Implementation vulnerabilities exist when developers make errors implementing software designs. Continuing with the previous physical example in Figure 1.1, while the developer's plans contained designs for every house to be equipped with door locks, the locks were installed either improperly or not at all by contractors. In such a case, instead of all homes

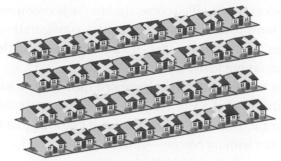

Design Vulnerability

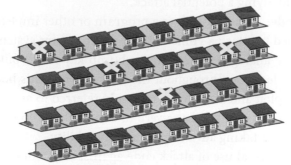

Implementation Vulnerability

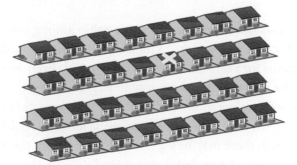

Configuration Vulnerability

FIGURE 1.1   Vulnerability types.

using the same plans that were vulnerable to break-ins, only those homes built by a certain contractor would be vulnerable. Implementation vulnerabilities in software can be difficult to find, but once discovered, they are often easy to fix with a software patch.

Configuration vulnerabilities occur when a user either configures the system incorrectly or uses system defaults. Continuing with the door lock example in Figure 1.1, this would be the case when design plans were correct and locks were installed correctly, but the homeowner fails to lock the door. The most common computer system configuration vulnerabilities occur when the user fails to change a default password, chooses a weak password, or elects not to use a password at all.

Exploit: An exploit is an unimplemented method or algorithm that is able to take advantage of a vulnerability in a computer system. Using the door lock example, an exploit might consist of knowing that if you made a bump key—a key with no notches—it will open certain locks, but you do not possess or know how to make the key. Therefore, an exploit is a potential threat underlying a potential attack.

Attack Code: An attack code is a program or other implementation of an exploit used to attack a vulnerability in a computer system. An attack code would be analogous to creating a bump key that would be able to open vulnerable locks. Throughout the remainder of this book, the coupling of an exploit and attack code is simply referred to as an exploit. The term *exploit* will also be used as a verb to denote the action of an attacker or malware when taking advantage of a vulnerability.

Attack: The actual use of attack code against a system or the exploitation of a vulnerability. This is the same as using a bump key to open a vulnerable door.

Figure 1.2 shows the chronological relationship among vulnerabilities, exploits, attack code, and attacks. Vulnerabilities often lay dormant in software programs for years before being discovered. Even when they are discovered, there may not be an easy way to exploit them. The time interval between when a vulnerability is discovered and an exploit is designed can be anything from days to months or even longer. Once the exploit has been identified, there may be a period of time before the attack code is created. Sometimes, the exploit is discovered directly through creation of attack code, and the time between exploit and attack code is thus zero.

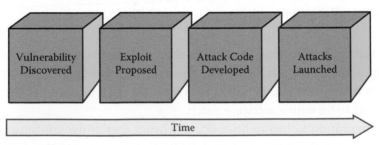

FIGURE 1.2　Relationship among vulnerabilities, exploits, and attacks.

The time between attack code production and widespread attacks can also vary depending on the attack code type and its distribution method.

As is often the case, attack code is made available on the Internet for other users to download, use, modify, and improve the original design. Attack code is like any other software that goes through a design process, and the attack code itself may ironically have vulnerabilities that can be exploited by other attack code. There are documented cases on the Internet for competing versions of malware, engaged in a virtual turf war, attempting to defeat the competition's malware by exploiting vulnerabilities in the adversary's software design. Therefore, even those that design and write attack code must be sensitive to writing secure software that strives to be free of vulnerabilities.

Zero-Day Exploit: When attack code is used to target a system before the vulnerability or exploit is discovered or known to exist by the security community (i.e., defenders or good guys), this action is known as a "zero-day" exploit. Zero-day exploits are particularly dangerous because security practitioners are often initially defenseless against such attacks.

It is a common misconception that attackers are sophisticated computer programmers with a deep understanding of computers and networks. While there are indeed many such people creating attacks, there are an even larger number of naïve attackers who simply use attack code created by others. Such attackers do not need to understand the vulnerability, the exploit, or the code itself. They simply visit a website, download a malicious program, and with a few clicks of the mouse, start attacking other computer systems. The ubiquitous nature of the Internet fuels this problem and allows naïve attacks to be easily launched against numerous computer systems.

The next four terms deal with quantifying the likelihood that a computer will be subjected to an attack and the resultant costs of such an attack.

Risk: Risk is a measure of the criticality of a situation—the likelihood of something being attacked. Risk is based on several metrics, as subsequently described. The risk of attack associated with a given situation consists of several factors, commonly described as *threats, vulnerabilities* (previously discussed), and *impact*.

Threat: Threat is a measure of likelihood that a computer system will be attacked or the confidentiality of information lost. For example, a web server placed on the public Internet may have a high probability of being attacked, while a web server located on a private corporate network not connected to the Internet would have a significantly lower probability of being attacked. Determining the threat of an attack can be difficult to quantify and is dependent on many factors. Consider a web server hosted on a private corporate network; the threat is low from an Internet-based attack. However, the threat might be much higher if the attack consists of a company employee determined to steal information from the internal web server to which he or she has access.

Impact: Impact is the measure of potential consequences if the computer system or the confidentiality of information was compromised as the result of a security breach or information leak. Impact is sometimes a hard-to-quantify factor based on the overall consequences of a security breach for a specific organization. Again, consider an attack in which a public web server is compromised. Such a loss might be considered to be low impact since the data hosted on the server is already public. However, if an internal server that contains employee or customer records were compromised, the impact would likely be very high.

In summary, risk is a combination of a system's vulnerability to attack, attack likelihood (threat), and attack impact. The relationship between these factors can be described using three examples. For the purposes of discussion, the presented examples are simplified since, as one might imagine, analysis of risk in a practical situation can be a complex process. A helpful way to understand these relationships is by considering examples in which one of the three factors (threat, vulnerability, and impact) is absent.

The first example is one in which a system is not vulnerable to a specific attack. Consider the case in which an Internet-connected Macintosh computer (i.e., Mac) running the OS X operating system is being attacked by attack code designed to exploit a vulnerability for the Windows operating system. In this case, because the considered attack code is ineffective against a Mac, the risk for the Mac computer is zero even though the attack may have a high impact if successful, and the threat of attack for the system is high.

The second example considers a situation in which the impact of an attack is zero, or at least very small. This example is less likely since there typically is some nonzero impact resulting from a successful attack. Often, the impact level is considered to be either high impact or low impact. A low-impact system would be one containing little important or private information. For example, because the disclosure of information found on a public web server is already public, the impact of such loss of confidentiality would be low. Thus, the overall risk would be low even though the system under consideration possesses a high threat of being attacked and may also be vulnerable to multiple types of attacks.

The last example is when the threat is zero. Although highly improbable, this occurs when a system cannot be attacked because of the manner in which it is connected or accessed. It has been said that "the only truly secure computer is one buried in concrete, with the power turned off and the network cable cut." Even if the system possesses many vulnerabilities and contains important information, if it cannot be attacked, then the risk is zero.

Risk Assessment: Risk assessment is a process or procedure in which the importance of a system or data is evaluated and a determination is made regarding how many resources must be devoted to its protection. The idea is that not all data must be protected at the same security level. Many books and other resources dedicated to risk assessment are available, and there are consulting firms engaged in the lucrative business of performing risk assessment for organizations. The goal of this book is not to provide an in-depth study of risk, but to give the reader insight into the nature of and the need for risk assessment.

1.5 CYBER ETHICS

The indirect nature of computers creates a tendency among computer users to act somewhat differently behind a computer screen than they might act in the physical world. For example, most people would not steal a CD off the shelf of a local music store. In the cyber world, however, it is not uncommon for people to download a file like a song or video that they clearly do not own. Although the reasons are many, there are people who generally feel that because such files are copies of "just data," that these files have no perceived monetary value. In addition, others feel that since they are just downloading a copy and the owner still has the original, that the act does not constitute stealing. Last, because people have little to no expectation of being caught for downloading copyrighted files, they do not fear any type of punishment for the action. The same mind-set seems to be present for attackers with respect to breaking into a computer versus breaking into a house.

The U.S. legal system does not help much with this issue. In many cases, the theft of information is treated differently from the theft of physical property, and breaking into a computer to steal information is treated differently from breaking into a house to steal a similar item. Many of the laws that deal with computer crimes do not provide penalties as severe as those for noncomputer crimes. This difference in perception, coupled with the relatively low probability of getting caught while engaging in data theft, adds to the problem of trying to keep your information protected.

If the C-I-A model is reexamined and each of its elements (confidentiality, integrity, and availability) is related to a physical act, one can see the contrast between cyber ethics and traditional ethics. The loss of confidentiality is the same as theft of a physical item. When the integrity of information is compromised, the action can be considered equivalent to forgery. Finally, the loss of information availability is analogous to destruction of property. While many people would not steal a physical item, illegally forge a document, or destroy others' personal property, the same ethics that dissuade such actions in the physical world do not always permeate into the cyber world.

Another aspect that makes cyber ethics seem different from traditional ethics is the ease of carrying out cyber attacks. As discussed, there are many attack tools available on the Internet that can be used by people with limited computer skills. These tools allow virtually anyone to become a "hacker," contributing to the attitude that using tools that are found on the Internet is not unethical. Obviously, however, just because someone can hack does not mean they should or should escape penalty if they do.

It should be pointed out that there are people, sometimes called ethical hackers or white-hat hackers, who are hired by corporations and get paid to attack computer systems and computer networks. They perform so-called penetration tests designed to test the security of systems. Penetration testers follow a strict set of guidelines and a well-defined code of ethics. The objective of penetration testers is to test security systems and to identify security problems or vulnerabilities before they are exploited. There is also a popular misconception that companies often hire reformed hackers for this purpose. While a few "reformed" hackers might find such jobs, most organizations will not hire someone with a history of malicious hacking activity and a criminal background.

1.6 THE PERCEPTION OF SECURITY

As has already been discussed, security is a matter of economics. This statement is also true for cybercriminals. A common misconception in computer security is that one type of computer system is inherently more secure than another. First, regardless of the make, model, or vendor, all computer systems, operating systems, and applications are vulnerable to attack and are capable of being compromised. Often, a system's potential for compromise is a function of its market share and overall volume of use. The Windows operating system, for instance, has a significantly larger market share than Mac OS X. As of May 2012, the Windows operating system composed 92.5% of all desktop computers, while Mac OS X represented only 6.5%. Cyber criminals are often thieves of opportunity and prefer to target computers for which there is a high probability of stealing or damaging something of value. This does not mean that Mac-based computers are fundamentally more secure than Windows-based computers, just that the Windows-based computers are targeted more often and thus more attack code exists for them because of their larger percentage of market share.

For the attacker, it all boils down to simple economics. The system that costs the least to attack and has the most potential to produce a reward is the prime target. A problem associated with the myth of a Mac's relatively lower vulnerability to attack is that people often believe they are safer using a Mac than they are a Windows-based computer. This perception has led to Mac users being less aware of their activities in the context of security and the use of insufficient security mechanisms (i.e., antivirus software) to protect themselves and their data. Malware does indeed exist for Mac computers, and its presence is expected to grow. The Flashback Trojan malware, which infected an estimated 600,000 Mac computers in 2012, is a prime example of the malware threat that Mac users face. In addition, as discussed in Chapter 11, many phishing attacks are not operating system specific, and users of Mac-based or Windows-based computers (or cell phones for that matter) are equally vulnerable to fall victim to these deceptive attacks.

1.7 THREAT MODEL

Previously, the concept of a threat was introduced as a determinant for deciding if information is at risk. A question many people ask themselves is, Why should I care about computer security if I do not value the information on my computer? Before this question is examined, it is first helpful to determine against just whom are the threat sources that seek to attack computers. Numerous labels have been attached to individuals and groups of people who attack computers. Although there are many ways to categorize malicious actors on the Internet, this section divides attackers into six groups (script kiddies, malicious insiders, hackers, hacktivists, cyber criminals, and nation-states) and examines each group's typical experience level, resources, and motivations.

Script Kiddies: As previously mentioned, there is a significant group of people who have little to no programming or security knowledge who are able to easily find software on the Internet with which to attack other computers. Such attackers are often called *script kiddies*, and the resources script kiddies need are often nothing more than a personal computer and a connection to the Internet. The goal of script kiddies is to find vulnerable computers and attack them for pleasure. Because these crimes are often associated with boredom, script kiddies seldom seek to profit from their attacks. Because script kiddies wage attacks against real systems, they can cause significant damage, even without realizing the result of their actions. Another problem with script kiddies is that they often try to attack reputedly secure computers or computers that, while not vulnerable to the attack, can raise false alarms in computer security systems, making individuals or organizations think they are being targeted and forcing them to deal with expensive nuisances.

Malicious Insiders: A malicious insider is a trusted person who either has or has previously had legitimate access to the targeted information. Malicious insiders can be current or former employees within a business setting, current or former friends in a personal setting, or even family members. Because malicious insiders are trusted persons, they often do not need special hacking tools since they have easy access to the targeted information and require few or even no resources to carry out an attack. The goals of a malicious insider can be profit (selling the information), or it can be to cause harm to the employer or (former) friend. Because a malicious insider is often a trusted person, this person can often gather information without raising suspicion, and subsequently these attacks are difficult to prevent and detect.

Hackers: The term *hackers* is a broad category often referring to individuals who are curious and knowledgeable about computers, networks, and security but not always malicious in intent. Although the term *hackers* was not originally considered malevolent, it now carries with it malicious connotations. Hackers are often credited with discovering vulnerabilities and creating the exploits used by script kiddies. The goals of a hacker can vary but are often driven by simply proving that something is possible. For example, among hackers, there is great prestige to be the first to exploit an unknown vulnerability. The last three groups (hacktivists, cyber criminals, and nation-states) often enlist or employ hackers to accomplish their objectives.

Hacktivists: A subgroup of hackers, often called hacktivists, is hackers typically targeting computer systems or websites with the motivation of making ideological, political, or religious statements, to name a few. Although often talented hackers, this group of malicious actors often compensates for their lack of resources by way of their strong convictions. The end game for hacktivists is to raise awareness about their cause or to embarrass their targeted adversaries.

Cyber Criminals: Cyber criminals are the digital equivalent of scam artists and represent organized crime on the Internet. Their goal is to make money through attacking computers and their respective users. Cyber criminals may be hackers or malicious insiders, or they may hire hackers or pay insiders for information. Cyber criminals may also use the same tools as script kiddies but with the goal of profiting from stolen information. This group of malicious actors represents the largest threat to individual computer owners. Its members look for information to enable stealing individual identities and then use such false identities to make money. In fact, the cumulative profits from cyber crime have recently skyrocketed and are now being considered in the same context as illegal drug trade. Many security professionals believe that once groups of hackers learned how to make money by attacking computers that the security landscape of the Internet was fundamentally changed, and that virtually everyone has now been put at risk.

Nation-States: Countries are becoming increasingly dependent on using computers to conduct many activities, ranging from national defense, media, and public utilities to online banking and integrated supply chains. This makes their computer systems prime targets during times of conflict. Most nation-states have active cyber-warfare groups with goals of both protecting themselves and attacking potential adversaries. Also, some nation-states use hackers to obtain trade secrets and other information from foreign companies and foreign governments with whom they have otherwise-friendly relationships. Most nation-states have virtually unlimited resources.

Now that the threat sources have been defined, the question of, Why should I care? can be answered by considering three general categories describing just what can happen to a victim as a result of a security breach. These general categories can be used to help make the point that information security can affect nearly anyone. Defending against these threats is discussed in further chapters.

The first category of threat is called **malware**. Malware is a broad category covering malicious software installed on a victim's computer without the victim's knowledge or consent. Many people are familiar with the term **computer virus**, a form of malware. Malware can cause loss of information (confidentiality), alteration of information (integrity), or even loss of the use of information or a computer (availability). Malware also has other functions, including using the victim's computer to mount attacks against other computers on the Internet. Chapter 5 discusses the many ways in which malware finds its way onto a computer.

The second threat category is disclosure of **private information**. There are many ways, including through malware, that information can be improperly disclosed. The impact arising from the loss of confidentiality of information depends on the type of information disclosed. Some information may have a monetary value, while other information may be personal in nature.

The third threat category is loss of **time, money, reputation, or resources**. With most attacks, recovery costs time and, depending on the severity of the attack, can also cost money. Loss of reputation is harder to quantify and, depending on the person involved, can have significant consequences like the loss of employment, for example. For companies, on the other hand, such loss of reputation can cause long-term harm and even lead to failure and bankruptcy. Loss of resources can range from short-term loss of Internet access or use of a computer to requiring the victim to start anew by reinstalling the computer operating system. Loss of resources also includes the deletion or accessing of personal or private data, such as pictures, tax return documents, and emails.

The last question that needs to be addressed when discussing threats is, What is the value of the resources that we seek to protect? Remember the security truism, "Security is a matter of economics." Each individual person needs to determine the value of his or her computing assets and information to be protected and subsequently to decide the cost of securing it. An easy way to perform such an assessment is to state how much you would be willing to pay to recover your information if, at this instant, all information on your computer were deleted. For many people, the information stored on their computers (i.e., pictures, songs, schoolwork, programs, financial documents, etc.) is irreplaceable and thus invaluable.

If you do not value your digital information, this does not mean that it is unnecessary to provide some level of security for your computer. After all, it is likely that you will use your computer to store confidential information like usernames and passwords or type a credit card number when shopping online—all information you would not want an attacker to learn. By the same token, malware can cause damage to others if installed on your computer. Malware can also result in your Internet service provider (ISP) restricting your Internet access or might even result in you being accused of a computer-based crime. The remainder of the book strives to provide you with the context to make informed decisions about computer security and to stay safe while using your computer when faced with numerous situations that you are likely to encounter in your everyday use of computers and the Internet.

1.8 SECURITY IS A MULTIDISCIPLINARY TOPIC

There is a misconception that only people who have studied computer engineering or computer science populate the field of computer or information security. This perception could not be further from the truth. Solving the problems of cyber security involves more than just dealing with technical issues; there are numerous social, political, legal, and economic issues to be addressed. As seen throughout the book, both attackers and defenders will use both technical and nontechnical methods to achieve their goals.

Disciplines involved in protecting computers range from hard sciences like mathematics, computer science, and computer engineering to other, "softer" disciplines like social sciences, business, and economics. The hard sciences are typically involved with the creation and maintenance of the technology used to protect information, and these are the disciplines involved in the bulk of the security workforce. Disciplines like business, statistics, and economics are involved in the determination of risk and the cost of attacks versus the cost of protection. They are also involved in developing appropriate business processes to help manage security. Disciplines like psychology, sociology, and political science focus on analyzing the social and political aspects of security. They study attackers to better understand why they attack and to help understand attacks against people. They also research the effects of attacks on individuals or society in general to improve understanding of how to better prepare individuals, corporations, or government entities to protect themselves.

1.9 SUMMARY

The prime objective of this book is to focus on the practical methods available to users wishing to protect the security and privacy of computer-based assets and personal information. While hackers and security companies are major external factors, we, the users, play the most significant part in determining the security of our information by the decisions we do or do not make.

- Information security is the process of protecting the confidentiality, integrity, and availability of personal data from the threats of hackers and malware.

- An objective of practical computer security is to raise the bar high enough to greatly reduce the number of threats able to mount a successful attack by employing the defense-in-depth strategy discussed throughout this book.

- The ubiquity of networking should make us concerned not only with data stored on our personally owned and controlled computers but also personal data that may reside on computer systems owned and controlled by others, either commercial entities like banks or shopping websites or personal computers owned and controlled by other individuals.

- Practical computer security consists of a number of truisms: Security is a matter of economics, security should be composed of layers of defenses, absolute security does not exist, security is at odds with convenience.

- Hackers and malware exploit vulnerabilities to gain access to computer systems and information.

- Risk is a combination of a computer's vulnerability to attack, the likelihood of attack (threat), and the impact of the attack.

- People's tendency to ethically act and react differently in computer-based environments than they typically have in previous noncomputer contexts has contributed greatly to the challenges of cyber security.

- The malicious actors on the Internet can be divided into six groups: script kiddies, malicious insiders, hackers, hacktivists, cyber criminals, and nation-states. Each of these groups has differing experience levels, resources, and motivations.

- Since potential computer security breaches are possible in virtually an unlimited number of areas where computers play a role, understanding and implementing appropriate safeguards require expertise in a broad range of fields beyond computer science, computer engineering, or similar technology-oriented specialties.

BIBLIOGRAPHY

Allsopp, A. 2011. Mac and mobile malware set to increase. *Macworld*. http://www.macworld.com.au/news/mac-and-mobile-malware-set-to-increase-37626/ (accessed March 22, 2012).

Bevan, K. 2012. Mac users may think they're safe from malware, but they're not. *The Guardian*. http://www.guardian.co.uk/commentisfree/2012/apr/19/mac-users-malware-flashback (accessed May 11, 2012).

Bishop, M. 2003. *Computer Security: Art and Science*. Boston: Addison-Wesley Professional.

Camm-Jones, B. 2012. 2011 "eventful year for Mac malware." *Network World*. http://www.networkworld.com/news/2012/012512-2011-eventful-year-for-mac-255312.html?source=nww_rss (accessed March 22, 2012).

Cheswick, W.R., Bellovin, S.M., and Rubin, A.D. 2003. *Firewalls and Internet Security: Repelling the Wily Hacker*. Boston: Addison-Wesley.

Dunn, J.E. 2012. Flashback Trojan horse still on 650,000 Macs, security company says. *Macworld*. http://www.macworld.com/article/1166523/flashback_trojan_horse_still_on_650_000_macs_security_company_says.html (accessed May 11, 2012).

Gahran, A. 2011. Report: 90% of Americans own a computerized gadget. CNN. http://articles.cnn.com/2011-02-03/tech/texting.photos.gahran_1_cell-phone-landline-tech-gadget?_s=PM:TECH (accessed March 23, 2012).

Goodin, D. 2010. Upstart crimeware wages turf war on might Zeus bot. *The Register*. http://www.theregister.co.uk/2010/02/09/spyeye_bots_vs_zeus/ (accessed March 22, 2012).

Grimes, R.A. 2011. Your guide to the seven types of malicious hackers. InfoWorld. http://www.infoworld.com/d/security-central/your-guide-the-seven-types-malicious-hackers-636?source=IFWNLE_nlt_sec_2011-02-08 (accessed March 23, 2012).

Mills, E. 2010. In their words: experts weight in on Mac vs. PC security. CNET. http://news.cnet.com/8301-27080_3-10444561-245.html (accessed March 23, 2012).

Net Applications. 2012. Market share. http://marketshare.hitslink.com/ (accessed March 23, 2012).

Parker, D. 1998. *Fighting Computer Crime: A New Framework for Protecting Information*. New York: Wiley.

Pettey, C. 2011. Gartner says PC shipments to slow to 3.8 percent growth in 2011; units to increase 10.9 percent in 2012. Gartner. http://www.gartner.com/it/page.jsp?id=1786014&source=email_rt_mc (accessed April 3, 2012).

Young, C. 2010. *Metrics and Methods for Security Risk Management*. Waltham, MA: Syngress.

Introduction to Computers and the Internet

2.1 INTRODUCTION

The goal of this chapter is to describe a typical computing environment to develop a common framework and foundation for subsequent chapters. The two main topics introduced are the **technology layers** comprising a typical computer (user, applications, operating system [OS], hardware) and the basic operational **components of the Internet**. An overall picture of the Internet and the vast collection of computers connected to it is provided to illustrate interactions in the collective system. Several fictitious security characters (role-players) are defined to assist in describing various security concepts. The diagrams and concepts presented in this chapter serve as a principal basis for the discussion of the security concepts presented in the remaining chapters.

2.2 COMPUTERS

The task of a computer is to perform a set of operations based on instructions provided by a software program. Computers come in many forms and are used in virtually every aspect of our lives. For example, a modern automobile typically has dozens of computers controlling everything from the braking system to the satellite radio. Although over 1 billion computing devices are produced every year, most of these computers do not represent targets for hackers or malware as these computers do not process or store confidential information. The concepts presented in this book narrowly focus on personal and nonpersonal computers that process our private and confidential information and therefore represent a security risk.

For the purpose of discussions about practical computer security, a general computer is considered to have the basic four-layer structure (hardware, OSs, applications, and users) shown in Figure 2.1. Each of these layers is subsequently described.

2.2.1 Hardware

The designation *hardware* refers to the collection of physical components used to create a computer. This collection may vary from computer to computer, depending on the computing device's intended use. Figure 2.2 depicts a diagram of the hardware components likely to be found in a typical computer. Correspondingly, Figure 2.3 shows the physical representation of the items presented in Figure 2.2.

As shown in Figures 2.2 and 2.3, the heart of the computer is the central processing unit (CPU), the "brains" of the computer responsible for executing the instructions provided by software. The CPU is connected to memory (i.e., RAM) that stores the instructions (i.e., software) to be executed by the CPU. In most computers, the CPU, memory, and other hardware devices are located on a physical structure called a motherboard whose printed-circuit configuration interconnects many of the hardware components used in the computer. The hard drive and the CD-ROM/ DVD drive are two other hardware elements found in a typical computer. The hard drive is used to store both collections of data (data files) and

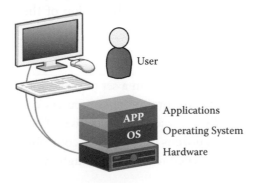

FIGURE 2.1 Technology layers of a computer.

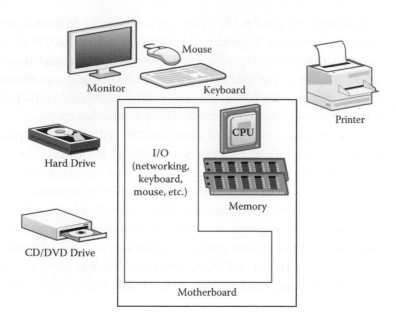

FIGURE 2.2   Basic diagram of computer components. I/O, input/output.

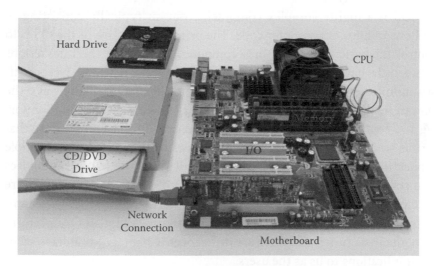

FIGURE 2.3   Actual computer components.

collections of instructions (program files). Both types of files can be written to or erased from the hard drive. The CD-ROM/DVD drive is used to provide long-term storage of data and programs. A CD-ROM/DVD disk can, at the user's convenience, be removed from the computer and replaced by another such disk, and information on the disk can either be permanent and not modifiable (read only) or capable of modification (read-write). Information transferred between a CD-ROM/DVD and other hardware elements is typically much slower than a similar transfer involving a hard drive. The user can interact with the computer through other devices, such as a keyboard, mouse, monitor, audio speakers, printers, and similar devices, interconnected via the motherboard.

Computers can also connect and communicate with other computers and devices through several common standardized interfaces. The USB (Universal Serial Bus) is used to connect devices like keyboards and printers to a computer. Bluetooth is a standard wireless interface used to connect wireless devices over short distances. Both a wireless keyboard and a wireless mouse are two examples of common hardware components that utilize Bluetooth. Other typical computer interfaces include networking capabilities for both wireless and wired Ethernet. Wireless network interfaces represent a specific and common security risk and are described in more detail in Chapter 9.

2.2.2 Operating Systems

The OS is a highly complex computer program typically consisting of millions of lines of computer code. The primary objective of the OS is to control the basic operations of a computer, namely, all the interactions between the hardware devices (i.e., hard drive, mouse, USB drives, memory, monitor, etc.), software applications, and the user. In many ways, the OS can be thought of as a traffic cop—charged with the task of monitoring and controlling multiple concurrent events within a computer so that it runs smoothly. The brokering of resources by the OS enables multiple applications to run simultaneously while all share the hardware devices connected to the computer. The Windows OS, Mac OS X, and Linux are examples of popular OSs for personal computers, and together they comprise well over 95% of the total OS market share. While all OSs perform the same basic functions, there are differences (Chapter 1) that have security implications to us as the users.

Because the OS presides over the operations of the entire computer, it is natural for hackers or malware to attempt to compromise the OS by exploiting vulnerabilities to gain control over a computer and thereby access all of its information. This is why OS vendors are constantly providing software patches/updates (Chapter 6), typically by way of Internet downloads, to reduce or eliminate vulnerabilities and thus protect computers from hackers and malware. The OS can also protect your computer by running applications like antivirus software and firewalls (Chapter 6) and, against being generally accessed by other users, by requiring a user-name/password combination to log in to the computer.

2.2.3 Applications

An application is a computer program that provides a specific function, such as word processing, web browsing, spreadsheet analysis, financial tools, and email. Some general-use applications typically are included with an OS, while other applications, more specifically focused on individual user needs, are purchased and then installed on the computer by the user. Applications can be obtained and installed from a number of sources, including the hard drive, CD-ROM/DVD, USB drives, and the Internet. While applications are typically thought of as installed or executed solely by a computer user, applications also possess the ability not only to run other applications but also to install other unwanted software, such as malware.

2.2.4 Users

A user can be anyone interacting with a computer, either directly or indirectly and whether permission is given or not. Direct interaction occurs when a user provides input to the computer (typically through a keyboard or mouse) or receives output from the computer via a screen display or a printed document. The most common type of direct interaction occurs with desktop or laptop computers. The user is the prime focus of this book because the actions a user does or does not take often have the most significant bearing on a computer's security and thus the user's security.

2.3 OPERATION OF A COMPUTER

To better understand how a computer can be manipulated by a hacker or malware, it is important to understand how a computer operates and even more specifically how a computer loads and runs an OS and its given applications. Since attacks against a computer can originate from running applications, it is necessary to examine an application's capabilities that permit such attacks to occur. The next three sections describe how a computer is started, how an OS loads and runs applications, and how applications interact with an OS and a computer's hardware.

2.3.1 Booting a Computer

When a computer is first turned on, it goes through a process called *booting* (hence the term *reboot* when a computer is restarted). Figure 2.4 shows the steps involved in the booting process.

In Step 1 in Figure 2.4, the user turns on the computer by pressing the "power button" or "on switch." This action causes the CPU to search for a specific program to execute. The motherboard (shown in Figures 2.2 and 2.3) is designed to provide a "hardwired" and relatively small program, called the Basic Input/Output System (BIOS), for the CPU to execute at power-on (Step 2). The BIOS contains a series of programs that provide basic access to the hardware and the initial configuration of the computer. One function of the BIOS is to load *boot code* (so-called because this is a sort of bootstrapping operation) from a storage device (Step 3). The

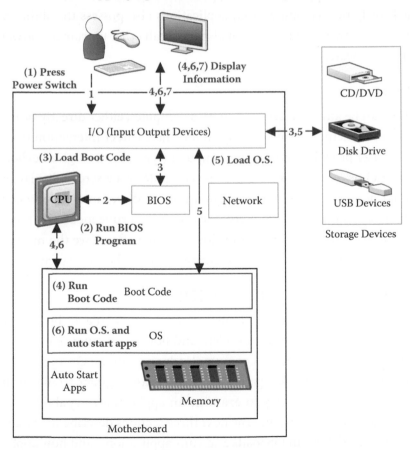

FIGURE 2.4 Booting a computer.

storage device housing the boot code is typically the hard drive, but can in some cases be a CD-ROM or a USB-connected flash drive. The boot code is specific to each OS and is designed to load the OS, from a storage device, into memory. Once the boot code is fully loaded into memory and running (Step 4), it begins to load the OS into memory (Step 5) from a storage device. After this action is complete, the boot code initiates execution of the OS program (Step 6), which will load other programs needed for the computer and OS to function. These programs are called *startup applications* and include applications like antivirus software, firewalls, calendars, and printer drivers. Once the OS has finished loading startup applications, the user can start to interact with the computer and the OS via the keyboard and mouse (Step 7). Depending on how a computer is configured, the OS may require entry of a username and password before giving the user access to the computer. Once successfully logged in to a computer, the user can start to use the computer and run applications, as described in the next section.

2.3.2 Running an Application

When using a computer, the user is primarily interacting with applications that logically execute "on top of" the OS, as depicted in Figure 2.1. In the Windows OS, the primary program that the user interacts with is called *Windows Explorer*, and for Mac OS X it is called *Finder*. Such programs allow a user to browse through the files stored on the computer and launch applications. Users typically start (or execute) applications by double-clicking on an application icon or by double-clicking on a file associated with an application; double-clicking on a word-processing document, for instance, will launch a word-processing application. Figure 2.5 illustrates a situation for which the user has started several applications (i.e., email, word processor, etc.). To run a web browser application, a user typically double-clicks on an application (Step 1). The OS processes the user request by accessing the storage device containing the application (typically the hard drive). The OS then loads the application into memory, and it begins executing (Step 2). Once the application is fully loaded, the application will be presented to the user on the monitor, in which case the user is then able to command and interact with the application (Step 3). One key function of an OS is to make it appear to the user that multiple applications are all running at the same time, even though a single CPU can actually be executing only one application at any instant. The OS performs this balancing act by letting each program execute for a short period

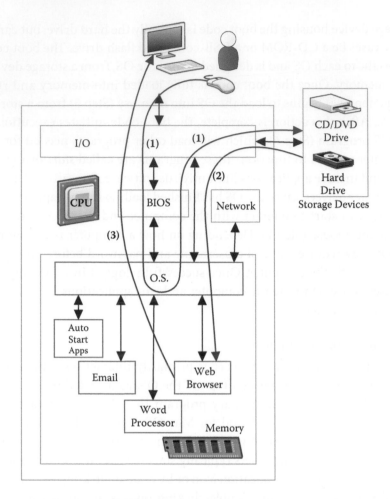

FIGURE 2.5 Starting an application.

of time and then cycling on to the next application, or time-sharing. Now that it is understood how an OS loads and runs applications, the functions that a running application can perform are examined next.

2.3.3 Anatomy of an Application

A running application has the ability to access any user-accessible file on a computer and may also access all of the hardware devices connected to the computer, as shown in Figure 2.6. To do this, an application may use OS resources to access file and hardware devices. Figure 2.6 demonstrates that the input or task from the user is first processed by the OS and then passed to the application. The application can also access files stored on the various devices, such as hard drives, CD-ROMs, or USB drives,

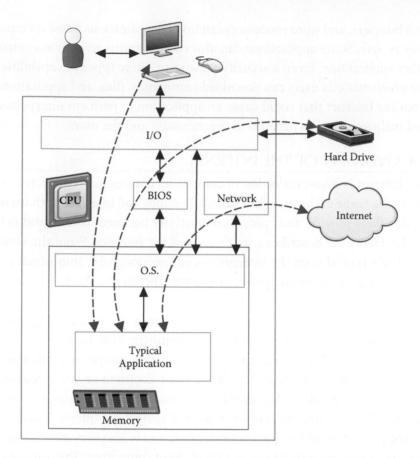

FIGURE 2.6 Anatomy of an application.

connected to the computer. Furthermore, because an application interacts with the computer through the OS, an application can also access network hardware and therefore the Internet, representing a danger discussed in Chapter 5. While an application can use the OS for good, it can also use it for bad. The OS can also protect specific files and devices from certain applications based on various permissions or access rules (e.g., who owns the file, meaning that not every application is able to read, write, or execute every file on a computer). Other protection methods enabled by the OS are the execution of applications such as firewalls and antivirus software (Chapter 6) that work with the OS to protect the computer from hackers and malware.

Applications can access files and hardware devices and can also execute other applications, sometimes without a computer user's interaction and knowledge. As will be seen in further chapters, applications like email, web browsers, and word processors can invoke applications based on input they receive. Some applications can also run programs written to control other applications. From a security viewpoint, these types of capabilities are problematic as users can download commands, files, and applications from the Internet that could cause an application to perform unexpected and malicious actions harmful to the computer and the user.

2.4 OVERVIEW OF THE INTERNET

The Internet is a vast collection of computing devices interconnected via networks. Some of these devices run applications and interface with users, while others provide and control connectivity between devices and networks. Figure 2.7 describes a user's view of the Internet. From the viewpoint of a typical user, the Internet is a connection point into which the user can plug in their computer, permitting the user to "talk" to anyone else connected to the Internet and to use a variety of services, such as the web, email, banking, and shopping. The Internet is typically diagramed as a cloud and thought of as a black box requiring little knowledge of its inner structure. From a security standpoint, the Internet is a black box from which attacks emerge. This is the most common security-oriented view of the Internet since a user is most often concerned about attacks against his or her specific computer and not against the Internet itself.

The perception of the Internet as a black box is also very contextually similar to understanding the function of cloud computing. The concept of

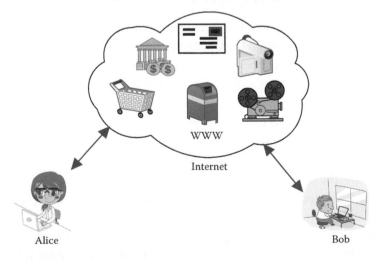

FIGURE 2.7   A user's view of the Internet.

cloud computing is essentially to store computer files or process information on a third-party's computer hardware (i.e., Apple iCloud, Amazon Cloud Drive, Microsoft Azure, etc.). A user typically accesses the cloud-based resources via an Internet connection, and the user often has little control or knowledge of where his or her files or computing resources are physically stored. Hence, the term *cloud* is used in the context of cloud computing: The cloud is a representation of a black box mentality when it comes to accessing, processing, and storing information.

Figure 2.8 provides a representation of the hierarchical structure of the Internet. The Internet consists of interconnected networks and networking devices managed by entities called Internet service providers (ISPs). These ISPs have an informal hierarchy, and at the highest level, national, international, and large regional ISPs are interconnected to create what is often referred to as the "backbone" of the Internet. Backbone ISPs are interconnected through dedicated high-speed and high-volume connections, and they carry the bulk of Internet traffic. At the next level, medium-size ISPs like those of corporate organizations connect to the backbone ISPs; this hierarchy continues with smaller ISPs and organizations connecting to the midtier ISPs. Finally, an end user or organization will be connected to

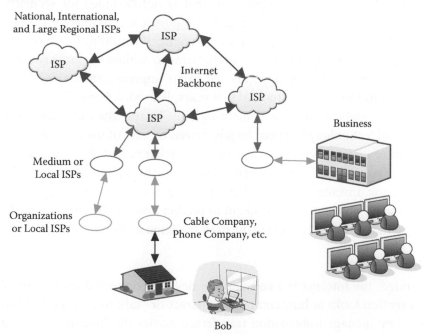

FIGURE 2.8 Hierarchy of Internet service providers.

the Internet through a midtier ISP. Often, the only information that a user knows about his or her ISP is its name, connection type, upload/download speed, and service cost. As seen in Figure 2.8, the Internet is not owned or operated by one single corporation but instead by multiple entities and ISPs distributed across the globe. Therefore, an email sent from a computer in Australia to a computer in the United States will likely traverse across many different ISPs en route to its final destination.

Before the Internet is discussed further, it is useful to examine its history. As seen in Figure 2.9, there have been vast changes since 1980, with both the size and complexity of networks increasing dramatically. Networks were initially designed to provide connectivity and did not focus on supporting security. The first networks in the 1970s interconnected a relatively small number of research organizations and universities. Everyone in this connected community was trusted, and security was not an issue. In 1988, the first major attack was launched against computers connected to the Internet, and to this day some of the same underlying methods used in that attack are still effective.

Vint Cerf, one of the founding fathers of the Internet, stated in reference to the modern-day Internet: "The engine of the world economy is based on this really cool experiment that is not designed for security" (Menn, p. 245). As chronicled in Figure 2.9, it took approximately 45 years from the invention of the phone to achieving 10 million. For Internet-connected servers, it took nearly half that time to achieve the same volume. Advancements in technology have led to an unprecedented growth. To achieve 1 million users, it took AOL 9 years, Facebook 9 months, and the cell phone application Draw Something only 9 days. The innovation and growth of technology has been largely driven by ease of use and interconnection of devices, with security taking a backseat, and this same shortcoming is observed (from a security viewpoint) throughout the remainder of the book. Inventors of technology do not generally have a disregard for security; it is just extremely difficult to predict how the invention of technology during its inception will be used maliciously in the future.

2.4.1 Protocols

As stated, the Internet is a collection of devices connected via networks. This section looks at how computers interact or "talk to each other" and how they manage information transferred across the Internet. The first concept to be introduced is that of a network protocol, that is, a set of rules used by computers to talk to each other. Whether they are aware or not,

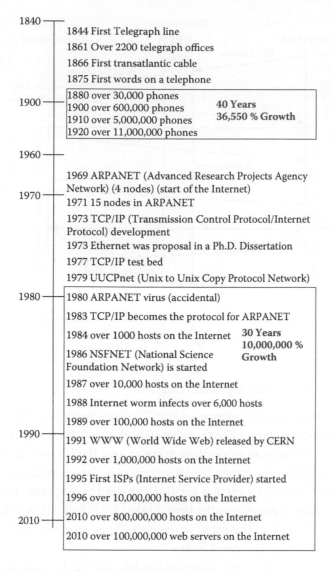

FIGURE 2.9 History of networking and the Internet.

people often use protocols as part of their everyday lives. For example, the telephone system can be viewed as having multiple protocols. One protocol is used to make a call using the phone system, and a second protocol is used to manage interactions between the two people talking. This would be analogous to one protocol used by a computer to obtain access to the Internet and a second protocol used to send email using that access. Figure 2.10 shows the protocol-managed exchange between devices in the phone system and the protocol-managed exchange between two users

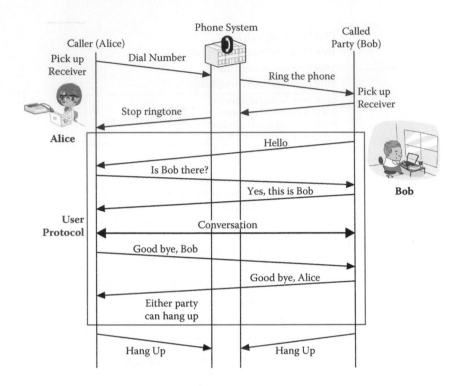

FIGURE 2.10   Phone system protocol diagram.

(Alice and Bob) of the telephone system. These exchanges can be described using a protocol diagram like that shown in Figure 2.10, where the vertical lines represent the communicating systems and the horizontal lines represent information exchange. The diagram can also represent a temporal element, with time progressing vertically down the diagram, and slanted horizontal lines representing the time it takes for information to flow from one side to the other. The gaps between the lines represent waits or processing times at each protocol layer.

In Figure 2.10, Alice, the caller on the left side of the diagram, begins by picking up the receiver. Alice listens for a dial tone (a part of the protocol), and after hearing the dial tone, Alice dials Bob's number. If the called party's phone (i.e., Bob) is not busy, Alice receives a ring tone, and Bob's phone rings. Once Bob picks up the phone, the connection between the lower layers is completed. Alice and Bob are then able to start a new protocol (user protocol) shown in Figure 2.10.

For the user protocol, Bob, the person answering the telephone, typically starts the interaction by saying "Hello," and the other person, Alice, responds. Alice and Bob will continue to talk (send data) in a back-and-forth manner until one of them terminates communication, most often by saying good-bye. At any time, Alice or Bob can also terminate a call by simply hanging up the receiver. One part of the protocol usually involves identification of one or more parties, using one of many different methods. There may be a system-provided method for identifying the calling device (caller ID). However, caller ID identifies only the phone number used by the caller and not necessarily the person using the phone, and no foolproof method for identifying either the actual calling or called parties is provided. One can imagine that this could lead to problems if a person wanted to use a phone for dishonest purposes. Even with caller ID, only the phone is identified, even though this feature primarily was added to support screening of incoming calls from individuals.

The phone system provides an example of connection-oriented communications, an approach in which a protocol exchange is used to establish a connection between the two parties (dialing the phone, picking up the phone). Once the connection has been established, the data flow between the two parties using the same route or path and are received in the same order as sent. At the conclusion of the data flow, the connection is broken.

Another method, called *connectionless communication*, can also be used to transfer data between two parties. The post office is a familiar example of a connectionless system. Each letter is handled independently and could conceivably follow a route different from other letters to get to a common destination. Each letter is self-contained and has its own address information. If multiple letters are sent from a given location to a given destination, there is no guarantee they will all be delivered at the same time and in the same order, that they will follow an identical route, or that they will be delivered at all. Like the mail system, the Internet operates in a similar fashion utilizing connectionless communication protocols. One of the main differences, however, is that data or files sent over the Internet are broken up into smaller chunks called packets, and each packet is handled separately as it is sent from one computer to another. When all packets are received at the destination address, the packets are then reassembled to create the original file again.

One common factor between both connection-oriented and connectionless methods is the requirement that users must be able to identify each other for the system to work fluidly. The phone system uses phone numbers to uniquely designate each individual phone within the system. The post office uses addresses printed on the outside of letters to identify destinations. In a similar way, the Internet uses addresses to identify every connected device. The next section describes how addressing is implemented on the Internet.

2.4.2 Internet Addressing

One of the key aspects of a network is the addressing method used to distinguish among interconnected devices. For example, addresses are used to identify each computer on a given network or to distinguish a particular instance of an application from another such instance or one protocol from another. Before Internet addressing is discussed, it is first useful to look at a nonnetwork example to appreciate the critical function of unique addresses within a communication system. Figure 2.11 shows a diagram describing two people using the postal system to communicate via letters.

As seen in Figure 2.11, Alice, who lives in a building at 101 Main Street in Los Angeles, wishes to send a letter to Bob, living in a building at 333 Elm Street in Washington, D.C. Alice will print her own address (return address) and Bob's address (i.e., recipient address) on the outside of the envelope, with both addresses containing several pieces of information like name, street, building, state, and zip code to identify each respective person. Alice then takes the letter to a mailbox, whose physical address identifies its street location. The physical address of the mailbox is not important to Bob and is only important to Alice because she needs to

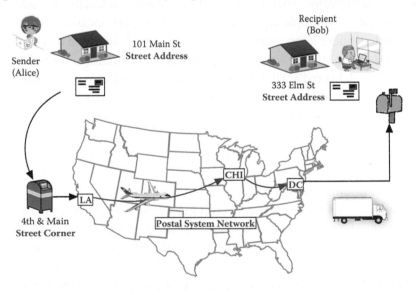

FIGURE 2.11 Postal addressing system.

know where to find it to get the letter into the postal system. Alice need not put the physical address of the mailbox on the envelope.

Once the letter is in the mailbox, the postal system will take over and route the letter to the recipient at the destination address. Although Alice needed to know a mailbox location to get the process started, she need not know anything about how the postal system works or the route taken by the letter to the destination. In this example, the letter is taken from the physical mailbox to a sorting center in Los Angeles. Note that Alice did not need to specify the location of the sorting center because the postal system knew where to take it after getting it from the mailbox. The sorting center in Los Angeles will read the recipient address and determine where the letter should next go; this is called *routing*. The letter is then placed on a plane and taken to the next sorting center, in this example in Chicago. Even though the Chicago sorting center has a physical address, neither the sender nor the recipient of the letter need know this address to success-fully mail a letter. Once the letter reaches the Chicago sorting center, the recipient address is read, and the letter is routed to the next sorting center, in the example in Washington, D.C. Again, the physical address of the sorting center is not important to the sender or the recipient.

When the letter arrives in Washington, DC, the recipient address is examined to determine which local mail carrier will deliver the letter to the building where the recipient lives. The local mail carrier will deliver the letter to the physical mailbox at the building indicated by the recipient address. The physical location of the mailbox (front porch, street cluster, etc.) was not on the envelope because that information is known by the mail carrier. Once the mail carrier places the envelope in the recipient's mailbox, Bob is able to retrieve his mail. Note that to successfully mail the letter, Alice's address was not used by the postal system, and in real-ity, Alice could have addressed the envelope with whatever sender address she desired (this is called *spoofing* and is discussed in Chapter 4). To the receiver, the sender address can be used to filter mail and determine which mail is important to open and read.

Reexamining this example, but this time considering when Alice and Bob use two computers to communicate, it can be seen there are many similarities between postal system addressing and how addressing works in a network like the Internet. Figure 2.12 shows Alice and Bob using com-puters to send and receive messages.

In Figure 2.12, Alice is at her computer and is running an email appli-cation. On the Internet, every directly connected computer has a unique

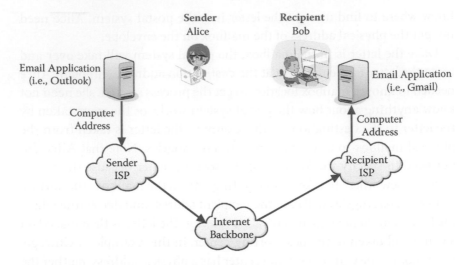

FIGURE 2.12   Computer network addressing.

address (i.e., IP address), similar to a unique postal address. The computer application will take the email message from Alice's computer and read the destination (recipient, Bob) address from the email message to determine where to send it next. The computer will send the message to Alice's ISP, which could be Comcast, Verizon, Mediacom, AOL, and others. The computer knows the physical address of this ISP, even though that information is not directly important to the user. The ISP will read the recipient address denoted in the email to determine the next location to send (i.e., route) the message. The ISP will send the message into the Internet, where the message will be routed until it reaches Bob's computer. For each step along the way, physical addresses of intermediate devices will be used to help route the message to the correct destination. When the message reaches the end computer, as determined by the destination computer address contained in the email message, the computer will examine the message and read the application address to determine which application should get the message. While there is not a one-to one-correlation between the postal system's activity and that of the Internet, it should be clear that there is a need for each element in the Internet to have a unique address.

2.4.3 Internet Protocol Addresses

Every device connected to the public Internet has an Internet Protocol (IP) address, and this IP address is globally unique. Before examining how packets (i.e., data) are moved through the Internet, it is helpful to understand how IP addresses are allocated and assigned. An IP address is a number between 0 and 4,294,967,295, or 2 to the 32nd power. For readability issues, an IP address is usually written as four decimal numbers separated by periods (for example, 192.168.1.1). Each IP address consists of two parts, a network part and a host part. Similarly to the way the different components of a phone number (area code, prefix, and a number) are used to help the phone system route traffic to the correct location, the two parts of the IP address are used to help route Internet traffic. One way to look at the Internet is as a collection of uniquely addressed networks, each containing some number of uniquely addressed hosts (a generic name for a computer or server). Figure 2.13 shows three networks and the address allocations for the networks and the hosts.

Figure 2.13 shows an XYZ Office Network with IP address 197.12.15.0. Networks are given addresses as a way to refer to them. Even though a person may never address a network by its numerical representation, devices connected to the network certainly will. The XYZ Office Network can have up to 254 connected devices, with addresses ranging from 197.12.15.1 to 197.12.15.254. Host address 0 is not allowed, and the address 255 is a reserved address. Similarly, Figure 2.13 shows 254 possible host addresses for the ABC Office Network as well as for Joe's Coffee Shop network.

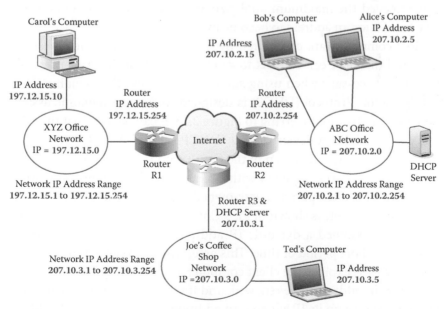

FIGURE 2.13   IP addressing example.

Unlike landline phone networks, IP addresses assigned to physically adjacent networks often have no numerical relationship. In Figure 2.13, Joe's Coffee Shop network and the ABC Office Network have numerically adjacent network address ranges, but the physical networks are not necessarily even in the same city.

As previously discussed, IP addresses are globally unique identifiers assigned to devices on the Internet. IP addresses are assigned in blocks to organizations, which in turn assign them to individual devices. For example, when a consumer purchases Internet service from an ISP like Mediacom, Mediacom assigns an IP address to its new customer's computer. The overall assignment of Internet IP addresses is controlled, and a few centralized groups allocate address blocks. There are two methods for IP address assignment: static and dynamic. In static assignment, an address is assigned to a device, typically through manual configuration, and that address is permanently "reserved" for that device. In dynamic assignment, the address is determined using a protocol during each Internet session, and a device's IP address may change from session to session. The dynamic method enables an ISP to maintain a pool of IP addresses smaller than its actual number of potential users and then allocate from this pool to users requesting use of the Internet at particular times. This could present a problem if the number of users requesting service exceeded the maximum pool size, in which case some users would have to wait for an address to become available.

Most computers are configured by default to use dynamic IP assignment and therefore can connect to a network without the prior-user configuration necessary when using static IP addresses. The Dynamic Host Configuration Protocol (DHCP) is designed to support dynamic assignment of IP addresses. Referring to Figure 2.13, it can be seen that the ABC Office Network has a device labeled "DHCP server." A DHCP server can be a separate device, as shown in the figure, and is responsible for assigning IP addresses to computers within a network. In a home network, a DHCP server is often part of a user-owned router that enables one to connect to the Internet, as shown in Joe's Coffee Shop network in Figure 2.13. A device is assigned a dynamic IP address, determined by the DHCP server, for a short period of time. This assignment is referred to as a *lease*. When the lease expires, the client computer automatically asks the DHCP server for the address to be renewed, and if the server rejects renewal, the device must give up its IP address. In addition to providing an IP address to the client, the DHCP server will tell the client computer the address of the router it should use and the address of a name server (the name server is discussed further in the chapter).

2.4.4 Public versus Private IP Addresses

Unique IP addresses on the Internet are called public IP addresses. Private IP addresses are also used in networking to create private networks capable of connecting to the public Internet. Every computer within the same private network must have a unique private IP address, but computers in different private networks can have identical private IP addresses. A device with a private IP address cannot be connected directly to the Internet but is connected to the Internet using a special router called a Network Address Translator (NAT). A NAT has two network connections: a public IP address for its Internet network connection and a private IP address for its non-Internet private network connection. NATs allow multiple computers in a private network to share a single public IP address. There are a couple of advantages to using a NAT. First, they allow a user to set up a home network with multiple computers using a single public IP address. The use of NATs has also allowed the Internet to have more computers than the allowable number of public IP addresses. As shown in Figure 2.14, Bob and Alice are both able to have the same private IP address but have different, and globally unique, public IP addresses. There are three private network ranges, namely:

10.0.0.0 to 10.255.255.255

172.16.0.0 to 172.32.255.255

192.168.0.0 to 192.168.255.255

The 192.168 network range is the most common private IP address network, and home routers often use this range. Figure 2.14 shows a typical home network setup with a router that functions as an NAT. Note that the router may provide both wireless and wired network connections to the home users' computers or devices. The home router is sometimes included as a cable modem if the ISP is a cable TV company or as part of a DSL (digital subscriber line) modem if the provider is a phone company. The ISP often provides such home routers, but a home user may instead purchase his or her own router from commercial vendors like Best Buy or Amazon. So-called hot spots or MiFi® adapters can also provide wireless connections to a similar collection of user computers, with the Internet connection

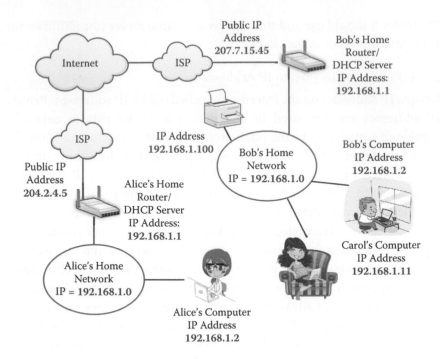

FIGURE 2.14   Home network example.

provided by another wireless service using the 3G or 4G cell phone protocol offered by vendors such as Verizon, Sprint, AT&T, or T-Mobile.

2.4.5 Finding an IP Address

For everyday computing tasks, users rarely need to know the numerical IP address for their computers or other network devices. If you do need to know an IP address or are just curious about what yours may be, there are methods for finding it. For the Windows OS. you can navigate to the control panel to produce a display like that shown in Figure 2.15. Alternatively, you can open up a command window (first click the Windows "Start" button, followed by clicking "Run," then type 'cmd' in the presented text dialog box and hit 'enter' to open the command window) and type "ipconfig." On a computer with a UNIX OS, you can similarly type ifconfig in a command window, and this also works for the Mac OS X OS. The ipconfig or ifconfig command will show you both the IP address of your computer and the IP address of the router you are using to connect to the Internet. The output produced by the ipconfig command is shown for Bob's computer in Figure 2.16.

FIGURE 2.15   Display of a computer's IP address.

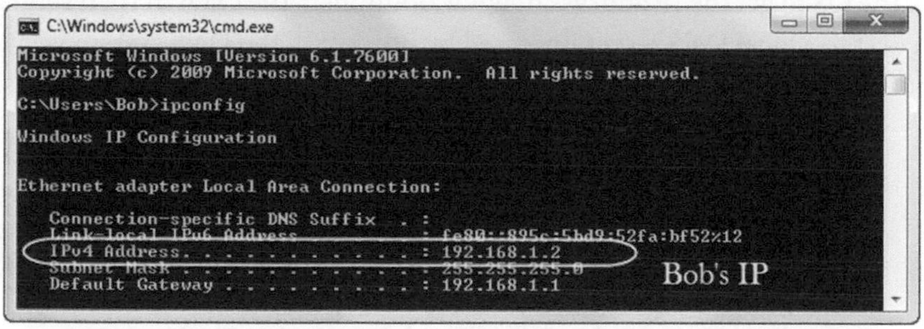

FIGURE 2.16   Using ipconfig to display an IP address.

2.4.6 Domain Name Service

Internet-connected devices use IP addresses for sending and receiving data. Most users, however, would not want the hassle of remembering or correctly typing numerical IP addresses to specify servers, websites, or applications to which they desire to connect. Instead, it is more convenient to use natural-language-based naming conventions for websites or domain names. For example, when a user sends an email message, he or she can specify a domain name (e.g., admin@dougj.net) as the destination address. A domain name (e.g., www.dougj.net) can also be specified when webpage access is desired. When an application sends a message into the Internet, however, it must provide the numeric IP address of the destination computer to send the message successfully across the Internet. Translation between host names and the numeric IP address is accomplished by a distributed application called Domain Name Service (DNS). Every computer has a local DNS application that communicates with DNS servers distributed on the Internet to translate between the full name of a host (host name + domain name) and its numeric IP address. Examining a typical name of a device on the Internet (such as a web server), it can be seen that this name consists of several parts. For example, www.dougj.net is the full name of a host. The name of the computer is www (i.e., subdomain), and the name of the domain is dougj.net. Dissecting a hostname is more thoroughly examined in Chapter 11. The DNS model is shown in Figure 2.17.

In the example shown in Figure 2.17, Bob wants to visit the website www.dougj.net. To do this, Bob will start his web browser application (i.e., Firefox, Chrome, Internet Explorer [IE]) and type www.dougj.net into his browser's web address bar. The web browser on Bob's computer will then ask the OS to get the IP address of www.dougj.net. The OS will then send a request to a local DNS server operated by Bob's ISP. The DNS system is laid out in a tree structure with a set of root DNS servers containing address

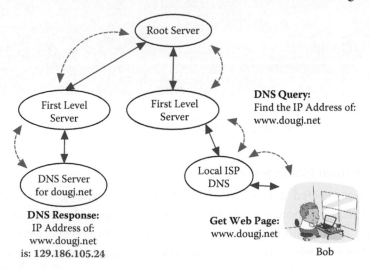

FIGURE 2.17 Hierarchical DNS model.

information about all top-level domain servers (like .com or .net). Such a server either has information about the IP addresses of every host within its domain or knows which DNS server within its domain to ask for such information. Such a hierarchical approach allows a DNS server to distribute knowledge based on administrative control of the name-to-IP address mapping. When a computer wants to know the IP address of a host, it asks its DNS server, which in turn will fetch the answer. The answer may already be in the DNS server's cache from previous queries, or it may have to ask the root server where to find it. This is also true for Bob's computer, which also has a cache of recently asked IP addresses and therefore may not need to ask the local ISP DNS server for the name-to-IP address mapping every time a webpage is requested. As Figure 2.17 shows, the request (represented by the blue dashed lines) propagates through the root server to a DNS server that knows the answer, and the response propagates back (shown by the red solid lines).

Every Internet application will query the DNS system when the user enters a host name. There are also applications that will query the DNS system and return the IP address. As mentioned, users do not typically deal with numeric IP addresses of computers. However, it can sometimes be useful to know how to find the IP address of a host. The easiest way to accomplish this in the Windows OS, Linux, or Mac OS X is to use a command prompt. The command to query the DNS is "nslookup." To use this command, type "nslookup hostname" (where "hostname" is something like www.amazon.com), and the IP address of the host will be returned. An example of output produced by such an nslookup command is shown in Figure 2.18. The DNS lookup for the host computer (www.doug.net) shows the name of the first DNS server (Unknown) and its IP address (192.168.1.1), and then the answer to the DNS lookup is the IP address 129.186.105.24.

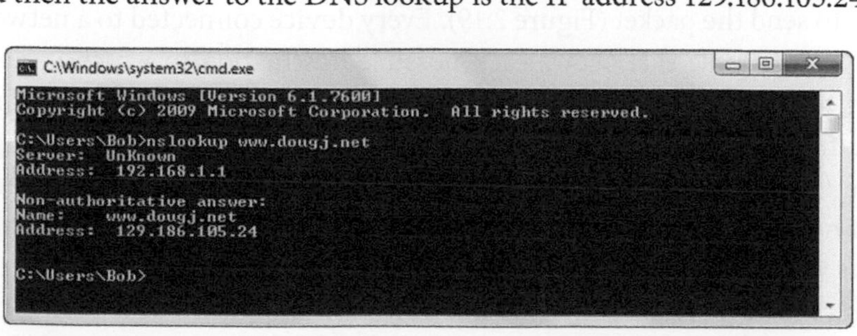

```
C:\Windows\system32\cmd.exe
Microsoft Windows [Version 6.1.7600]
Copyright (c) 2009 Microsoft Corporation.  All rights reserved.

C:\Users\Bob>nslookup www.dougj.net
Server:  UnKnown
Address:  192.168.1.1

Non-authoritative answer:
Name:     www.dougj.net
Address:  129.186.105.24

C:\Users\Bob>
```

FIGURE 2.18   Obtaining an IP address with nslookup.

2.4.7 Network Routing

Previous sections discussed how devices on the Internet are addressed and how this addressing convention of the Internet is comparable to the postal system in which data is routed from one location to another until it arrives at its final destination. This section takes a closer look at routing—how data is moved through the Internet. One key function of the Internet is its ability to route packets (message fragments) from source to destination across multiple networks and networking devices, each owned or controlled by a different organization. For the sake of brevity, routing in this context is described as a simple function provided by a set of interconnected networking devices called routers. It is assumed that routers provide methods for determining where to send packets to get them to their correct destinations. Before examining routing on the Internet, it is useful to look back at some of the history of routing in earlier networks.

The first networks were based on the same basic concepts as the telephone system, in which a route was first established between source and destination before any traffic could pass, and all traffic for a given transaction followed this same established path. This connection-oriented approach made it easy to send and receive data, particularly since the data arrived in a sequential order. Undesirable complexity associated with this type of network results from the requirement to achieve a global view of all devices to establish a route. In such an approach, intermediate devices are not required to know about the network since they only react to commands given by the global network management system.

The Internet uses a connectionless approach in which each packet of a transaction is handled separately by each individual router. Packets are sent from a source device to any next device capable of handling them. That next device then queries its local route table and determines where next to send the packet (Figure 2.19). Every device connected to a network has a route table that shows each possible destination to which it could next send the packet. In this table, potential next hops (i.e., routers) are specified by IP addresses and an interface (routers, for example, might have two or more interfaces). At first glance, if every possible destination needs to have a route entry, this might seem to require a very large route table. Perhaps the easiest way to look at how routing tables avoid this requirement is to look at the possible destinations for the packet. Each destination is represented by a network address consisting of an address and a network mask. The network mask is used to show which part of the IP

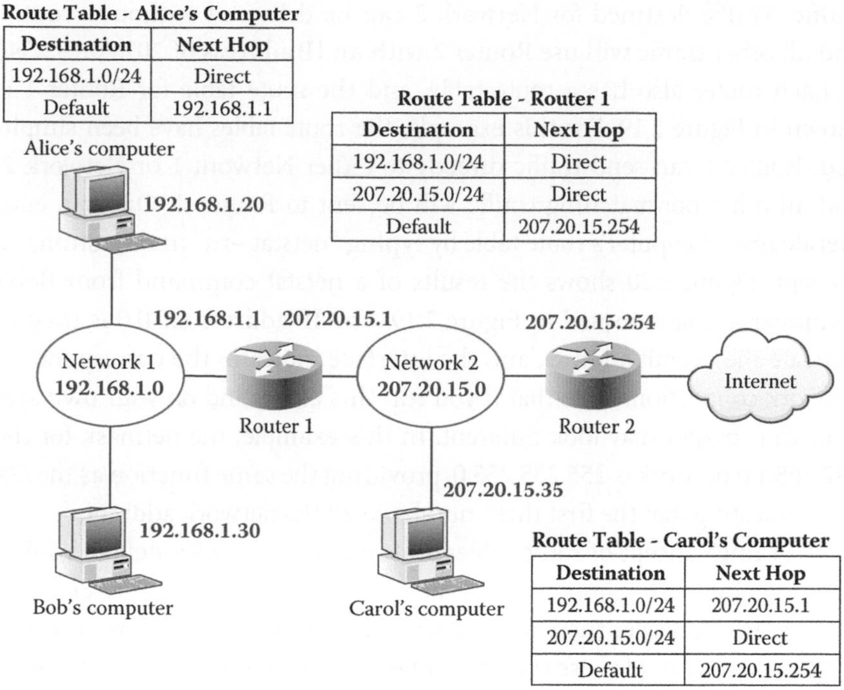

Route Table - Alice's Computer

Destination	Next Hop
192.168.1.0/24	Direct
Default	192.168.1.1

Alice's computer

Route Table - Router 1

Destination	Next Hop
192.168.1.0/24	Direct
207.20.15.0/24	Direct
Default	207.20.15.254

192.168.1.20

192.168.1.1   207.20.15.1   207.20.15.254

Network 1
192.168.1.0   Network 2
207.20.15.0   Internet

Router 1   Router 2

207.20.15.35

192.168.1.30

Bob's computer   Carol's computer

Route Table - Carol's Computer

Destination	Next Hop
192.168.1.0/24	207.20.15.1
207.20.15.0/24	Direct
Default	207.20.15.254

FIGURE 2.19   Network routing example.

address is the network address and which part represents the host address. Figure 2.19 shows a network and the routing tables for several devices.

As can be seen in Figure 2.19, Alice's and Bob's computers are connected to Network 1. Each of these computers has two choices for destinations, either to other computers connected to Network 1 or to someplace else. The routing tables for these computers thus have two entries. The first entry is for a destination address matching any computer on Network 1 (192.168.1.0). The /24 entry indicates that the network address to match is 192.168.1. The computer can thus send a packet directly to any computer on Network 1 without a router. The second choice is any computer not on Network 1. This is the default route to be taken when there are no matching destinations in the table. In this case, the default route is through Router 1 with an IP address of 192.168.1.1.

Examining Carol's computer in Figure 2.19 shows three possible destinations: computers on Network 1, computers on Network 2, and someplace else as there are three entries in the route table for Carol's computer, corresponding to these three choices. Traffic destined for Network 1 (192.168.1.0) uses Router 1 with an IP address of 207.20.15.1 to route the traffic. Traffic destined for Network 2 can be delivered without a router, and all other traffic will use Router 2 with an IP address of 207.20.15.254.

Each router also has a route table, and the route table for Router 1 is shown in Figure 2.19. For this example, the route tables have been simplified. Router 1 can send traffic directly to either Network 1 or Network 2, and all other nonmatching traffic will be sent to Router 2. One can enumerate their computer's route table by typing "netstat –rn" in the command prompt. Figure 2.20 shows the results of a netstat command from Bob's computer as diagrammed in Figure 2.19. The IP address 0.0.0.0 is used to indicate the default address, and the interface indicates the corresponding network connection. Note that if you run this command on your own system, your output may look different. In this example, the netmask for the 192.168.1.0 network is 255.255.255.0, providing the same function as the /24 and indicating that the first three numbers are the network address.

The same concept of route tables and routers, each with default routes, is carried out throughout the Internet. In between your computer and a particular web server there may be several routers owned by many different ISPs, and each of these routers contains its own respective route tables. To enumerate a possible path that Internet traffic could take from your computer to a destination computer one can use the command "traceroute hostname" (on UNIX or Mac OS X) or "tracert hostname" (on the Windows OS), where "hostname" is the name of a website, such as "www. cnn.com." As shown in Figure 2.21, a "tracert www.cnn.com" command is

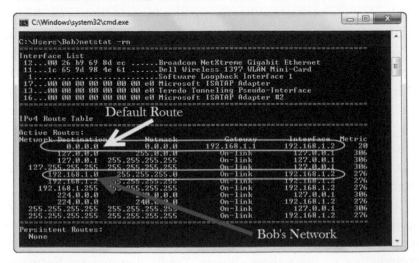

FIGURE 2.20   Route table displayed using netstat.

```
C:\Windows\system32\cmd.exe                                                    - □ x

C:\Users\Bob>tracert www.cnn.com

Tracing route to www.cnn.com [157.166.255.19]
over a maximum of 30 hops:

  1    <1 ms    <1 ms    <1 ms   192.168.1.1
  2    10 ms     71 ms     1 ms   router-129-186-105-0.iastate.edu [129.186.105.254]
  3     2 ms    <1 ms    <1 ms   b31gb1-vlan254.tele.iastate.edu [129.186.254.131]
  4     6 ms    <1 ms    <1 ms   b31gb2-438.tele.iastate.edu [192.245.179.52]
  5     5 ms     4 ms     4 ms   te-1-3-212.car2.KansasCity1.Level3.net [4.53.34.13]
  6     5 ms     4 ms     4 ms   ae-11-11.car1.KansasCity1.Level3.net [4.69.135.233]
  7    14 ms     13 ms    13 ms   ae-5-5.ebr2.Dallas1.Level3.net [4.69.135.230]
  8    18 ms     24 ms    24 ms   ae-62-62.csw1.Dallas1.Level3.net [4.69.151.129]
  9    13 ms     14 ms    14 ms   ae-63-63.ebr3.Dallas1.Level3.net [4.69.151.134]
 10    33 ms     33 ms    33 ms   ae-2-2.ebr3.Atlanta2.Level3.net [4.69.134.22]
 11    41 ms     33 ms    40 ms   ae-63-63.ebr1.Atlanta2.Level3.net [4.69.148.242]
 12    34 ms     33 ms    33 ms   ae-11-51.car1.Atlanta1.Level3.net [4.69.150.3]
 13     *         *         *     Request timed out.
 14     *        ^C
C:\Users\Bob>
```

FIGURE 2.21   Route path enumerated with tracert.

issued on Bob's computer and the resulting path between Bob's computer and the destination computer (i.e., www.cnn.com) is presented. Listed in Figure 2.21 are 12 distinct routers between Bob's computer in Ames, Iowa, and CNN's web server in Atlanta, Georgia.

The request issued from Bob's computer for CNN's web server traverses many states and miles on its way to its destination. As illustrated in Figure 2.22, each time that Bob requests CNN's homepage or clicks on a hyperlink on CNN's website, the request and subsequent reply are routed from Ames, Iowa, to Kansas City, Missouri, to Dallas, Texas, and finally to Atlanta, Georgia; all of this happens in the blink of an eye. While the given example provided one possible path between Bob's computer and CNN's web server, this path certainly is not permanent. Depending on the route tables of supporting routers, Bob's request to CNN's web server could just have easily been routed to Chicago, Illinois, and then to Lexington,

FIGURE 2.22   Geographical diagram of route path.

Kentucky, on its way to Atlanta, Georgia. The next time a webpage loads slowly, remember that your web browser could literally be requesting different web content from web servers hundreds or thousands of miles away and that are perhaps located around the globe. Try a "traceroute www.bbc. com" command on your computer to enumerate the path between your computer and BBC's web server in London, England.

All computers on the Internet are essentially interconnected through a vast array of ISPs and networking devices. Because each computing device connected to the Internet has the capability to communicate with any other Internet-connected device, this configuration promotes tremendous connectivity and interaction but also has its downfalls. While it is extremely convenient to be able to engage in a video chat with a spouse halfway across the country or host a website to be viewed from all seven continents, these same Internet capabilities also allow a hacker to attack a bank, electrical grid, or any other Internet-connected device with ease and without leaving the comfort of the hacker's own home. Past strains of malware have exploited this connectivity and were able to infect millions of computers in a very short time. The same Internet that enables tremendous innovation also facilitates unprecedented opportunities for those who seek to do harm.

2.4.8 World Wide Web

The Internet is often confused with the World Wide Web (WWW) because WWW is the most common Internet-based entity with which users can directly interact. The WWW (or the web) is actually only a part of the Internet and consists of a large number of servers, each identified by a hostname. Each server contains documents that can be accessed using a document address. The web has had the largest impact of any Internet-based entity, and its development has driven many of the newest technological changes. In many ways, the web has been the catalyst for the pervasive Internet access that we now experience and has transformed the Internet from a network used by researchers and academicians to a network for the masses.

Because of its large number of servers and even larger number of users, the web has also become a primary target for hackers. Before we can look at protecting ourselves, we need to understand the basic structure of the web and the applications that support it. Figure 2.23 shows how a document is addressed within the web.

As seen in Figure 2.23, a Bob provides a document address, called a Uniform Resource Locator (URL), using the hostname of the server and

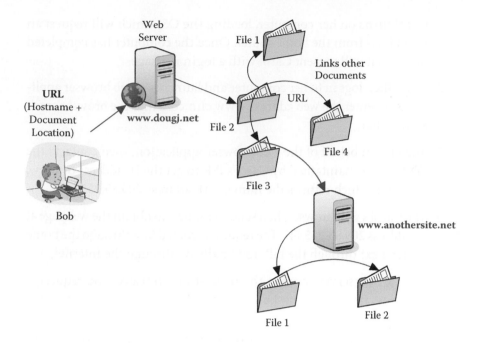

FIGURE 2.23   Document addressing in the World Wide Web.

the location of the document within that server; that is, the URL uniquely identifies a document within the web. Documents can contain links, called hyperlinks, to other URLs as well as to other documents. A web designer uses hyperlinks to create a path or series of paths that provide a way for the user to navigate freely through the documents stored on the web server. Hyperlinks can also link to files on other web servers. The web was not designed to have a central index to keep track of the location of documents, and as a result and to fill this need, popular search engines like Google Search and Bing provide this function. A search engine visits websites, examines documents, and catalogs their contents and may follow hyperlinks to gather additional content. The information gathered may be searched to provide answers to user queries. Search engines are thus websites that produce a list of hyperlinks to web documents to match a user's query.

2.5 COMPUTERS AND THE INTERNET

Figure 2.24 ties together the many concepts presented in this chapter. The diagram in Figure 2.24 shows Carol using her computer to read news from CNN's website. Steps involved in getting to CNN's homepage are outlined as follows:

1. Carol turns on her computer, loading the OS, which will request an IP address from the home router. Once the computer has completed booting, it will present Carol with a login message.

2. Carol then logs in to her computer and launches a web browser application to enter the web address www.cnn.com into the browser's web address bar.

3. The OS, on behalf of the web browser application, then contacts the DNS server maintained by Carol's ISP to get the IP address of www.cnn.com, which returns the numeric IP address 209.85.255.147.

4. The Carol's web browser then sends a request to obtain the webpage at IP address 209.85.255.147. The request is routed first through the home router, next through the ISP, and finally on through the Internet.

5. CNN's web server receives the request and retrieves the requested webpage from its own hard drive. The web server then sends this webpage back to Carol using the IP address of Carol's router (207.45.15.10). Carol's router then routes the reply to Carol's computer at IP address 192.168.1.10.

6. Once received, the web browser on Carol's computer displays the webpage from CNN.

A similar series of steps is used for every communication operation on the Internet.

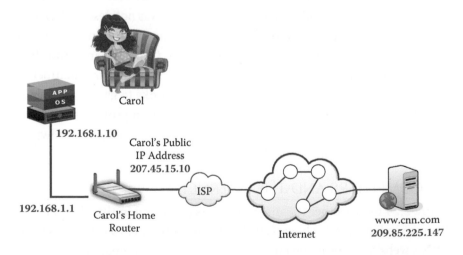

FIGURE 2.24 Accessing a webpage on the Internet.

2.6 SECURITY ROLE-PLAYING CHARACTERS

As various security-oriented scenarios are examined throughout the book, it is helpful to introduce role-playing characters to give these scenarios something of a real-life aspect. There will be two groups of such characters, the good characters and the bad characters. The good characters are named Alice, Bob, and Carol, and the bad characters are named Eavesdropper Eve, Malicious Mallory, Phishing Phil, and Intruder Trudy.

Figure 2.25 depicts the interactions between the good and bad security characters. The scenarios are illustrated to show a network diagram of Internet-based attacks. Even though Malicious Mallory is associated with Alice in this figure, this interaction is not exclusive as Mallory could just as well send a malicious message to Bob or Carol.

As shown in Figure 2.25, Eavesdropper Eve can intercept or eavesdrop on the messages that Carol sends over a coffee shop wireless network (a wireless network is denoted by dashed lines). Therefore, if Carol is having

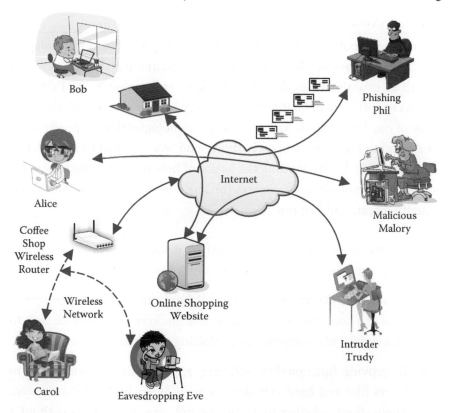

FIGURE 2.25   Security role-playing characters in action.

a conversation with Bob or communicating with an online shopping website, Eve has the ability to passively monitor these interactions (Chapter 9). The objective of Malicious Mallory is to send malicious messages (i.e., emails or instant messages) to Alice with the hopes that Alice clicks on a hyperlink or opens a document attached to Mallory's malicious messages. The goal of Mallory is to infect Alice's computer with malware (Chapter 6). Intruder Trudy is a skilled hacker and has the ability to hack into computers like an online shopping web server to steal confidential information. Last but not least is Phishing Phil, who sends deceiving (phishing) emails or messages to Bob. Phishing Phil hopes that Bob either responds to his requests for personal information or clicks on hyperlinks to fake websites created by Phishing Phil and then errantly enters his username and password. Throughout the remainder of the book, Alice, Bob, and Carol battle the evil forces of Eve, Malory, Trudy, and Phil.

2.7 SUMMARY

Although computers and the Internet are often thought of as technologies that help make peoples' lives better, the same technology that affords such amenities can also be exploited by hackers and malware. As President Obama so aptly said in his 2009 Cyber Policy Review speech: "It's the great irony of our Information Age—the very technologies that empower us to create and to build also empower those who would disrupt and destroy" (Obama, 2009). Understanding the basics of how these technologies work provides the much-needed context for more in-depth discussions about security threats and best practices.

- A general computer is composed of a basic four-layer structure: hardware, operating system (OS), applications, and the user.

- Because the OS has control over all hardware and software operations of a computer, it is common that hackers and malware seek to gain control of a computer by exploiting OS vulnerabilities.

- To provide functionality, software applications are often able to access files and hardware devices such as an Internet connection. Applications, whether malicious or not, can often do so without a user's knowledge or interaction.

- The Internet is a vast network of billions of geographically dispersed computers located around the world and networked together by several tiers of ISPs.

- The Internet is often conceptually thought of as a black box, with information flowing from the user's computer into the box as well as from the box back to the user's computer. Practical computer security is principally concerned with security attacks that originate from the Internet and threaten individual computers rather than attacks against the Internet itself.

- The Internet and its supporting technologies were not invented with security as a top priority, and it was not envisioned that the Internet would evolve to its current capacity.

- Using globally unique IP addresses, computers are able to connect to each other via the Internet by way of standardized networking protocols.

- The addressing of computers and the routing of Internet traffic are analogous to the postal system.

- Since people work better with meaningful names rather than long numerical IP addresses, Domain Name Servers (DNSs) translate numerical IP addresses (129.33.22.1) into names like ebay.com, google.com, iastate.edu, for example.

- The Network Address Translation (NAT) devices, often found in home routers, create private networks and expand the number of devices able to connect to the Internet.

- When web requests are routed through the Internet, they are literally routed through several geographically disperse routers that lie in between the requesting computer and the destination server.

- The World Wide Web is a single component of a much larger set of services that compose the Internet. Because it is so widely used, the WWW is a prime target for hackers and cyber criminals.

- Since all computers are connected to the same Internet, they all technically possess the capability to be able to communicate with each other and thus also possess the capability to attack each other.

BIBLIOGRAPHY

Cheswick, W., Bellovin, S., and Rubin, A. 2003. *Firewalls and Internet Security: Repelling the Wily Hacker*. Boston: Addison-Wesley Professional.

Damien, J. 2011. *Introduction to Computers and Application Software*. Sudbury, MA: Jones & Bartlett Learning.

Jacobson, D. 2009. *Introduction to Network Security*. Boca Raton, FL: Chapman & Hall/CRC.

Kurose, J., and Ross, K. 2006. *Computer Networking: Complete Package*. Boston: Addison-Wesley Longman.

Menn, J. 2010. *Fatal System Error*. New York: PublicAffairs.

Motavalli, J. 2010. The dozens of computers that make modern cars go (and stop). *New York Times*. http://www.nytimes.com/2010/02/05/technology/05electronics.html?_r=1 (accessed April 3, 2012).

Net Applications. 2012. Market share. http://marketshare.hitslink.com/ (accessed March 23, 2012).

Remarks by the president on securing our nation's cyber infrastructure. 2009. http://www.whitehouse.gov/the-press-office/remarks-president-securing-our-nations-cyber-infrastructure (accessed April 23, 2012).

Tanenbaum, A.S. 2003. *Computer Networks*. Englewood Cliffs, NJ: Prentice Hall.

Vance, A. 2010. British chip designer prepares for wider demand. *New York Times*. http://www.nytimes.com/2010/09/20/technology/20arm.html?pagewanted=all (accessed April 3, 2012).

Yu, E. 2012. Zynga confirms Draw Something acquisition. ZDNet. http://www.zdnetasia.com/zynga-confirms-draw-something-acquisition-62304260.htm (accessed April 3, 2012).

CHAPTER 3

Passwords Under Attack

3.1 INTRODUCTION

Just as a lock and key are used to protect against unauthorized access to a home, passwords provide the same type of access control for computers and online accounts. Like the possession of a key, the secrecy of a password is often the only barrier that separates the private and confidential information found in bank, personal email, and online shopping accounts, to name a few, from those who seek to do harm. With so much valuable information protected by knowledge of a single password, it should come as no surprise that passwords are routinely attacked and from every conceivable angle. These attacks can be both creative and effective, targeting not only the passwords but also password owners, who are often susceptible to errantly disclosing their passwords. Being aware of password threats and having the ability to identify threats that you and your passwords will encounter is essential for the safe everyday use of information technology (IT).

When tasked with creating a password, many people are accustomed to rules such as those shown in Figure 3.1. A common misconception is that, by following these rules, one has effectively mitigated all password threats. While these rules are certainly important, they alone are not sufficient to achieve sound password security. In fact, these rules are only a small piece of a much larger, but seldom discussed, body of knowledge that composes practical password security. This chapter examines the many password threats, how to keep passwords secret, how to choose strong passwords, and last but not least, methods to assist in effectively managing the many passwords that one needs to remember to function in everyday life.

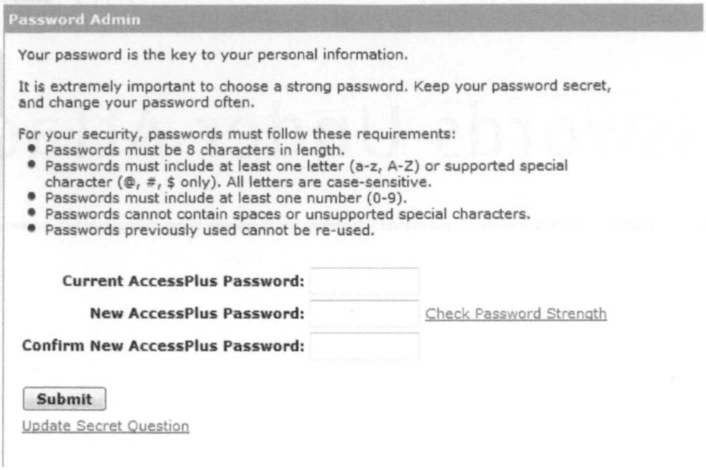

Password Admin

Your password is the key to your personal information.

It is extremely important to choose a strong password. Keep your password secret, and change your password often.

For your security, passwords must follow these requirements:
* Passwords must be 8 characters in length.
* Passwords must include at least one letter (a-z, A-Z) or supported special character (@, #, $ only). All letters are case-sensitive.
* Passwords must include at least one number (0-9).
* Passwords cannot contain spaces or unsupported special characters.
* Passwords previously used cannot be re-used.

Current AccessPlus Password:

New AccessPlus Password: Check Password Strength

Confirm New AccessPlus Password:

Submit

Update Secret Question

FIGURE 3.1   Password creation rules.

3.2 AUTHENTICATION PROCESS

For accessing computers, Internet-based services, and mobile devices, the coupling of a username and a password forms a digital identity. Authentication is the process of proving one's right to assume this identity. Access is granted to an account if one can respond with the correct username and password when challenged by a login screen. This granting of access is what makes password security so essential. An attacker, armed with the knowledge of your username and password, can assume your digital identity and perform actions with all of the same privileges that you have as the account owner. In other words, the attacker becomes you (i.e., identity theft). To provide a foundation for better understanding password security and the many threats that passwords face, the mechanics of the authentication process are examined in the context of accessing an online shopping website.

Interacting with websites involves the sending and receiving of information through the Internet. As a result and as shown in Figure 3.2, any information, such as a username and password, submitted by Alice on a given online shopping website is routed through the Internet to the computer (i.e., web server) that hosts a given website. Although the authentication process is initiated on Alice's computer, the actual verification of the username and password combination takes place on the online retailer's web server. Thus, such a web server (or underlying systems) is responsible

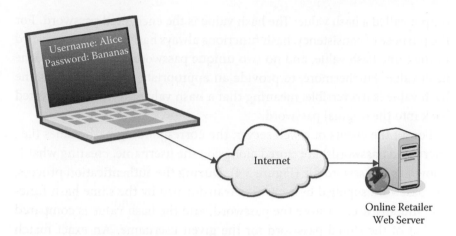

FIGURE 3.2   Authentication network diagram.

for both storing clients' passwords and determining if a password and username combination is correct for each authentication attempt.

When creating a web-based account for an online shopping website, for example, Alice is prompted to supply a username and a corresponding password. While the username, a unique identifier, is generally not regarded as a secret, the password most certainly is. To allow Alice to log in to the account at a later time, the online retailer (e.g., amazon.com or overstock.com) must store not only Alice's but also its other clients' passwords on their servers for future use. To keep their clients' passwords secret from both bad guys (i.e., hackers, malicious insiders) and good guys (i.e., system administrators), passwords are encrypted by means of a hash function during the initial password creation process, as seen in Figure 3.3. A hash function is a one-way transformation of data that produces a random

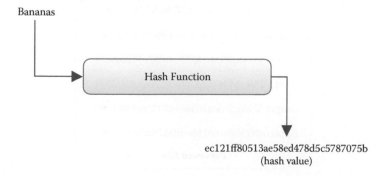

FIGURE 3.3   Password hash example.

output called a hash value: The hash value is the encrypted password. For the purpose of consistency, hash functions always hash the same password to the same hash value, and no two unique passwords result in the same hash value. Furthermore, to provide an appropriate level of security, the hash value is irreversible, meaning that a hash value cannot be converted back into the original password.

For all the clients of a web server, the corresponding hash values (i.e., encrypted passwords) are stored alongside the username, creating what is known as a password file (Figure 3.4). During the authentication process, the password supplied by a client is transformed by the same hash function initially used to store the password, and the hash value is compared to that of the stored password for the given username. An exact match indicates that the correct password has been entered and thus represents a successful authentication. As seen in Figure 3.5, even a slight deviation in the password creates a completely different hash value that does not match the stored value, indicating that an incorrect password has been entered.

From an attacker's perspective, there are three primary ways to defeat this type of authentication system. The first method is for the attacker to guess the password for a given username using the publically accessible online login webpage. The second method is for the attacker to steal the password file from the web-based service provider and, if the passwords are encrypted with a hash function, employ the services of a password-guessing program. These programs are also known as password crackers because they "crack" the hashed values to reveal the plaintext passwords

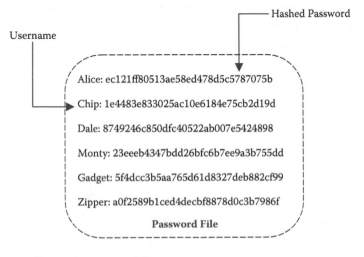

FIGURE 3.4   Example password file.

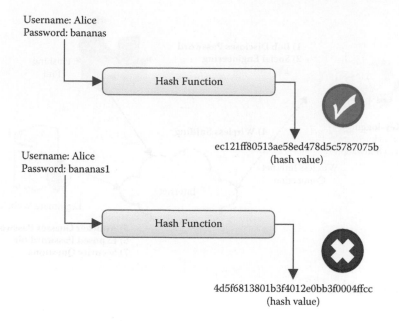

Username: Alice
Password: bananas

Hash Function

ec121ff80513ae58ed478d5c5787075b
(hash value)

Username: Alice
Password: bananas1

Hash Function

4d5f6813801b3f4012e0bb3f0004ffcc
(hash value)

FIGURE 3.5   Password hash comparison.

(more on this later). The third method is for an attacker simply to learn, steal, observe, or trick the owner of the password into inadvertently disclosing a password in plaintext (i.e., not encrypted). The next section of this chapter examines the ways in which these threats are realized.

3.3 PASSWORD THREATS

There is a distinct difference between choosing a strong password and keeping that password confidential. A *strong* password is chosen in such a way that neither a human nor a computer would be likely to successfully guess the password in any reasonable amount of time. While strength is a necessary condition for a secure password, password strength alone is not sufficient. Preserving the *secrecy* or not providing an accidental revelation of a password to an attacker are just as important, if not more so, than choosing a strong password.

The following section describes the many threats passwords face, so one should pay close attention to which of these threats are mitigated by password strength and which are mitigated by password secrecy. Figure 3.6 provides a graphical depiction of the common ways through which attackers guess, steal, learn, or observe passwords. This figure serves as a guide for the examination of password threats and best practices.

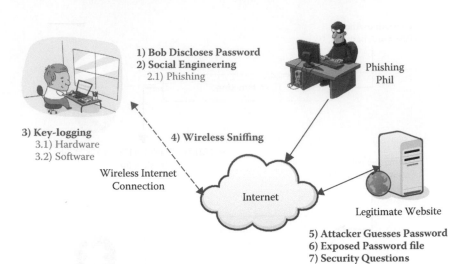

FIGURE 3.6   Common password threats.

3.3.1 Bob Discloses Password

Passwords by their very nature are secrets, and when such a secret is revealed to another person, the knowledge cannot be directly controlled or unlearned—thus it is no longer a secret. A common way of losing password secrecy is simply to tell it or allow it to be discovered by another person. For many reasons, it is best never to reveal your personal passwords to anyone— not a friend, girlfriend, boyfriend, uncle, classmate, coworker, or stranger requesting your password over the phone. If you are unable to keep your password a secret, how do you expect someone else to do the same?

The same advice goes for emailing or texting a password to another person. Once you have created and given away a copy of your password, there is no way to effectively manage the recipient's copy or knowledge of the password. Furthermore, as discussed in Chapter 4 (on email) and Chapter 9 (on wireless Internet security), passwords sent via email are typically sent in clear text and can often be observed by eavesdropping (i.e., sniffing) on an unsecure wireless connection. It is also good security practice never to write a password on a sticky note and place it on a monitor, underneath a keyboard or office chair, or in an unlocked desk drawer. Such practices defeat the purpose of the password, and both attackers and corporate security auditors are smart enough to look in such places. If you do either purposefully or inadvertently disclose your password to someone else, you should change it immediately.

There is an ongoing debate over whether to better manage passwords by writing them down in a notebook, for example. Some security experts say to write your passwords down, while others cautions against it. Neither is totally correct or incorrect. Password management is a pragmatic exercise for which there are no absolute rules. If writing passwords down in a list allows you to choose stronger, more secure passwords and if that list can be stored in a safe place, then it might in some cases be beneficial. However, if a password list were at all in danger of being exposed, found by a roommate, or accidentally left in a coffee shop, conventional wisdom would suggest that an alternative password management technique would be more effective (Section 3.5).

3.3.2 Social Engineering

In many cases, it is actually much easier for an attacker simply to ask the user for a password than it is to attempt to compromise a computer system or perform a guessing attack. In such activity, known as social engineering, an attacker will often call an unsuspecting victim, perhaps posing as a corporate IT worker in a pickle or as a graduate student from Yale conducting research for a dissertation. After providing a convincing backstory to match the fake identity, the attacker then claims to need the victim's password for one reason or another. If the victim is fooled and reveals the password to the attacker, the password is no longer a secret.

Legitimate companies will never phone or email customers to ask for their login credentials. Just as you would not give the keys to your home to a person sitting next to you on a bus, you should not give your password away to a stranger who solicits it, no matter how convincing his or her story may be. Phone-based solicitation of passwords is just one example of a much larger class of social engineering attacks. With respect to practical computer security, social engineering and its many types of attack require a chapter of their own (Chapter 11).

3.3.2.1 Phishing

One of the most prevalent and effective ways for a cyber criminal to steal a person's username and password is through a phishing attack—a form of social engineering. Phishing is similar to its homophonic counterpart, fishing, in the sense that the attacker sends out "bait" in the form of phishing emails that appear to come from trusted institutions like a bank. As shown in Figure 3.7, Phishing Phil sends a phishing email to Alice supposedly from her bank claiming that Alice needs to "Reset your password" (Step 1). Phishing

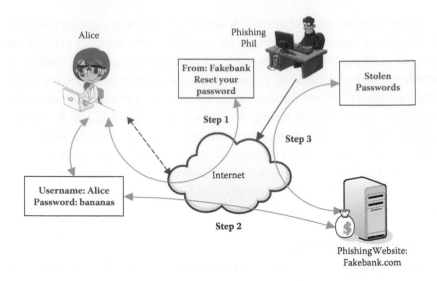

FIGURE 3.7 Phishing attack steals password.

Phil hopes that Alice will be fooled by the fake email, take the bait, and click on a misleading hyperlink. As the result of clicking on the hyperlink in the phishing email, Alice is taken to a phony website (fakebank.com)—usually an impressive mimic of an authentic site—and is asked to verify her username and password for her online bank account. However, when Alice submits her login credentials, they are not sent to her bank's website, but instead to Phil's phishing website (Step 2). Phil's phishing website then records these stolen passwords. Every so often, Phishing Phil logs in to his phishing website and collects the stolen passwords. Phishing Phil can then either sell this information or use it for his own malevolent purposes (Step 3).

Phishing attacks can be quite sophisticated and hard to detect. As a general rule, one should never enter a password on a website after clicking on a hyperlink in an email, instant message, or advertisement. While not all hyperlinks result in phishing attacks, it is best to get into the habit of going directly to websites requiring authentication by personally typing in the website address or by using a trusted bookmark in your web browser.

In addition to directing users to phony websites, phishing attacks may seek to obtain passwords by having victims reply to a phony email with their password. As a result, it is never good security practice to email (or text) a password to anyone for any reason. Again, once a password has been emailed to another person—attacker or not—you lose control of how that information is handled and disseminated.

3.3.3 Key-Logging

Keystroke logging, or *key-logging*, is the act of maliciously and covertly recording keystrokes made on a computer keyboard. On the surface, this threat might appear to be taken straight out of a spy movie. However, the threat of key-logging is actually quite real, and this method of attack is quickly increasing in popularity among hackers because of the value of the sensitive information that can be obtained in this way.

Keyboard loggers can be implemented and deployed both as hardware and as software. A hardware key-logger is a small, inconspicuous device—similar-looking to a USB (Universal Serial Bus) flash drive—that is inserted between the keyboard and a computer (Figure 3.8). The task of a key-logger is simply to record every keystroke typed on the keyboard. Because the hardware key-logger sits in-line with the cord that connects the keyboard to the computer, the key-logger is able simply to record keystrokes as they are typed, an action that is undetectable by a user or the computer. Typically, such hardware devices are quite difficult to spot with an untrained eye. When placed on a computer in high-volume login areas such as a library, hotel lobby, or a public coffee shop, these devices can be quite devastating, capturing hordes of passwords and sensitive

FIGURE 3.8 Hardware key-logger.

information in a matter of hours. Adding to the threat, hardware key-loggers possess enough storage to record keystrokes for up to a year's time.

Software key-loggers, on the other hand, are malicious software programs that perform the same function of recording keystrokes but instead insert themselves into a computer's operating system as spyware. In comparison to their hardware counterpart, software key-loggers are not restricted to external keyboards connected via cords and thus are also threats to laptop users. Furthermore, unlike hardware key-loggers that require the attacker to physically insert and remove the device, software key-loggers can be installed and used to relay stolen information back to the cyber criminal via the Internet. The attacker can thus avoid being in physical proximity to the crime scene.

The threat of key-loggers is the motivation of why you should strongly refrain from typing passwords or other sensitive information on computers that you do not control or trust. This statement is valid for any computer found in a store, library, hotel lobby, or coffee shop and pertains to friends' or coworkers' computers. The same is true for your own computer if you believe it to be infected with malware (more on malware in Chapter 5). There is no telling what type of key-logging malware might be installed on an unsecure or untrusted computer, and typing a password on such a computer could likely result in a loss of password secrecy.

3.3.4 Wireless Sniffing

Analogous to discovering a secret by eavesdropping on a telephone conversation, the act of *sniffing* captures data as it travels to and from a computer over a wireless Internet connection (Chapter 9). In a sniffing attack, hackers are able to use a laptop and readily available free software programs to enable the laptop to become a listening device for all wireless Internet traffic to and from a given wireless router (Figure 3.9). Attackers are able to see both what is submitted to a website (i.e., username and password) and what web requests may return (i.e., the contents of an email). To the attacker who is sniffing wireless Internet traffic, it is almost as if the attacker is sitting behind you, watching every move you make on the web over your shoulder. If such an act were, however, carried out in a more literal sense—an attacker was able to physically watch a victim type their password—this loss of password confidentiality is known as *shoulder surfing*. The threat of shoulder surfing, especially in busy coffee shops or on an airplane, is a real danger as some people are adept at this skill.

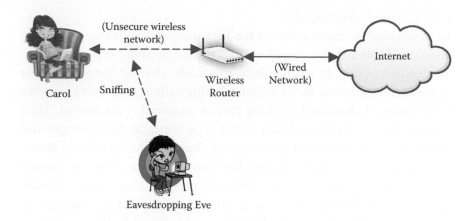

FIGURE 3.9   Sniffing for sensitive information.

Unlike key-logging, which records every stroke on the keyboard whether the computer is connected to the Internet or not, a sniffing attack is limited only to data that travels to and from the Internet. Offline actions performed on a computer, such as editing a word-processing document, for example, are not vulnerable to sniffing attacks since they are not transmitted over the Internet.

The primary objective of this type of attack is for the attacker to passively observe data in the hope of capturing passwords and other types of sensitive information like credit card or Social Security numbers. Usually, sniffing attacks occur over unsecure wireless connections like those found in public libraries, coffee shops, or hotels. The threat of sniffing is why it is never a good idea to submit confidential information over such a presumably unsecure wireless Internet connection. Chapter 9 describes this type of attack in more detail.

3.3.5 Attacker Guesses Password

Because online login webpages are accessible to anyone with a computer and an Internet connection, there always exists the threat that a password for a given username can be randomly discovered by means of a guessing attack. In respect to guessing passwords, there are typically two types of attacks employed by attackers: brute force and dictionary attacks. Each of these attack types is discussed in the context of practical password security. This discussion implicitly provides a foundation for understanding how to better choose or construct passwords resilient to such attacks.

3.3.5.1 Brute-Force Guessing

Brute force is the name given to the first password-guessing attack discussed, and this attack is played out exactly as one would expect from the self-descriptive title. In a brute-force attack, the attacker simply attempts to guess the password to an account by logically trying every possible combination of characters until the correct password is discovered. Time becomes the most limiting factor in this type of attack. As the length and complexity of the password increase, and thus also the number of guessing attempts that a successful attacker must make, so does the amount of time taken to guess all conceivable sequences of characters. Consider Figure 3.10, which shows the time required to guess every password of a given length and with varying character combinations. In this example, it is assumed that the attacker is capable of guessing 1 million passwords per second—an incredibly ambitious assumption for a web-based login site. As in Figure 3.10, increasing the password length and character diversity exponentially increases the amount of time necessary to guess every password.

Many corporations providing web-based services are well aware of this type of attack and install authentication defense mechanisms. A popular type of defense is to lock an account after three—or some other relatively small number—of failed login attempts. This defensive scheme to prevent guessing attacks is similar to one used in ATMs that consume a debit card after three failed login attempts. While this effectively limits brute-force attacks for web logins, it provides a potential complication for users who have trouble remembering passwords—an example of how security can be at odds with convenience.

Another defense mechanism used to prevent automated attacking on websites is using a **C**ompletely **A**utomated **P**ublic **T**uring test to tell

Length of the Password (in characters)	Lowercase Letters Only	Uppercase and Lowercase Letters Combined	Uppercase and Lowercase Letters Combined with Numbers	All Characters
<= 4	Instantly	7 seconds	15 seconds	1 minute
5	12 seconds	6 minutes	15 minutes	2 hours
6	5 minutes	5 hours	16 hours	7 days
7	2 hours	12 days	41 days	2 years
8	2 days	2 years	7 years	177 years
9	63 days	88 years	430 years	16500 years
10	4 years	4580 years	26600 years	1530000 years

FIGURE 3.10   Relative password strength (approximate times).

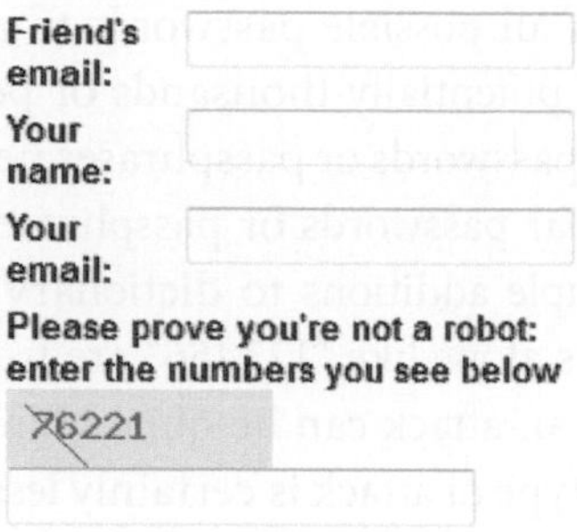

Friend's
email:

Your
name:

Your
email:

Please prove you're not a robot:
enter the numbers you see below

76221

FIGURE 3.11   Example CAPTCHA.

Computers and **H**umans **A**part, more briefly known as a CAPTCHA. Encountered by most Internet users, a CAPTCHA distinguishes computers from humans by asking a user seeking authentication to solve a puzzle or correctly identify a set of distorted characters like those seen in Figure 3.11. CAPTCHA puzzles are designed to be simple for humans to decipher and difficult for computers to interpret correctly. While it is debatable how easy these puzzles actually are for users to solve, this type of security mechanism is often able to successfully prevent automated brute-force attacks carried out by computers, but again at the expense of user convenience.

As seen in the results of the brute-force attack scenarios described in Figure 3.10, a password composed of all possible character types and eight or more characters in length would take on average more than a lifetime to crack with a brute-force attack using today's technology. The lesson to be learned from the discussion of such attacks is that it is infeasible for an attacker to randomly guess a password given that the user chooses a strong, eight-character password. Well aware of the amount of time required for a successful brute-force attack, hackers have adapted their methods to increase the likelihood of successfully discovering a password in significantly less time. In what is known as a *dictionary attack*, the attacker tries to systematically guess commonly used and weak passwords, knowing that strong passwords are virtually unguessable.

3.3.5.2 Dictionary Attacks

Despite the fact that the choice of a password is often a private undertaking, it has been shown time and time again that people tend to follow very similar conventions when selecting a password, and many users tend to choose the same passwords as one another. A dictionary attack, a more sophisticated adaptation of the brute-force attack, preys on this tendency by narrowing the scope of the attack from all possible passwords to a carefully crafted list. This list is composed of potentially thousands or perhaps millions of specifically chosen common passwords or passphrases people are known to use on a regular basis. Popular passwords or passphrases like "password," "iloveyou," or "letmein"; simple additions to dictionary words like "password123"; and plain numbers alone like "123456" are frequently used. The potential for success of such an attack can be quite high in comparison to brute-force attacks, and this type of attack is certainly less time consuming.

The methodology of brute-force and dictionary attacks can also be extended to include information that an attacker can accumulate about a specific user beyond that of what is known about the password habits of the general population. With the aid of specialized software, the attacker can attempt to guess passwords to an account by using specific knowledge obtained either through their personal relationship with the victim or through information gleaned from public disclosures on social networking sites or even by way of search engine queries of the target's name. Stop and think; could someone conceivably guess your password based on information about you posted on a social networking site or from the information returned by a simple web search? If so, your password may not be as strong as you thought.

3.3.6 Exposed Password File

There is no such thing as absolute security, and as a result, legitimate websites and corporations large and small are susceptible to hacking incidents that can result in loss of their customers' passwords. As a user of a web service, not only must you be responsible for your own password management practices, but also you must be security conscious toward those managing your passwords. This section presents three case studies of password files being stolen. In the first case, the client passwords were not encrypted with a hash function, and in the second two cases they were. As discussed, even encrypted passwords do not guarantee secrecy.

3.3.6.1 Password File: Not Encrypted

In December 2009, the website of social media services provider RockYou was breached, and the passwords of 32 million users were stolen by a wily attacker. In this incident, a single hacker was able to compromise the RockYou password database. Unfortunately for RockYou's users, their passwords were not encrypted by a hash function, and the list of usernames—the users' email addresses—and corresponding plaintext passwords were posted on the web for all to see. To date, this is one of the single largest public disclosures of passwords, and the incident has provided security professionals and attackers alike with a unique glimpse of the most frequently chosen user passwords. Figure 3.12 lists the 32 most common passwords leaked from this incident, collectively accounting for nearly 1 million of the 32 million total passwords. At first glance, this list appears quite humorous; the passwords are relatively trivial and lack complexity. With the prevalence of password advice and increased public awareness of identity theft and cyber crimes, why do so many people continue to choose such simple passwords? One explanation—an optimistic one—is that the users of this website do not view RockYou as a high-security account warranting a complex password. On the other hand, this password list could also be viewed as a representation of the current state of password security or lack thereof.

It can be argued that this list of passwords may not be representative of the habits exhibited by all cyber citizens, but it does provide interesting and helpful insights into what would otherwise be considered secret knowledge. Password lists such as the one revealed in the RockYou incident are often used in dictionary attacks because they provide a useful summary of common passwords. If the password to your bank account or any other sensitive account appears on the list in Figure 3.12, it would be wise to act

Rank	Password	Rank	Password
1	123456	17	michael
2	12345	18	ashley
3	123456789	19	654321
4	password	20	qwerty
5	iloveyou	21	iloveu
6	princess	22	michelle
7	rockyou	23	111111
8	1234567	24	0
9	12345678	25	tigger
10	abc123	26	password1
11	nicole	27	sunshine
12	daniel	28	chocolate
13	babygirl	29	anthony
14	monkey	30	angel
15	jessica	31	FRIENDS
16	lovely	32	soccer

FIGURE 3.12   Most popular RockYou passwords.

immediately to change your password as soon as you are finished with this chapter because these are the passwords attackers will try first.

Corporations and websites alike have and will continue to be susceptible to hacking incidents that result in the disclosure of their clients' passwords. Some of these incidents have been made public, while others have not. The RockYou incident is a prime example of why it is good security practice to change passwords to your accounts from time to time. Even if a password is exposed, by changing the password you are limiting the time window during which the password can be successfully used.

3.3.6.2 Password File: Encrypted

Similar to the RockYou incident, in January 2012 hackers were able to compromise the servers of online retailer Zappos and stole 24 million user names, email and billing addresses, phone numbers, partial credit numbers, and password hashes. Unlike RockYou, however, the Zappos passwords were encrypted using a hash function as described in Section 3.2. Although hash functions provide encryption, certainly better than storing passwords in plaintext, hash functions only provide secrecy for strong passwords. To crack password hashes, attackers use what is known as a password cracker—a software program that discovers passwords for known hash values.

Although hash values are irreversible, this does not stop an attacker from hashing known passwords and comparing them to the hash values found in a stolen password list. The hash functions used to encrypt passwords are known to the world, meaning that anyone—good guy or bad guy—can obtain a hash value for a given password with the same hash function used by Zappos. Based on this knowledge, and with the aid of software, password cracking is the process of discovering which password hashes are transformed into which hash values. As shown in Figure 3.13, password cracking is similar to the authentication process; however, instead of comparing a password hash value for a single username, the password-cracking software compares the test hash value to all hash values in the password list. If a test password hash is the same value as a hash value found in the password list, the password has been learned.

There are many free, legal to own, and downloadable software cracking programs able to take a password list as an input and output plaintext passwords. Even though these programs exist, all is not lost for those whose username and hash values are exposed. As previously discussed, hackers perform two types of guessing attacks: brute-force and dictionary attacks.

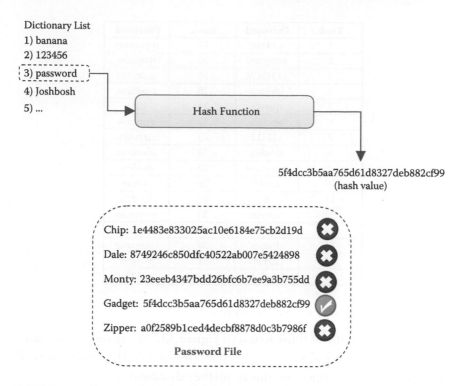

FIGURE 3.13   Password-cracking dictionary attack.

It should be no surprise that password-cracking software like John-the-Ripper, L0phtCrack, or Cain and Abel employ the exact same methodology. Often, password-cracking attempts will first perform a dictionary attack using known and popular passwords. In 2010, this is how the hackers who breached Gawker Media's password file containing 1.3 million hashed passwords for online services like Lifehacker and Gizmodo were able to crack, and post on the Internet, nearly 200,000 cracked passwords soon after the hacking incident occurred. Similar to the results from the RockYou incident, Figure 3.14 lists the most popular passwords discovered in the Gawker breach.

In addition to that of a dictionary attack, a password cracker often will use a brute-force attack to discover passwords that may not be in the dictionary list but are short enough to guess. In this scenario, Figure 3.10 is more applicable since password-cracking software is typically able to guess hundreds of thousands—if not more, depending on the computers used—of passwords per second. For strong passwords, however, brute-force guessing still takes a great deal of time. To avoid falling victim to password-cracking software, it is important not to pick a password

Rank	Password	Rank	Password
1	123456	17	superman
2	password	18	iloveyou
3	12345678	19	gizmodo
4	lifehack	20	sunshine
5	qwerty	21	1234
6	abc123	22	princess
7	111111	23	starwars
8	monkey	24	whatever
9	consumer	25	shadow
10	12345	26	cheese
11	0	27	123123
12	letmein	28	nintendo
13	trustno1	29	football
14	dragon	30	computer
15	1234567	31	f---you
16	baseball	32	654321

FIGURE 3.14   Most used Gawker passwords.

remotely close to any of those found in Figure 3.12 or Figure 3.14 and also to choose a password of at least eight characters in length that contains all character categories (more on this in further discussion).

In addition to choosing a strong password, it is important to choose a *unique* password. As exemplified with the two password guessing attacks, even if a password is strong enough to prevent brute-force guessing, if that same password happens to have been used by another user and finds its way onto a dictionary list, the password will be easily cracked. Thus, uniqueness is a quality of password strength that must also be taken into account. For example, the password "TouchThemAllKirbyPuckett1991" may appear to be resistant to brute-force guessing, but to fans of the 1991 Minnesota Twins such a password may be common and thus such a password is not "strong."

The rules shown in Figure 3.1 are provided to help prevent against dictionary and brute-force guessing attacks. However, without the context of these password-guessing attacks, it is difficult for one to infer exactly what these rules are protecting against. Further, the RockYou, Zappos, and Gawker Media examples show why it is never a good idea to use the same username and password combination for multiple websites. Even though the users in each of the case studies did nothing wrong, their login credentials, quite possibly the same credentials used for multiple websites (email, bank, social networking, etc.), were exposed by hackers, with many of these passwords being posted on the web for all to see. By choosing different passwords for different websites, a victim can effectively limit the impact of a single exposed password.

3.3.7 Security Questions

One side effect of having to choose and remember many passwords for multiple accounts is that people forget passwords from time to time. To automate password recovery, many websites offer a manual mechanism allowing a user either to recover or to reset his or her own password. While the mechanics of such password recovery systems differ from site to site, they typically share a common secondary form of authentication through use of a security question (Figure 3.15). Just as the primary password provides access to an account, the answer to a security question provides a second form of authentication for recovering a forgotten password. If the security question is answered correctly, some websites display the user's forgotten password directly on the webpage, while other websites may either require the user to reset the password or will email a new password to the user's registered email account.

From a convenience standpoint for the account owner, having the option to enter a secondary password based on an easy-to-remember question is a simple password recovery method. It is not surprising that hackers also find this retrieval method convenient. Instead of attempting to compromise a strong, 12-character password, it is much simpler for an attacker to learn or reset a password by performing a web search for the elementary school of a target's hometown or to browse public information on a social networking website for the name of a potential victim's dog. In fact, this is exactly what happened to the 2008 Republican vice presidential candidate, Sarah Palin. An amateur hacker was able to access Palin's Yahoo!

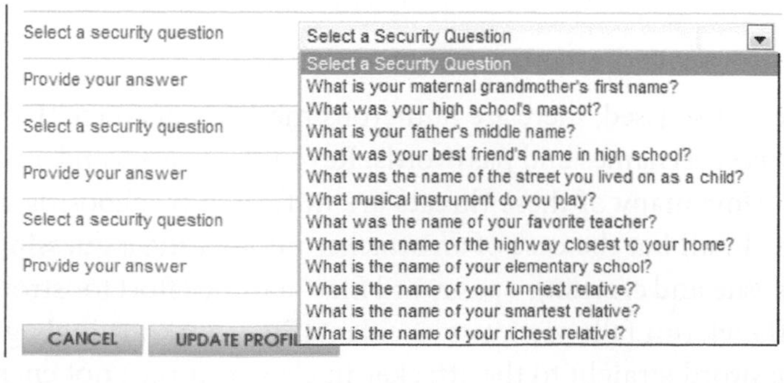

FIGURE 3.15 Security question prompt.

email account by providing her birthday and zip code as well as information about where she met her spouse (Wasilla High), which was the security question for her account. Using the results of a simple Google search, the attacker was able to gain access to all of the correspondence stored in Palin's Yahoo! account. Furthermore, the attacker locked Palin out of her own email account by changing her account password to "popcorn."

Keeping this example in mind, it should be apparent that the term *security question* is a bit of a misnomer. Although it provides a convenient means for password recovery, providing a predictable or publicly available response to a security question actually decreases the overall security of an online account that it is meant to protect. Instead of cracking the strong password that a user has established, the hacker is challenged only with answering a trivial question within which a clue is provided for finding the answer.

How should one proceed when confronted with the task of establishing the answer to a security question? The safest strategy, from an account security standpoint, is simply to lie. There is no penalty for answering the security question untruthfully. The objective of choosing a security question and answer is to avoid choosing a response that is easier to guess than the account's primary password. It is best to observe the same best practices when choosing the answer to a security question as you would for choosing a password in the first place.

For all those pranksters and aspiring hackers eager to attempt to guess the answer to a security question with intentions of accessing an account of a friend, relative, coworker, or celebrity, let this be your warning *not* to attempt to do so. The potential legal consequences are significant because this action may be a felony. The amateur hacker in the Palin example was caught and convicted of misdemeanor computer intrusion as well as obstruction of justice and sentenced to 1 year in custody and 3 years of probation.

3.3.8 Stop Attacking My Password

As has been discussed, there are numerous methods of attack that seek to compromise usernames and passwords. Revisit Figure 3.6 and answer the question: How many of these threats are mitigated by choosing a strong password? In all but the case of an attacker performing a guessing attack on the website and cracking a password file—a futile effort for strong passwords—the victim falls victim or accidentally or unknowingly gives his or her password straight to the attacker in clear text (i.e., not encrypted). In these cases, it does not matter how strong the password is because it is no longer a secret if the attacker learns the password directly through a key-logger, phishing attack, or stealing an unencrypted password file. While choosing a strong password is a necessary condition for password security, it has been shown that password strength is clearly not sufficient. Although this is seldom discussed, keeping a password a secret is just as important, if not more so, than picking a strong password in the first place.

3.4 STRONG PASSWORDS

The objective of creating a strong password is to prevent against many types of guessing attacks like brute-force or dictionary attacks. Before the construct of a strong password is discussed, keep in mind that a password must also be familiar and remembered easily enough to be recalled and typed accurately at a later time. Certainly the password "UW1llBv!@v31c0meD;" is strong and would be virtually unguessable; however, it would be difficult not only to remember but also to type accurately. Forgetting a strong password or accidentally locking oneself out of an account due to too many unsuccessful authentication attempts tends to increase the potential of choosing a less-secure and more easily remembered password as a replacement.

3.4.1 Creating Strong Passwords

Choosing a password is a pragmatic process, and an optimal solution does not exist for creating a password that is easy to recall when needed but strong enough that it cannot be easily guessed or cracked. The suggestions for generating a strong password presented in this chapter are meant to serve as a set of guidelines and provide an illustration of what is generally accepted as best practice for achieving password strength. Knowing that one must be able to recall a password at a later time, it is often convenient to start creating a password with a word or phrase in mind that is meaningful, such as a favorite location (i.e., Cape Cod) or band (i.e., Beach Boys). If the meaning behind the creation of the password tells a story, it is likely to be easier to recall at a later time, even if the final password deviates from its original form as a simple name or phrase (i.e., Cape Cod transformed into $$C@pe99C0d!).

- **Composition:** To protect against guessing attacks, use a mix of lowercase letters (a–z), uppercase letters (A–Z), numbers (0–9), and special characters (!@#$%^&*). As seen in Figure 3.10, intermixing these character types increases the strength of the password.

Example: "$$Cape99Cod!" or "($33)(BEeach78BOys)"

Note: Remember; let the password tell a story. For example, perhaps you attended a Beach Boys concert in 1978 and, remarkably, front row tickets were only $33. This is an easy story to remember, and the inclusion of all character groups adds strength to the password and provides resilience against brute-force attacks.

- **Substitution:** Substitute letters with similarly shaped numbers or special characters.

  Example: "$$Cape99Cod!" → "$$C@pe99C0d!"

  Note: This technique is effective, but be careful because it is well known to attackers that passwords such as "p@ssw0rd" and "m1cr0$0ft" are often used and thus are likely found in password lists for dictionary attacks. Instead, replace one or two letters from a complex phrase as shown in the previous example.

- **Acronyms:** Using a favorite set of song lyrics, a poem, or quotation, extract the first letter from each of the words in the passage, creating a string of seemingly random characters.

  Example: "All the single ladies, all the single ladies" → "Atslatsl"

  Note: Use the acronym method to create a base for your password, then use the substitution method to increase the password's strength and uniqueness.

  Example: "Atslatsl" → "@t$l@T$L"

- **Phonetic Replacement:** Replace parts of a word or phrase with a phonetic equivalent.

  Example: "I love to laugh" → "EyeLuv2L@ff"

  "How much money do I have?" → "#m$$du1H4ve?"

- **Encapsulation:** Use symbols or numbers to separate or encapsulate words or phrases.

  Example: "sunGlasses4" → "(sun)Glasses4"

  "footballTD" → "22football22*TD*"

- **Length:** The password length should be a minimum of eight characters. As seen in Figure 3.10, adding additional characters and increasing the diversity of the characters adds to the strength of the password.

- **Passphrase:** In contrast to creating a password, which suggests that the secret token consists of a single word, one could create a passphrase instead. A passphrase is a combined string of words that, taken together, forms a password. For example, maybe you grew up in northern Minnesota, are a Star Wars fanatic, and enjoy watching soccer. A possible resulting passphrase could be 10000LakesChewyDempsey. From a brute-force standpoint, such a passphrase would be virtually unguessable in one's lifetime, and it would be highly unlikely that such a passphrase would be found in a dictionary attack list. To add more strength to the password, one could add a few numbers, capitalization, or special characters. Perhaps easier to remember than a cryptic eight-character password, the length and randomness of the combined words provides a sound alternative and, at times, easier-to-remember option to use than a traditional password.

Example: Minnesota11trout11soccer or NewYork(Hotdog)Cannoli

Now that a series of conventions regarding how to choose strong passwords has been reviewed, the concentration now focuses on observing some important rules to avoid falling victim to common password pitfalls. A 10-character password composed of all 4-character groups is not automatically guaranteed to be a strong password.

- **Do NOT use trivial passwords.** Trivial passwords may be convenient to remember and type, but they are also convenient to guess. Any password listed in Figure 3.12 or Figure 3.14 or anything remotely close to those passwords is a weak password.

- **Do NOT use a password from an example of how to choose passwords.** Hackers are very well aware of the tendency of the general public to reuse passwords on popular password advice websites or in books. These passwords are often used as part of a dictionary attack. Consequently, then, all of the password examples used verbatim from this book are considered weak simply because they have been published.

Example: $$Cape99Cod! (weak) or ($33)(BEeach78BOys) (weak)

- **Do NOT create a password based on easily guessable personal information.** Although doing so may make your password easy for you to remember, the tendency of users to choose passwords based solely on the name of a pet, family birthdays, favorite sports teams, and children's names is well known, and choosing these easy-to-remember passwords may make it easier for an attacker to guess them. Likewise, a password should not be easily guessable based on information found on one's social networking page.

  Example: Vikings1998 (weak) or jessica111680 (weak)

- **Do NOT base a password solely on a dictionary word (in any language), popular phrase, or acronym.** The simple "base" + "suffix" technique of password creation in which the base is a dictionary word or phrase and the suffix is a series of numbers is well known to attackers.

  Example: password1 (weak) or letmein123 (weak)

- **Do NOT use keyboard patterns or a series of sequential numbers.** As seen in Figure 3.12 and Figure 3.14, "123456" was the most commonly used password in both the RockYou and Gawker incidents. Keyboard patterns such as "asdf," "qwerty," and "987654" are equally susceptible to attack. Similarly, do not construct passwords by shifting your hands to the left or right on a keyboard and then typing a common word or known password—attackers know people do this.

  Example: asdf (weak), qwerty (weak), 987654 (weak), [sddeotf (weak)

With a newly created password in hand, how does one measure the actual strength of the password? Microsoft provides a confidential online tool that allows users to check the strength of a password (https://www.microsoft.com/protect/fraud/passwords/checker.aspx). It should be noted that this service does not guarantee password security or uniqueness, but it does provide a good indication of the relative strength of a password.

3.5 PASSWORD MANAGEMENT: LET'S BE PRACTICAL

A typical web user has on average 25 different accounts requiring a user name and password. It is neither realistic nor expected that one would be able to create strong, unique passwords for every account as well as change these passwords every 6 months to a year, as many security tip websites suggest. With so many accounts requiring passwords, it is normal to feel the effects of *password fatigue.* In the face of password fatigue, a typical reaction is to choose a few semisecure passwords and reuse these passwords across many accounts. Although easy to remember, this type of password strategy is vulnerable to a slippery slope of compromised accounts: If an attacker learns the password username and password for one account, the attacker has access to many accounts. This is especially true if the attacker is able to gain access to a personal email account—the digital Rolodex for account registration emails.

Instead of succumbing to password fatigue, it is suggested that you rank your accounts into three categories: (1) most secure (bank account, personal email, retirement account); (2) secure (social networking), and (3) least secure (online newspaper, etc.). For your most secure accounts, choose unique strong passwords and be diligent about changing your passwords for these accounts every 6 months to prevent against any accidental disclosures of your password. Create a few strong passwords for your secure accounts that can be easily remembered and circulated between accounts, changing your password on a yearly basis. For your least-secure accounts, those that would not significantly impact you if compromised, choose one strong password to reuse across multiple websites. The basic key to this method of practical password management is not to choose the same username and password combination for a less-secure website as you would for your most secure accounts. Containment of a compromised password is essential to limiting the damage if a cyber criminal ever learns a password.

If memorization is a problem, there are a number of other password management techniques that one could use. As previously stated, writing passwords down in a notebook or on a piece of paper is effective if the secrecy of the password record can be secured. But, instead of explicitly writing down the account site, username, and password, include some obfuscation, such as including hints to your password so that if the secrecy of the password list is compromised, all is not lost.

Another technique of password management is to use a specifically designed desktop application such as KeePass (http://keepass.info/) or web browser add-on LastPass (https://addons.mozilla.org/en-US/firefox/addon/lastpass-password-manager/) to manage passwords on your behalf. On logging in to your web-based email account, for example, LastPass provides the capability simply to autofill the username and password fields with your unique username and password. This obviates the need for typing a password and all but mitigates the threat of key-loggers. Many password management applications will also generate strong, random passwords on the user's behalf. The advantage of using an application like LastPass is that unique and strong passwords can be created and changed often for each of your accounts and with little effort. The largest downside to using a password management program is that it becomes a single point of failure. Often, a single password may be used to gain access to the software program managing all of a user's passwords. If the single password is forgotten or compromised, all the user's passwords are subsequently lost or compromised.

Last, many popular web browsers also provide the services of password management. As shown in Figure 3.16, when a username and password are submitted to a particular website, the web browser prompts the user and asks if the web browser should remember the username and password on the user's behalf. If the password is remembered, the web browser will automatically populate the username and password in the appropriate fields when the user next visits the same website (Figure 3.17). This alleviates the need for the user to remember the password and it is hoped facilitates the creation of a strong password. While effective in certain respects, this type of management system has its downfalls. First, the password management application contained in the web browser is often restricted to the computer on which it resides. Therefore, a user wishing to access a personal email account on a different computer must either remember the password or create and bring a written reminder. Second, access to such a computer would need to be highly restrictive as anyone able to open the

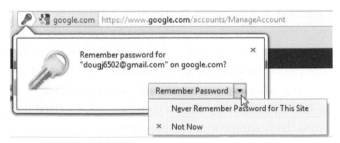

FIGURE 3.16   Web browser prompt to save a password.

FIGURE 3.17   Username and password populated by a web browser.

web browser would have access to all a user's accounts for which saved passwords exist.

A further risk of allowing a web browser to manage passwords is that by default anyone with access to the web browser can navigate through the browser's setting options and actually enumerate the saved usernames and passwords in plaintext as shown in Figure 3.18 for the Firefox web browser.

For this reason, when using a web browser as a password manager, it is important to enable a "master password" (Figure 3.19) to control access to the many passwords a browser is tasked to remember. Enabling the master password has two distinct security benefits. First, it requires that anyone wishing to view the saved passwords as illustrated in Figure 3.18 know

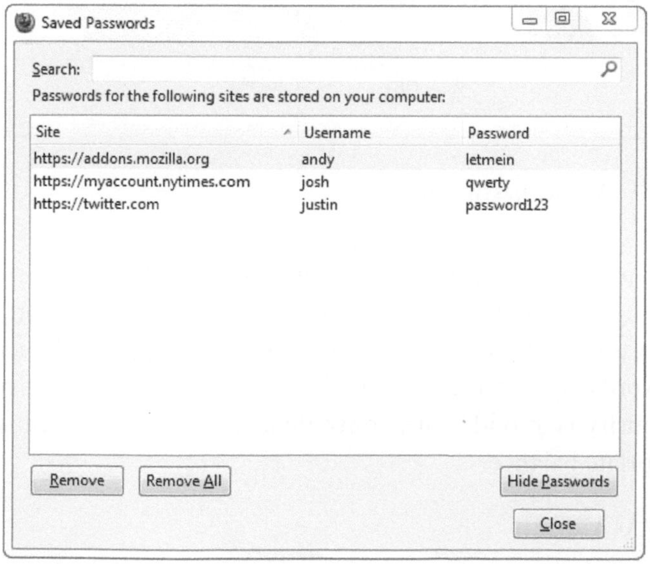

FIGURE 3.18   Saved passwords enumerated.

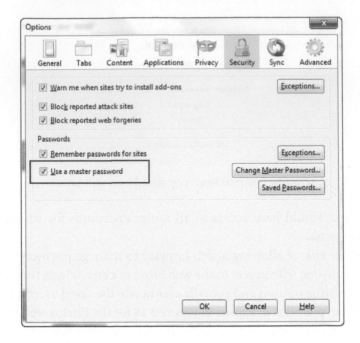

FIGURE 3.19   Preference options for enabling master password.

FIGURE 3.20   Master password.

the master password (Figure 3.20). Second, it prevents unauthorized users from logging in to remembered websites as the master password must be supplied at the beginning of each web session to populate the usernames and passwords automatically. As is the case with many security mechanisms, security is at odds with convenience, and each user must choose the appropriate balance.

3.6 SUMMARY

Passwords are an inescapable part of our digital lives. While there are many technologies that seek to replace the common password, it is unlikely that any of these alternative solutions will supplant passwords any time in the near future. As a result, it is best from a practical computer security standpoint to understand the threats passwords face, observe the security best practices discussed in this chapter to keep your strong passwords secret, and exhibit secure password management practices.

- The knowledge of a password is often the principal barrier preventing unauthorized access to sensitive and confidential information.

- A secure password is one that is strong (cannot be guessed) and one that is a secret (only known by the password owner).

- Authentication is the process by which a user proves his or her right to assume a digital identity by providing the correct username and password pair.

- A hash function is a one-way transformation of data that is used to encrypt and store passwords.

- The primary ways in which password confidentiality is lost are through the user disclosing a password, social engineering, key-logging, shoulder surfing, sniffing, guessing and cracking attacks, stolen password files, and security questions.

- Password choices and password management techniques are a pragmatic exercise in which there are many effective strategies.

- If an attacker is able to steal, sniff, social engineer, key-log, or observe a plaintext password, the strength of the password is irrelevant.

- Security-conscious companies will never initiate a phone call or email requesting sensitive information like a password.

- There are two primary password-guessing attacks: brute force and dictionary.

- While a brute-force attack will theoretically guess the correct password at some point in time, the time complexity of iterating through every conceivable password limits the effectiveness of this guessing strategy.

- Dictionary attacks are not guaranteed to crack every password, but they are often effective at cracking weak and commonly used passwords.

- To protect against online guessing attacks, many online websites limit the number of failed attempts before an account is locked or use graphical puzzles like CAPTCHAs to distinguish between a human and an automated program tasked to guess passwords.

- Despite decades of password advice, security breaches, and identity theft, many still choose common and easy-to-guess passwords.

- Although the length and character diversity of a password may appear to give the password resilience against a guessing attack, if the password is not relatively unique, such a password could be contained in a dictionary list and thus be considered weak.

- An objective of structuring a strong password is to create one that is strong while being relatively easy to remember and type accurately.

- Strong passwords often consist of lower and uppercase letters, numbers, and special symbols and are not largely based on personal information or dictionary words.

- Even though the term *password* suggests a single word, passphrases (i.e., multiple words pieced together) also provide a secure alternative to traditional password formation and have the potential for being easier to remember.

- Creating unique passwords for each high-security account and changing these passwords every six months limits the security risk if a user or the online service provider has exposed a password.

- There are a number of different types of software programs (i.e., web browser features, web browser add-ons, and desktop applications) that assist in the task of managing strong, unique, and secret passwords.

- Although password managers are convenient, they have their faults and limitations. Ultimately, each individual person must choose his or her own acceptable balance between password security and convenience.

BIBLIOGRAPHY

Acohido, B. 2012. Hackers swipe Zappos data; customers should change password. *USA Today*. http://www.usatoday.com/tech/news/story/2012-01-16/zappos-security-breach/52605292/1 (accessed April 8, 2012).

Bishop, M. 2003. *Computer Security*. Boston: Addison-Wesley.

Buley, T. 2010. Online password tips and tricks. *Forbes.* http://www.forbes.com/2010/03/03/hacker-rockyou-imperva-technology-security10-password.html (accessed April 8, 2012).

Danchev, D. 2008. Attacker: hacking Sarah Palin's email was easy. ZDNet. http://www.zdnet.com/blog/security/attacker-hacking-sarah-palins-email-was-easy/1939 (accessed April 8, 2012).

Denning, D. 1999. *Information Warfare and Security.* New York: ACM Press.

Engebretson, P. 2011. *The Basics of Hacking and Penetration Testing: Ethical Hacking and Penetration Testing Mad Easy.* New York: Elsevier.

Ferguson, N., and Schneier, B. 2003. *Practical Cryptography.* New York: Wiley.

Florencio, D., and Herley, C. 2007. *A Large Scale Study of Web Password Habits.* Banff, Alberta, Canada: Association of Computing Machinery, Inc.

Florencio, D., Herley, C., and Coskun, B. 2007. Do strong web passwords accomplish anything? Usenix HotSec, Boston. Association of Computing Machinery, Inc.

Garfinkel, S., Spafford, G., and Schartz, A. 2003. *Practical Unix and Internet Security.* Sebastopol, CA: O'Reilly Media.

Google. 2012. Keeping your account secure. http://support.google.com/accounts/bin/answer.py?hl=en&answer=46526 (accessed April 8, 2012).

Google. 2012. Telling humans and computers apart automatically. http://www.google.com/recaptcha/captcha (accessed April 8, 2012).

Greenberg, A. 2012. Zappos says hackers accessed 24 million customers' account details. *Forbes.* http://www.forbes.com/sites/andygreenberg/2012/01/15/zappos-says-hackers-accessed-24-million-customers-account-details/ (accessed April 8, 2012).

Hadnagy, C. 2010. *Social Engineering: The Art of Human Hacking.* New York: Wiley.

KeePass. 2012. KeePass password safe. http://keepass.info/ (accessed April 8, 2012).

LastPass. 2012 LastPass password manager. https://addons.mozilla.org/en-US/firefox/addon/lastpass-password-manager/ (accessed April 8, 2012).

Leyden, J. 2010. RockYou hack reveals easy-to-crack passwords. *The Register.* http://www.theregister.co.uk/2010/01/21/lame_passwords_exposed_by_rockyou_hack/ (accessed April 8, 2012).

Lucas, I. Password recovery speeds. 2009. http://www.lockdown.co.uk/?pg=combi (accessed April 8, 2012).

McClure, S., Scambray, J., and Kurtz, G. 2009. *Hacking Exposed 6: Network Security Secrets and Solutions.* New York: McGraw-Hill.

Moscaritolo, A. 2009. RockYou hack compromises 32 million passwords. *SC Magazine.* http://www.scmagazine.com/rockyou-hack-compromises-32-million-passwords/article/159676/ (accessed April 8, 2012).

Paul, I. 2010. Gawker media hack. Everything you need to know. *PCWorld.* http://www.pcworld.com/article/213438/gawker_media_hack_everything_you_need_to_know.html (accessed April 8, 2012).

Richmond, R. 2009. How to create strong P@$$word$. *New York Times.* http://gadgetwise.blogs.nytimes.com/2009/05/22/four-ways-to-strengthen-a-password/ (accessed April 8, 2012).

Robinson, S. 2002. Human or computer? Take this test. *New York Times*. http://www.nytimes.com/2002/12/10/science/human-or-computer-take-this-test.html (accessed April 8, 2012).

Schneier, B. 2009. Security questions. http://www.schneier.com/blog/archives/2009/05/secret_question.html (accessed April 8, 2012).

Seward, Z., and Sun, A. 2010. The top 50 Gawker Media passwords. *Wall Street Journal*. http://blogs.wsj.com/digits/2010/12/13/the-top-50-gawker-media-passwords/(accessed April 8, 2012).

Smith, M. 2012. Zappos customer accounts breached. http://www.usatoday.com/tech/news/story/2012-01-16/mark-smith-zappos-breach-tips/52593484/1 (accessed April 8, 2012).

Stross, R. 2010. A strong password isn't the strongest security. *New York Times*. http://www.nytimes.com/2010/09/05/business/05digi.html (accessed April 8, 2012).

Vamosi, R. 2008. Social engineering cracked Palin's e-mail account. CNET. http://news.cnet.com/8301-1009_3-10045969-83.html (accessed April 8, 2012).

Vance, A. 2010. If your password is 123456, just make it HackMe. *New York Times*. http://www.nytimes.com/2010/01/21/technology/21password.html?_r=1 (accessed April 8, 2012).

Whitney, L. 2011. Scammers turning to phone calls to gain PC access. CNET. http://news.cnet.com/8301-1009_3-20071568-83/scammers-turning-to-phone-calls-to-gain-pc-access/?part=rss&tag=feed&subj=News-Security (accessed April 8, 2012).

Wired. 2010. Choosing a strong password. *Wired*. http://howto.wired.com/wiki/Choose_a_Strong_Password (accessed April 8, 2012).

Wu, A. 2012. Keeping your online accounts safe. CNN. http://money.cnn.com/2012/01/11/technology/online_security.moneymag/index.htm (accessed April 8, 2012).

Yegulalp, S. 2012. Review: 7 password managers for Windows, Mac OS X, iOS, and Android. *Network World*. http://www.networkworld.com/reviews/2012/032812-review-7-password-managers-for-257717.html (accessed April 8, 2012).

Zetter, K. 2010. Sarah Palin e-mail hacker sentenced to 1 year in custody. *Wired*. http://www.wired.com/threatlevel/2010/11/palin-hacker-sentenced/ (accessed April 8, 2012).

CHAPTER 4

Email Security

4.1 INTRODUCTION

Email is one of the most common Internet applications and is widely used for both business and personal communications. As email has become an integral part of our daily lives, it has also given attackers a means to easily target and contact many potential victims, often by sending emails pretending to be someone they are not. The first goal of this chapter is to introduce the underlying concepts and various components of basic email systems on the Internet. With this knowledge in hand, this chapter explores common ways in which the email system can be used to target potential victims and how these attacks can be mitigated through security best practices. In addition, a handful of email privacy concerns is also discussed.

4.2 EMAIL SYSTEMS

Email is one of the earliest network applications and one of the first to gain widespread use on the Internet. In comparison to the present day, early email systems were initially simple programs that restricted users to the options of creating, sending, and reading short text messages without supporting file attachments—much like modern-day text messaging. Furthermore, early email systems were proprietary and generally did not communicate well with each other. As the popularity of email grew and the demand for functionality and interoperability increased, the email system evolved into the familiar systems of today. Figure 4.1 depicts the two primary components of contemporary email systems: the Message Transfer Agent (MTA) designed to store and transport email messages

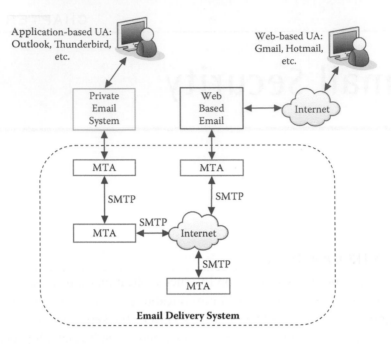

FIGURE 4.1   Email system components.

across the Internet and the User Agent (UA) that enables users to manage email messages.

4.2.1 Message Transfer Agent

Because the electronic mail system was patterned after the ordinary postal mail system, an understanding of the email system can be gained through comparison. As shown in Figure 4.2, MTAs are similar to mailboxes in that they are responsible for both sending and receiving email messages. In place of postal carriers, MTAs communicate with each other using the Simple Mail Transfer Protocol (SMTP), and an email may be routed through several MTAs on its journey from sending MTA to destination MTA. Each individual MTA also maintains its own file storage system for inbound email not yet picked up by the receiver and for outbound mail waiting to be delivered. Except for spam filters and antivirus scanners, MTAs do not need to open emails to route a message to its final destination.

Like a mailbox or post office box, MTAs hold user emails until they can be delivered or picked up by the user. This type of storage system enables email users to receive and accumulate emails even when they are not logged into their email accounts. Just like the need for a key to a post office box, a user must first authenticate to the MTA by providing a correct

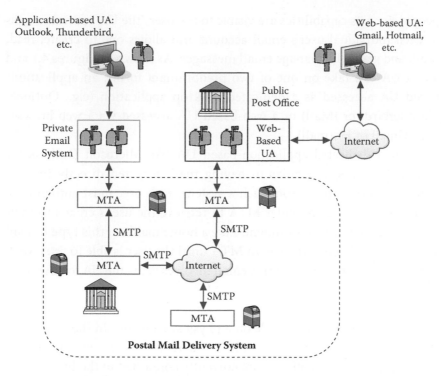

FIGURE 4.2   Email versus postal system.

username and password. The use of authentication provides confidentiality by preventing unauthorized users from accessing one's emails.

The sending of an email is also very similar to putting a letter in a mailbox. As in the postal system, outbound email is not authenticated, meaning that one does not need to supply a username and password to send an email from an MTA. Furthermore, one can place a letter in a mailbox with a return address not that of the sender for both conventional mail and email. Some, but not all, MTAs check the validity of an email's return address, that is, whether it matches the sender's address, before an email is sent. If this check is not performed, the ability to forge the sender email address is created, and from the email receiver's perspective, it is difficult to verify the authenticity of emails by examining the "from address" alone (more on this in further discussion).

4.2.2 User Agents

Another major component of an email system is the User Agent (UA), whose function is to support interaction between the user and the MTAs. The UA is generally the most familiar aspect of the email system for many people since its capabilities are visible to the user. The UA controls access to each individual user's email account and allows one to create, read, send, and generally manage email messages. As shown in Figures 4.1 and 4.2, a UA can take on one of two predominant forms: an application-based UA accessed as a dedicated desktop application (e.g., Outlook, Thunderbird, or iMail) or a web-based UA accessed via a web browser (e.g., Gmail or Hotmail).

Using a dedicated application-based UA like Microsoft Outlook (or Outlook Express) is similar to having mail delivered directly to your home. To access email from such a system, each user must authenticate to the email service provider MTA to retrieve the user's emails to their desktop computing environment. Like a home mailbox, this type of mail system will hold one's mail at an MTA until the user is able to retrieve it. In this case, the retrieval of one's email involves using the UA to download emails to one's computer. This type of UA also maintains local storage to help each user manage email messages offline on his or her own computer. Because retrieved emails reside on a physical computer in the user's own space, an application-based UA allows one to access already downloaded emails even if the computer is not currently connected to the Internet.

The second common method for accessing a UA is through use of a web browser. In this case, the UA is not an application running on a computer, but instead resides on a server owned and operated by an email service provider (e.g., Gmail) accessed via the Internet using a web browser like Internet Explorer or Firefox. Gaining access to a web-based UA requires that the user first provide authentication (username and password) to his or her email service provider. Using this type of UA is similar to having your mail delivered to a centrally located post office box and gaining mail access by requesting one message at a time, much like requesting a web page. Unlike the desktop application version of the UA, emails in this system do not reside locally on your computer but are instead stored on the email service provider's servers (i.e., in the cloud). This provides the capability to view one's emails from many different Internet-connected computers. It should also be noted that web-based email accounts provide support and access to application-based UAs.

The UA often provides the user with many useful capabilities that, as will be discussed, have security implications. Examples include capabilities for attaching documents to outbound email, viewing documents attached to inbound email, saving documents on the user's computer, and addressing, replying, and forwarding messages.

4.2.3 Email Addressing

Just like conventional mail, the email system is based on a system of unique destination and return addresses. An email sender specifies the address of the recipient in the format "username@email_domain_name" and typically provides his or her email address as the return address. However, as in the conventional mail system, the sender's email address typically plays no role in the process of transferring an email message from the sender to the receiver. Like the sender's address on an envelope, the sender's email address is included in the email message and is displayed to the recipient by the UA, even though it does not have to be the address of the actual sender of the email message. In this situation, the action of pretending to be someone else is known as *spoofing* and allows a sender to pretend to be virtually anyone, including your bank or an online shopping website.

To transfer an email from one MTA to another, it is necessary for the sending MTA, using the recipient address (email_domain_name), to obtain the IP address of the MTA from which the receiving user will retrieve email. The sending UA may either directly contact the recipient's MTA or instead contact an intermediate MTA (typically the MTA it itself uses for email). The sending UA will send the message to this MTA using the SMTP protocol. If the UA sends the message to an intermediate MTA, that MTA will forward the email to the next MTA based on the recipient's email address. As discussed in the next section, each MTA appends to the email message information about itself and the message it handled during this transmission. When the recipient's MTA receives the email message, it will use the recipient's email address to determine into which email box the message should be placed.

4.2.4 Email Message Structure

The first email systems were designed to transmit text messages only and were incapable of sending or displaying embedded pictures, specially formatted text, or attachments. Present-day systems have evolved, with UAs now using MIME (Multipurpose Internet Mail Extensions) to enrich the appearance and functionality of emails. MIME is used to tell UAs what type of data is embedded in or attached to an email message as well as the data's encoding scheme. The email message may contain many different data formats, including web-based data, hyperlinks, pictures, text files, sound, and video in various formats. UAs display the content in a format that the user can directly interact with or see. For example, the UA can display embedded pictures sent as part of the email message. Although MIME provides convenience and other aesthetic benefits, it also can be used as a vehicle for attackers to send viruses, worms, and other types of malware directly to the user in the form of email attachments.

Following the postal system analogy, the basic message format used by the email system is similar to many surface mail systems that allow one to track a package as it is transported from sender to receiver. Each time the package, in this case an email message, is received by a UA or MTA, tracking information is appended to the email message in a header format. As shown in Figures 4.3 and 4.4, an email message is composed of a message body and a list of headers that describe the UA and MTAs that were used to transfer the email message from source to destination. Figure 4.3 illustrates a typical email message containing the user's message and headers added by each component of the email system that handles the message. These headers are not interpreted by the MTAs involved in the message transfer but can be used by the recipient's UA to help decode the message's contents. The email headers can also be used to determine the origin of the email and the path of the email from sender MTA to receiver MTA, including all intermediate MTAs.

Figure 4.4 illustrates an example in which Alice sends a message containing a picture of a palm tree and the text "Hello Bob" to Bob@dougj. net. Alice creates the message using her UA, which formats the message using MIME and adds a MIME header to indicate that the email contains pictures and text. Alice's UA also adds a header containing information about the UA itself, including the sender's email address (alice@iseage.net),

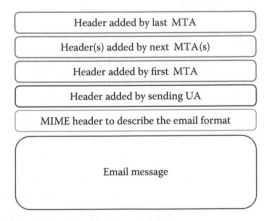

FIGURE 4.3   Email message and header format.

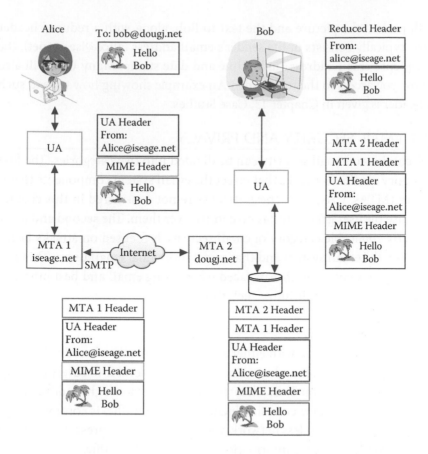

FIGURE 4.4   Email header information.

the subject of the message, the date and time the message was sent, and other information that might possibly be useful to the recipient. Alice's UA will send the message to an appropriate MTA, where it will be sent forward through a sequence of MTAs and ultimately to the destination MTA. Each time a MTA receives a message, it will append a header entry to the front of the message (Figure 4.3). This header entry contains the date and time that the message was received by the MTA, the IP address and machine name of the sender, and the email address of both sender and recipient. In the example provided in Figure 4.4, two MTAs handle the email message. Although examining headers can be useful in tracking the sender of an email message, most UAs do not display all of the header information by default, making email easier to read by reducing clutter. Bob's UA will interact with MTA 2 to retrieve the message and inform Bob that he has mail. When Bob selects the message from Alice to be viewed, his UA will present the picture and the text to Bob, along with a reduced header that typically consists of the sender's email address (alice@iseage.net), the recipient's email address, and a time and date stamp. Many UAs will also allow you access to the full header. An example showing how to read such a header is given in Chapter 13, Case Studies.

4.3 EMAIL SECURITY AND PRIVACY

Discussions of email security can be divided into two categories. The first category considers attacks that target the email system components themselves (MTAs, UAs, etc.). These attacks are not considered in this chapter because the user generally has no control over them. The second and more directly applicable category of email security is focused on attacks facilitated by the email system and that target individual email users. This section explores common threats faced when using email and best practices that can be used to minimize such threats.

4.3.1 Eavesdropping

When communicating with either a web- or application-based UA, both a user's login credentials and email content are vulnerable to eavesdropping. As mentioned previously in Chapter 3 and more thoroughly addressed in Chapter 9, when Internet traffic (including email traffic) is communicated over an unsecure wireless network, there exists an ever-present threat that an attacker can observe information comprising the traffic.

Figure 4.5 illustrates a network diagram in which a user interacts with a web-based UA over a wireless Internet network—similar to a user accessing a Hotmail account in a coffee shop. Since this involves using a web browser to access the email service provider's UA, the user must first provide a username and a password. Once authenticated, the user can send and receive emails. If the wireless network is unsecure, an attacker could potentially observe each of these actions. For this reason and to thwart

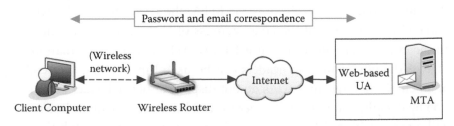

FIGURE 4.5   Web-based UA network diagram.

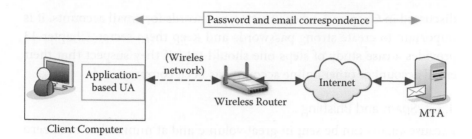

FIGURE 4.6 Application-based UA network diagram.

eavesdropping in general, many reputable email service providers encrypt interactions between the user and the web-based UA using HTTPS (more on this in Chapter 7).

While many web-based UA's encrypt all web interactions, the same cannot be said for a UA that resides as a desktop application on the user's computer, as shown in Figure 4.6. In such a case, to check for or retrieve new emails the user must provide authentication to their email service provider's MTA, requiring transmission of the user's username and password over the unsecure wireless connection. Subsequently, any emails sent or received are also sent via the unsecure wireless network to the MTA. While some application-based UAs provide support for encryption of traffic to and from an MTA, others do not, and such traffic is thus vulnerable to eavesdropping. Accordingly, it is best not to check one's email over an unsecure network unless one can ensure that email traffic is being encrypted by either the UA or by means of a virtual private network (VPN) (Appendix C). Otherwise, one should assume that an attacker could learn one's password and view the user's personal email correspondence.

In many ways, the security needs of one's primary email account should be considered equal to or even more important than one's online banking or other highly valued accounts. It follows that one should use caution in protecting the secrecy of an email password. Email inboxes are typically filled with account registration information, other usernames and passwords, purchase details, and hoards of personal and private information that can be used to steal identities. While online banking accounts are insured against fraudulent activity, email accounts are typically not afforded the same protection. With access to an email account, the attacker has the ability to search through, read, or worse yet, download all of your email correspondence for later access. Also, once authenticated, an attacker can send and receive emails from the victim's account. As discussed in Chapter 3, when creating passwords for email accounts, it is important to create strong passwords and keep them secret. Chapter 13 provides a case study of steps one should take if they suspect that their email account or other online account has been compromised.

4.3.2 Spam and Phishing

Because emails can be sent in great volume and at minimal or even zero cost to the sender, it should come as no surprise that the email system also suffers from unwanted junk mail, much like the postal mail system. Often called *spam email*, such unsolicited email messages typically attempt to entice the recipient into purchasing some sort of product or medicine. A spammer will send out thousands or millions of emails in hope that a few people will respond. In many cases, spam emails are more of an annoyance than anything else. Similar to spam, phishing emails are used to pose as messages from legitimate companies or banking institutions to trick people into disclosing private or financial information. Phishing attacks are often categorized as a type of social engineering and, as previously discussed, are covered in more detail in Chapters 11 and 13.

Both UAs and MTAs have built-in tools that attempt to identify and block spam and phishing emails from reaching your inbox, often placing them in a special folder (e.g., a spam folder). It should be noted that these spam and phishing filter tools are not perfect, and as a result, one should not assume that a particular email in the inbox is legitimate, and the email filtered to a spam folder should not be completely neglected.

4.3.3 Spoofing

As described previously, by spoofing the sender address of an email, the sender does not have to really be who they claim to be and could therefore pretend to be anyone, including a legitimate corporation or a bank. By providing a false email address in the "From" field, the email creator does not expect to receive an email back from the victim. Instead, the attacker may desire that the victim somehow interact with the email by clicking on a hyperlink, opening an email attachment, or calling a phone number provided in the email. One of the most common purposes of email spoofing is to misdirect an email recipient to a phony or malicious website as part of a phishing attack. Such an email may be disguised to look like it comes from a friend, a legitimate company, or an identity of the attacker's choosing. Figure 4.7 provides an example of a spoofed email. In this email, the sender, villain@hotmail.com, was purposefully chosen so

FIGURE 4.7   Spoofed email example.

that the spoofing was quite obvious. However, replace villain@hotmail.com with customer_service@insert_your_bank_name.com and one can see how spoofing an email address can contribute to the deception of a phishing email. Chapter 13 includes a detailed case study example showing how one can identify the true sender of a spoofed email address: The key is to examine the header list discussed in Figure 4.3.

4.3.4 Malicious Email Attachments

In addition to spam and phishing, attackers use emails to distribute malware: malicious software (i.e., viruses, worms, Trojan horses, etc.). The same functionality that UAs provide to make emails more accessible and useful can also be used for malicious objectives. In such a case, the focus of the attacker is to attempt to deceive the email user into clicking on a hyperlink or opening a malware-infested email attachment.

As previously described, UAs can permit email messages to include attachments—files that can be viewed or executed by a UA or an external program or saved to one's computer. Because email attachments are a popular method for sharing information, attackers have used them to exploit people's familiarity with opening email attachments, thus carrying out the attackers' malevolent deeds. As discussed in Chapter 2, computer programs like UAs possess capabilities for viewing, opening, or executing other programs. In the context of email, a UA can execute or view a file it receives as an attachment. When the attached email file is malicious in nature, this action may cause problems for the victim because the executing program has the potential to access the victim's computer and all of his or her data. This access also enables the action of opening an email attachment to install harmful software (i.e., malware) on the victim's computer. Chapters 5, 6, 11, and 13 deal with this issue at more length.

As shown in Figure 4.8, attackers will often use a combination of trickery—often referred to as social engineering (Chapter 11)—and email

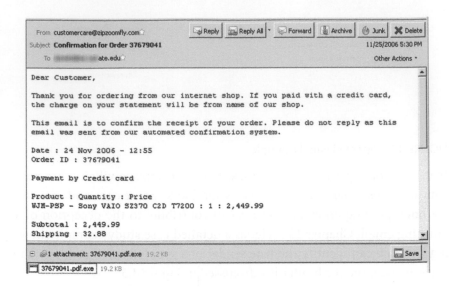

FIGURE 4.8 Email with malicious attachment.

attachments to infect a user's computer. In this example of a phony email, a PDF document is attached to the email and is cunningly name "37679041. pdf.exe." The hope of the attacker is that the email user will somehow be intrigued and open the email attachment out of curiosity. Opening such a file can enable malicious code in the email attachment to be executed on the victim's computer, potentially leading to a malware infection. This is why it is best not to open an email attachment unless you are specifically expecting it from a known email sender. If you are in the habit of opening a majority of email attachments you receive, beware that you are greatly increasing your risk of infecting your computer with malware. Although many MTAs do possess tools that detect and prevent the emailing of malicious attachments, attackers often have ways to circumvent these efforts.

4.3.5 Replying and Forwarding

The UA provides the user with the ability to *reply* to an email, further allowing the user to append to the original message and send the entire dialog back to the original sender (Figure 4.9). There is also a *reply all* function that allows the receiver to reply to everyone addressed on the original email, not just the sender. While "replying all" itself is not a direct security risk (i.e., contracting malware), it certainly can be a privacy risk when the response is meant only for the sender. Stories of someone accidentally "replying all" to an email when they intended to reply to the sender only

FIGURE 4.9   Email recipient options.

are plentiful and often have caused embarrassment. Be cautious when deciding which of these options to choose and always double-check the intended recipients of an email before sending.

Another feature provided by the UA is the ability to *forward* a message received from one user to another user or users. Again, use of this feature represents more of a privacy concern than a security concern, but you should be aware that an exact copy of an email could be copied verbatim and emailed to as many people as the recipient desires. This process could further continue, attributing your name to an email that could reach hundreds if not thousands of people. The ability to quickly and easily forward information via email is also a good reason why one should limit the personal and private information disclosed in an email message or be selective regarding recipients of such information since once the information is sent, the sender has no control on how the information may be further disseminated.

4.3.6 To, Carbon Copy, and Blind Carbon Copy

Unlike when mailing a letter, email allows one to send the same message to multiple people by crafting a single message and addressing it to many people. The conveniences that are afforded in being able to and easily disseminate correspondences quickly comes at the cost of protecting the privacy of those who have emailed us and those to whom we intend to email. When composing an email message, there are typically three text fields: To, Cc, and Bcc (Figure 4.9), into which one can enter email addresses for intended recipients. Each of these fields has a distinct purpose, and understanding each purpose will better help you observe best practices for email privacy. The central issue here is whether a recipient of an email can or should also be able to see other recipients.

When sending an email directly to one or more people, the "To" field is typically where one will enter the recipients' email addresses. As shown in Figure 4.9, any email addresses included in the "To" field will be viewable to all of recipients of the email.

The carbon copy (Cc) field is commonly used in an email message to include people who should have knowledge of the email's contents but to whom the email is not directly targeted. For example, if you were emailing multiple people on your work team about a recent project development, you would enter those email addresses in the To field and perhaps you would include your boss or another project leader's email address in the "Cc" field as an FYI (for your information) indication. When using the Cc field be aware that everyone addressed in both the To and the Cc fields will be able to see email addresses of others who were addressed in each of these respective fields.

The blind carbon copy (Bcc) field is used to send emails to multiple people without direct recipients of the email knowing who else was included in the Bcc field and therefore received the email. For example, if you were sending an email to your landlord and wanted to copy your lawyer on the email without indicating to the landlord that the lawyer was privy to it, then you would put the landlord's email address in the To field and your lawyer's email address in the Bcc field. Bcc is also used to preserve privacy when emailing to a large group of people. This field allows the sender to email numerous people without revealing identities of others receiving the email. To protect the privacy of their clients, businesses and corporations commonly perform this type of email best practice when sending mass emails.

4.4 SUMMARY

Email on the Internet has become pervasive and is now the preferred method of communication for a great majority of businesses and individuals, and for that reason it has become a preferred target for attackers. Because the mechanics of the email system enable an attacker to perform phishing attacks, spoof email addresses, and distribute malware via attachments with ease, education and caution are necessary to protect oneself when using email. Many such precautions are discussed in the next several chapters.

- As an email message travels from sender to receiver, it travels through a sequence of MTAs (Mail Transfer Agents) in much the same way that conventional mail may pass through a sequence of post offices.

- UAs (User Agents) are software applications linking email senders and receivers to MTAs to provide a multitude of user functions (receiving, sending, editing, saving, forwarding, etc.).

- UAs may use the MIME (Multipurpose Internet Mail Extensions) protocol to support a variety of email data types (text, pictures, video, audio, etc.). MIME is also a tool used by malicious attackers.

- As an email message travels from sender to receiver through a sequence of MTAs, each MTA attaches its own identifying header to the message.

- Like passwords, email messages are also vulnerable to eavesdropping as these correspondences often contain personal and private information.

- Spam is unsolicited email widely proliferated by unknown senders and usually composed of nuisance advertising messages.

- Phishing is an activity by which malicious users send messages disguised as legitimate email, usually containing requests for personal information or hyperlinks to phony websites, both means that lead to identity theft.

- Similar to writing a deceitful return address on an envelope, spoofing enables an attacker to craft an email message appearing to originate from a trusted entity like a bank or online retailer.

- Malware distributed via email attachments has been and continues to be a very effective propagation method. Great caution should be taken when opening email attachments, even when they are sent from someone the receiver already knows and trusts.

BIBLIOGRAPHY

Appel, E. 2011. *Internet Searches for Vetting, Investigations, and Open-Source Intelligence*. Boca Raton, FL: CRC Press.

Borghoff, U.M., and Schlichter, J.H. 2000. *Computer-Supported Cooperative Work: Introduction to Distributed Applications*. New York: Springer.

Cassel, L.N., and Austing, R.H. 2000. *Computer Networks and Open Systems: An Application Development Perspective*. Sudbury, MA: Jones & Bartlett Learning.

Flynn, N., and Flynn, T. 2003. *Writing Effective Email*. Independence, KY: Cengage Learning.

Grimes, R.A. 2001. *Malicious Mobile Code: Virus Protection for Windows*. Sebastopol, CA: O'Reilly Media.

Habraken, J.W. 2003. *Absolute Beginner's Guide to Networking*. Indianapolis, IN: Que.
Jakobsson, M., and Myers, S. 2006. *Phishing and Countermeasures: Understanding the Increasing Problem of Electronic Identity Theft*. New York: Wiley.
Smith, R. 2011. *Elementary Information Security*. Sudbury, MA: Jones & Bartlett.
Wood, D. 1999. *Programming Internet Email*. Sebastopol, CA: O'Reilly Media.

CHAPTER 5

Malware: The Dark Side of Software

5.1 INTRODUCTION

Gaining awareness of and comprehending the vocabulary of information security are important steps in learning how to better protect your computer and private information. These steps are especially important for the understanding of the peculiar and at times anti-intuitive terminology that is used to describe the topic of malicious software (i.e., malware). Start with the term *malware*, for instance; the simple use of the word causes confusion for many. When one goes to the store or shops online for a product to keep their computer clean of malicious software, they typically purchase antivirus software. A common point of confusion is whether antivirus software protects against just viruses—as the name suggests—or if it protects against all types of malware like spyware and Trojan horses, to name a few.

The literal interpretation of the term *antivirus* is technically an incorrect use of computer security terminology. In the past, the use of this term in such a context was correct. Today, however, the malware landscape has expanded drastically, and *antivirus* is simply a marketing term that has persisted because its familiarity resonates with many people, and a relabeling would cause confusion. When popular antivirus products are examined more closely, it is found that they protect against not only viruses, but also spyware, Trojan horses, and other malware.

It is not uncommon to hear both technically savvy and nontechnical people alike errantly calling a particular type of malware a virus when it may be, in fact, a worm or vice versa. This distinction may seem nit-picky, but there are subtle differences between the many different types of malware, and knowing these differences will help you to understand how malware spreads and which security mechanisms prevent against which types of malware. When one becomes sick, the treatment for the ailment depends largely on which illness has been contracted. It certainly does not make sense to treat strep throat with antibiotics that are typically used to treat ear infections caused by other bacteria. By the same token, when one hears about an airborne flu epidemic on the news, they do not proceed to venture out in public places thinking that by simply washing their hands they will be protected from a noncontact illness. The comparison between human ailments and malware is an apt one; as it turns out, there exist a number of commonalities between these two types of phenomena that can be used to illustrate the ways in which malware works and what we can do to protect ourselves against it.

This chapter explores the many different types of malware, how a computer can be infected, and what malware does once it gets onto a computer. After establishing a solid understanding of malware, we then learn more about the defense mechanisms that protect us from such vile software in Chapter 6.

5.2 WHAT IS MALWARE?

Simply put, malware is an all-encompassing term for **mal**icious soft**ware**. Just as the term *software* is used as an umbrella term for operating systems (OSs), applications, device drivers, and so on, malware is used in a similar way. The term *malware* describes all software having a malicious objective. Historically, the term has encompassed a number of types of commonly known threats, such as viruses, worms, and Trojan horses. Unfortunately, these are no longer the only types of malware that must concern us. Malicious software like ransomware, scareware, malicious adware, and spyware all fall under the umbrella of malware and also require our attention and understanding.

It should come as no surprise that when the first malware program (i.e., a virus) was written in 1982, it was done as a joke between friends. However, since this date, malware has become anything but a joke. To put the present-day malware epidemic into perspective, it is estimated that there are more malicious software programs than there are legitimate software programs currently being created. This is a staggering proclamation when one considers how much legitimate software is currently under production. Needless to say, malware is going to be an ever-present threat and one that is going to be a part of everyday life for years to come.

The functional objectives of malware are quite simple. First, earning itself the use of the Latin root *mal*, meaning "bad" or "evil," malware by definition contains a malicious function or act that the malware performs once it is executed on a computer. The malicious deed, whether it be formatting a hard drive or monitoring keystrokes, is the means by which it harms a system. The second functional objective of malware is to propagate between computers. Without the act of spreading, the threat of malware would not be held in the same regard. The challenge for malware creators is how to get malware to a victim's computer and how to get the malicious program executed. The more efficiently this process happens, the greater the success of the attacker. As will be seen, the progression of such tactics to achieve this task coincides directly with the evolution of technology and ways in which people use computers and the Internet.

To use a simpler description, malware is simply computer code (i.e., software) that is executed on a computer, resulting in unintended and malicious consequences for the victim. Just as legitimate software programs are composed of hundreds, thousands, or even millions of lines of code that are executed every time a computer is booted, a word-processing document is opened, or one double-clicks on a game, so does malware operate. The challenge for the malware writer is how to get the malicious lines of code to be executed on the victim's computer. There are three primary ways this happens:

1. The victim intentionally executes a malicious program without the knowledge that it is, in fact, malware.

2. By way of a software vulnerability (i.e., software flaw/bug), malware imbeds itself into legitimate code, and the victim unintentionally executes this code when performing a seemingly normal operation: opening a word-processing document, viewing a webpage, or inserting a USB (Universal Serial Bus) drive into a computer, for example.

3. Malware creeps onto a computer over a network connection and, by way of a software vulnerability, is able to execute itself, resulting in a malware infection.

For the most part, malicious lines of code are most often executed on a computer as a result of an action that we, the users, take as described in Items 1 and 2. Malware infections of the nature described in Item 3, however, are not the result of a user action but instead a result of some type of inaction. In many cases, the lack of taking a proactive stance to security, for example, failing to install software patches or not enabling a firewall, leaves a computer vulnerable to malware infections. The importance of taking protective measures against malware is discussed further in Chapter 6. Although it is not always the case, the success of malware is most often contingent on decisions that we do or do not make. This means that we, the users, play a significant role in preventing malware infections. Understanding how a computer actually becomes infected with malware aids in this effort.

5.3 HOW DO I GET MALWARE?

This section discusses the many different ways in which a computer can become infected with malware. The purpose of this section is not to use scare tactics to compel you to take immediate actions or drastically alter your computer habits, but instead to highlight what is possible, how malware spreads, and what actions could result in a malware infection. In the context of the nondigital world, the knowledge that there is an increased risk of contracting a biological illness by touching public door handles does not stop many of us from performing such actions. However, it certainly does help to understand the risks that we are taking and the most effective way with which to deal with these risks.

5.3.1 Removable Media

Before it became commonplace to connect computers together to form networks, the Internet being the largest network of all, the primary means by which malware was passed from computer to computer was by way of floppy disks. Malware of this nature did not spread as a file stored on the floppy disk but instead as malicious code resident in the floppy disk that was executed every time a computer loaded or "booted" the floppy disk. Known as a *boot-sector virus*, the first type of malware the digital world came to know (outside the environment in which it was written) was created by a teenager as a prank. Written by 15-year-old Richard Skrenta in 1982, the first virus targeted Apple II computers and was named "Elk Cloner" after the poetic message it displayed on the victim's computer every 50th time the infected computer was booted (Figure 5.1).

```
Elk Cloner:
    The program with a personality

It will get on all your disks
It will infiltrate your chips
Yes, it's Cloner!

It will stick to you like glue
It will modify RAM too
Send in the Cloner!
```

FIGURE 5.1   Elk Cloner poem.

The propagation of such a virus worked as follows: When an infected floppy disk was shared between two people and booted by a previously uninfected and vulnerable computer, the virus would replicate itself and spread from the floppy disk to the computer, resulting in contamination. On insertion of a new, vulnerable, and previously virus-free floppy disk into an infected computer, the virus would then seek to infect the new disk and so on. As one can imagine, viruses of this nature did not spread with blazing speed and were confined to much smaller circles than most types of modern-day malware. It was not until 1986 that the first virus was created that targeted a Microsoft OS. Also a boot-sector virus like Elk Cloner, the first Microsoft-based virus was dubbed "Brain" because it changed the name of each infected floppy disk to that of Brain.

It was no coincidence that Len Adelman would coin the term *virus* in 1983 to describe this type of malicious code. Just like biological viruses, *computer viruses* are dependent on a host to survive as well as humans to propagate. In the case of the Elk Cloner and Brain viruses, and in many viruses to follow, the virus (i.e., a parasite) required a floppy disk (i.e., a host) and a human to take an action, such as transferring a floppy disk between computers. The characteristic of seeking to infect a host file or device and their reliance on human action distinguishes viruses from other types of malware.

Since the creation of the boot-sector virus, many different forms of removable storage, like the comparatively sleeker and higher-capacity USB flash drives that are predominantly used today, have replaced the outdated floppy disk. Even though the technology has changed, the threat of spreading viruses by way of external storage devices remains. Like a floppy disk of years past, now the simple act of plugging a USB flash drive into a computer is enough for a virus to spread from one to the other. It is suspected that this very means of propagation was responsible for a malware infection on the International Space Station in 2008. USB drives have also been suspected as the cause of a number of other high-profile malware infections, such as the Stuxnet malware attack on the Iranian nuclear plants in 2010, the downing of Spainar flight 5022, and numerous attacks on U.S. government and military computer systems. During 2008 and 2009, the danger of malware infections by way of external media was such a formidable threat to U.S. military and government computer systems that USB flash drives were forbidden from use on any computer connected to a military network by order of the Department of Defense.

The simplicity of spreading viruses via USB flash drives, when coupled with their popularity and capability for easy concealment, make these devices a formidable obstacle for corporations as well. In one example of social engineering (Chapter 11), a security-auditing team (known as penetration testers) was hired to test the susceptibility of a credit union to security threats. One test used social engineering techniques to target the potential weakness of employees with respect to introducing malware onto the corporation's computer systems. To do this, the penetration testers scattered a number of USB flash drives in the company parking lot and around the smoking area near the credit union. As employees came to work in the morning and noticed the USB drives on the ground, they did what any benevolent human would do: They brought them inside and plugged them into their computers to discover to whom they belonged. In doing this, the employees unknowingly installed a benign form of malware on their computers—one that allowed the penetration testers to monitor the success rate of the attack. Of the 15 USB drives that were found by the credit union employees, all were plugged into a corporate computer.

Due to the threat of a malware infection, caution should be taken when deciding whether to plug a rogue USB flash drive into your computer or your USB flash drive into an untrusted computer. For the sake of practical computer security, an untrusted USB drive should be treated like an abandoned fountain soda found in a mall food court. Just as one would not take a sip of the soda to discover its flavor, one should also strongly curtail curiosity and refrain from inserting a rogue USB flash drive into their computer as such an action could result in a malware infection.

5.3.2 Documents and Executables

Just as viruses can reside in the startup code on a USB flash drive, they can also imbed themselves in computer files, such as word-processing documents, PDFs, and executable programs. Not only are USB flash drives able to transfer malware to uninfected computers, but also they possess the capability to transfer infected documents. Remember that a virus is dependent on two factors to be able to propagate and infect new computers: a host and a human action. In this case, the host is a document or an executable program, and the human action is the opening of the document or the execution of the program.

Modern word-processing documents are much more than simply text files. They possess a number of features provided by *macros*, which are small programs embedded in the document that allow their creators to embed functionality such as autofill capabilities, error checking, and drop-down options into the document. While macros are convenient, they also have introduced vulnerabilities that have been exploited by viruses. On exploitation, the virus infects the host computer and attaches itself to similarly vulnerable files. Known as a *macro virus*, this particular type of malware was first introduced in 1995 and has infected millions of computers over the years. The result of infection from macro viruses has ranged from being a petty annoyance slowing down a computer to damaging files or even deleting entire hard drives. In one peculiar case, the Beast virus would randomly open and close the CD-ROM door of an infected computer.

If a word-processing document (host) is infected with a virus (parasite) and is transferred to an uninfected computer, the computer is not immediately infected. Not until the document is opened (human action) and the malicious code is executed does the virus have the ability to infect. Otherwise, unexecuted, the virus remains dormant, waiting patiently in the document either to be opened, and thus executed, or to be detected by antivirus software. Aware that word-processing documents and spreadsheets contain macros that can harbor malware, software applications that open these files often prompt users to ensure that they do indeed understand the risk and want to open the document (Figure 5.2).

Macro viruses are not specific to word-processing or spreadsheet documents. They can infect all types of files, including PDF documents. In fact, PDF documents have recently supplanted Microsoft Office documents as the preferred attack vector for malware writers. This is in large part due the increasing number of vulnerabilities found in Adobe Acrobat Reader as compared to Microsoft Office applications.

Viruses can also infect executable programs (files typically with EXE or COM extensions; i.e., virus.exe) in much the same way they do to word-processing document files. Appropriately dubbed *file-infector viruses*, this type of malware exploits a software vulnerability and implants itself into the code of an executable program, which can be anything from an

FIGURE 5.2   Warning message for macro virus.

application to a game or even a utility. When the infected program or application is executed on a computer, the virus is able to spread to the computer and replicate itself in order to infect similar types of programs.

Just as many different kinds of human ailments can be transferred from one person to another by sharing a can of soda, kissing, shaking hands, breathing in close proximity, and the like, so can viruses spread between computers by sharing removable media, documents, and executables. This knowledge should not stop us from opening documents, executing applications, or sharing USB devices, but one should employ similar scrutiny with respect to objects in the digital world that can transfer computer viruses as you do with objects in the physical world that can transfer biological viruses. If you would not share a can of soda with a stranger on the street then you should not share documents with a stranger via email or insert a stranger's USB flash drive into your computer.

5.3.3 Internet Downloads

It has been seen that viruses can be spread to computers via external storage and in different types of computer files. In the case of the latter, this category of viruses can be transferred between computers via email attachments, shared network drives, and downloads from peer-to-peer (P2P) sharing networks. It is also reasonable to suspect that such viruses can also be downloaded from the Internet. While downloading viruses will always be a threat, this category of malware is not the only type of threat one must consider when surfing the web.

Downloading files from the Internet spurred another classification of malware known as *Trojan horses*. To entice their victim into downloading and executing this type of malware, a Trojan horse uses a façade such as a screen saver or useful utility application to present itself to the user. This type of malware finds its way onto a computer when a user believes that he or she simply is downloading a file such as a screen saver. They are, in fact, acquiring a new screen saver, but as they do so they are also unknowingly downloading malware hidden within the screen saver, hence the name *Trojan horse*. The name *Trojan horse* is fittingly derived from the tale of the Greek army concealing soldiers in a giant wooden horse to fool the Trojans. The cleverness of this type of malware distribution preys on the desire of Internet users to acquire flashy or intriguing "free downloads" online. P2P software applications have been historically notorious for being a Trojan horse for different types of malware like spyware and adware.

A significant difference in the classification between a virus and a Trojan horse is that a Trojan horse does not seek to propagate to other computers by attaching itself to a host file or external storage device. This type of malware is perfectly content with carrying out its malicious deed on the computer it infects. Furthermore, the inclusion of the malicious code within infected programs as a façade is not an accident, and it is not typically the result of a software vulnerability, as is the case with a virus. The malware creator carefully, and intentionally, hides the malicious code within the Trojan horse program.

5.3.4 Network Connection

The two classifications of malware that have been considered thus far (viruses and Trojan horses) both require some sort of human interaction for the victim computer to become infected. Whether plugging a USB drive into a computer, opening an infected PDF document, or errantly downloading and executing a Trojan horse disguised as a screen saver, the user plays the role of infector in each case. This is positive news for users since they often can control the performance of these actions. Malware writers have recognized the limits of the different types of malware that spread through human action and have consequently evolved their tactics to develop types of malware that are not reliant on humans or tethered to host files.

When malware no longer depends on the actions of a human to propagate from computer to computer or reliance on a host file or program, it is called a *worm*. Worms are autonomous programs that seek to replicate and propagate themselves from computer to computer over a network, such as the Internet. Complete independence from human action makes worms incredibly dangerous, as they can spread around the world, infecting millions of computers in a matter of hours. Like viruses, worms also exploit vulnerabilities in software to propagate. On infecting a computer, worms will actively scan other computers on the same network as the infected computer to search for other computers that also have exploitable vulnerabilities. When such a computer is found, the worm will exploit the vulnerability and replicate itself to a new computer. The worm on the newly infected computer will then also start to scan for vulnerable computers on the new victim's network. The actions of a worm on an infected computer often include a malicious function as well, which is discussed further in the next section.

The first worm was written by Robert Tappan Morris, Jr., in 1988 and is known as the Morris Internet worm. In a few hours, the worm reportedly crashed approximately 6,000 Internet-connected UNIX computers. This is a staggering statistic when one considers that 6,000 computers represented approximately 10% of the computers connected to the Internet in 1988. After the Morris worm, there have been a number of similar high-profile worms that have spread through the Internet, each with its own unique moniker. The Code Red worm that surfaced in 2001 was named for the type of soda that the researchers who first discovered the worm were drinking on that particular day. It took the Code Red worm approximately 9 hours to infect well over 250,000 computers, resulting in an estimated $2 billion in damage. Other popular noteworthy worms include Melissa (1999), the Love Bug (2000), Ramen (2001), Nimda (2001), SQL Slammer (2003), and Conficker (2009).

Today, there are security mechanisms on personal computers that can help to prevent attacks from such worms. Having both a firewall that resides between your computer and the Internet and applying software patches that fix vulnerabilities needed by worms to propagate as soon as they are released will help to protect your computer from this type of ravenous malware. These type of security mechanisms are further discussed in Chapter 6.

5.3.5 Email Attachments

Just as artists are not confined to a single color or medium when creating a work of art, malware writers are not restricted to creating malware with a single propagation method or malicious function. Many types of current-day malware are hybrids of viruses, Trojan horses, and worms. They combine the best (or worst) attributes of each category and contain multiple attack vectors. When such capability is coupled with a little social engineering, the results can be quite devastating. Shown in Figure 5.3 is a phishing email with an attached ZIP file likely to be infected with a virus. Although it is not the most deceiving of phishing emails, the labeling of the PDF document as "password.zip" is done to trick or intrigue the user into opening the ZIP file and thus executing the malware embedded in the document on the victim's computer.

The ease of being able to send numerous email messages easily in a matter of seconds coupled with the social aspects of email (receiving a potentially malicious email from a trusted friend, relative, coworker, or spoofed banking institution) has made email attachments one of the most successful ways of spreading malware between computers. When compared to the laborious transfer of a virus by way of a USB flash drive or even tricking a user to download a Trojan horse, malware that can spread as an

FIGURE 5.3   Phishing email with malicious attachment.

email attachment can infect many computers in a relatively short amount of time.

A famous example of combining the characteristics of different types of malware is that of the Love Bug virus/worm, which, for the sake of brevity, will simply be referred to as a worm. This particular type of malware was sent as an attachment in an email and was titled "LOVE-LETTER-FOR-YOU.TXT.vbs." Users, curious to see what the "love letter" contained, opened the email attachment (human action—virus). The result of this action infected the computer with malware. The malware infection then replicated itself and sent the same email (over a network—worm) with the malicious attachment to the first 50 contacts in the victim's email contact list. As one can imagine, this type of social engineering was quite effective. The people who received the Love Bug email were curious to read a love letter from a friend, acquaintance, coworker, or family member. When the worm was released, it literally traveled around the globe within 24 hours as people awoke, read their emails, and propagated the worm. By one estimate, the Love Bug worm infected 50,000,000 computers around the globe in 1 week's time.

5.3.6 Drive-By Downloads

Just as there is much more than meets the eye to word-processing documents and PDF files, so are modern-day webpages and websites more complicated than they at first appear to be. When graphical web browsers first surfaced in the early 1990s, websites were nothing more than simple text and pictures. Today, web browsers are practically OSs unto themselves with add-ons and plug-ins functioning as applications (Chapter 7). The complexity and functionality that web browsers afford users and developers also provides malware writers a new vector with which to distribute malware. As is the case with macro viruses, this increased functionality in web browsers can also introduce software vulnerabilities that malware is able to exploit.

As discussed in further detail in Chapter 7, a webpage is simply a document (composed of computer code) requested over the Internet that is interpreted (i.e., executed) by a web browser on a computer. The inclusion of malicious code within a webpage allows for this code then to be executed on a computer as the result of simply clicking on a hyperlink in an email, for example. Malware that is distributed via executing a webpage is known as a *drive-by download* or *drive-by install*. As seen in Figure 5.4,

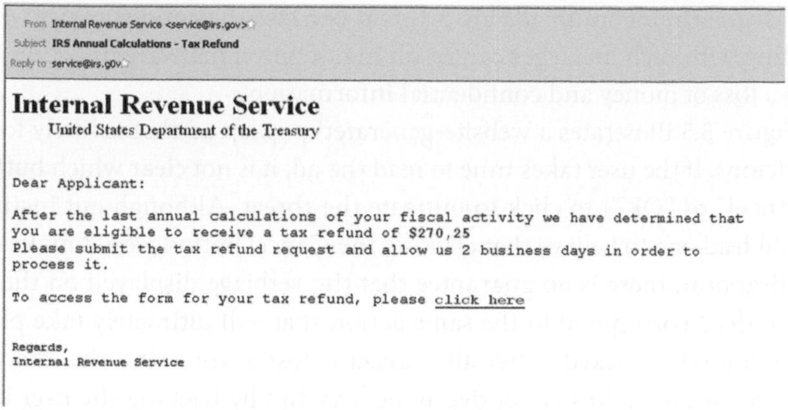

From Internal Revenue Service <service@irs.gov>
Subject **IRS Annual Calculations - Tax Refund**
Reply to service@irs.g0v

Internal Revenue Service
United States Department of the Treasury

```
Dear Applicant:

After the last annual calculations of your fiscal activity we have determined that
you are eligible to receive a tax refund of $270,25
Please submit the tax refund request and allow us 2 business days in order to
process it.

To access the form for your tax refund, please click here


Regards,
Internal Revenue Service
```

FIGURE 5.4 Malicious hyperlink.

simply clicking on the malicious hyperlink could potentially result in a drive-by download.

As discussed in the beginning of this chapter, malware is simply code that is executed on a computer and seeks to perform a malicious act. With the increased popularity and societal reliance on the World Wide Web (WWW), computer users are frequently executing code that has been sent to them in their web browsers from untrusted sources. While most people are generally aware that it is poor security practice to download an untrusted application from a website and execute it on their computer, there is less awareness that the simple act of viewing a webpage can produce similar results. In fact, drive-by downloads were the main cause of infection for the Mac Flashback Trojan in 2012, which infected 600,000 Mac computers. The Flashback Trojan was particularly successful because Mac computers contained a zero-day vulnerability for which a patch had yet to be released.

5.3.7 Pop-Ups

In addition to being annoying, pop-up ads can also serve as a vector to initiate an action that results in a malware infection. Malicious pop-up ads can appear on a computer screen in two ways. First, the pop-up may have been created by malware *already installed on the computer*. The second method occurs as the result of visiting a website that generates the pop-up ad. The content presented in a pop-up ad can be wide ranging, from misleading advertisement messages (i.e., *malicious adware*) to deceiving messages that alert the user his or her computer is infected with malware (i.e., *scareware*). Pop-up ads are a threat because the actions taken when dealing with such messages can result in not only a malware infection but also a loss of money and confidential information.

Figure 5.5 illustrates a website-generated pop-up ad that is likely to be malicious. If the user takes time to read the ad, it is not clear which button ("Cancel" or "OK") to click to mitigate the threat. Although gut instinct would lead one to believe that clicking the Cancel button would make the ad disappear, there is no guarantee that the verbiage displayed on the ad will indeed correspond to the same action that will ultimately take place if the button is clicked. After all, Cancel is just a word, and the attacker has no ethical qualms about deceiving a victim by tricking the user into clicking a misleading button. Often, clicking on either of the two buttons will result in the user unknowingly consenting to travel to a website containing a drive-by download or initiating a download of malware. When confronted with such a pop-up, first and foremost, do not trust or click on any of the buttons or hyperlinks on the ad. The safest course of action is simply to close your web browser without interacting with the pop-up message and then take care to never travel back to that webpage again.

Creators of malicious pop-up ads have become much more devious than merely trying to trick a user into clicking a purposely mislabeled button or hoping the user will errantly click on a button to "GET A $1,000 FREE CASH MONEY!!!" One of the more recent and effective scams that has been sweeping through the Internet are pop-up messages indicating that your computer has just been "scanned" by antivirus software—moments before you did not know the antivirus software existed—and that your computer is infected with malware (Figure 5.6). This type of ploy is known

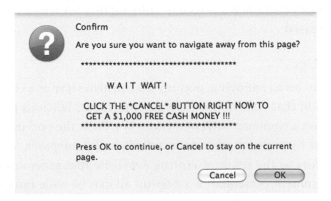

FIGURE 5.5   Malicious pop-up ad.

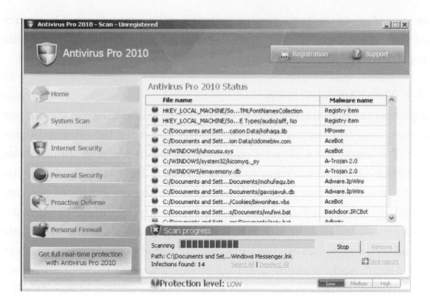

FIGURE 5.6   Scareware example.

as *scareware* or *fake antivirus* and can originate from both malware that is already installed on the victim's computer or by visiting a malicious website. The prime objective of this type of ruse is to con the victim out of money, financial information, or other confidential information.

Scareware uses social engineering tactics to "scare" the user into thinking that he or she has numerous malware infections on his or her computer. Figure 5.6 is a classical example of scareware. Not only does the scareware message appear to be scanning a computer (complete with a progress bar), but also it identifies and lists 14 infections found. By clicking on the pop-up message, the user may inadvertently download malware onto his or her computer, a somewhat ironic result because the user most likely thought that he or she was actually getting rid of malware by performing such an action. However, it is more likely that the user will be taken to a website and be asked to pay a certain amount of money to "get full real-time protection" to remove the phantom malware from the computer. Unfortunately, by purchasing such software, the newly found malware does not go away, and it is likely that by purchasing and installing "Antivirus Pro 2010" (in this example), the user has instead infected his or her computer with malware. It is highly likely at this point that the victim has suffered a loss of money and potentially personal and financial information as well. Simply put, do not trust or click on anything in pop-up ads, regardless of their cunning messages. Furthermore, the only program that should be scanning your computer for malware is the antivirus software that you purchased or installed from a legitimate software vendor.

5.3.8 Malicious Advertising

Subjecting users to unsolicited advertisements while they are viewing or listening to a free service is a concept that pre-dates the personal computer. For years, TV and radio stations have been injecting commercials amid their program offerings to make a profit. The user voluntarily listens to or watches free programming, and the station generates revenue by selling interspersed advertisements. When similar practices are used on Internet-connected computers, such schemes are classified as *adware* (i.e., **ad**vertising soft**ware**). For example, the use of online services such as Bing, Gmail, and Facebook grant users free access to these applications in exchange for viewing web-based adware posted within, above, or adjacent to the application's main content area. This basic concept has allowed companies like Google, Facebook, and others to generate billions of dollars in profits. In such cases, user exposure to adware is an inevitable consequence of using free computer services, and users generally regard it, at most, as an inconvenience.

At first glance, adware may appear to be much more annoying than harmful. *Malicious adware*—as opposed to legitimate adware—works in the same basic advertising framework as legitimate ads one may be used to viewing. However, malicious adware instead displays deceitful or malicious ads. Malicious web-based adware (also called malvertising) is presented to the user as an embedded ad within a webpage. Malicious adware creators have actually found it profitable to pay to have their malicious ads displayed on reputable websites using popular ad distribution networks like Microsoft's adCenter network or even by purchasing ad space on sites like NYtimes.com. The act of clicking on malvertising ad can result in a drive-by download or being taken to a website that cunningly tries to sell a phony product to steal personal and financial information. Because such ads appear on respected, well-known, and trusted websites, these ads tend to lull users into a false sense of security.

5.4 WHAT DOES MALWARE DO?

So far, we have discussed how malware infects computers and how it propagates between computers, but we have yet to describe what malware does once it has a foothold within a computer. This section addresses the more common malicious deeds that malware performs.

Long gone are the days in which the sole purpose of malware was to mischievously display irritating messages, delete files, erase hard drives, crash a system, or annoyingly slow down a computer. More often than not, the motivation of today's malware creators is distinctly monetary in nature. A high priority for malware programmers is for their malware to avoid being detected at all costs. If you are lucky enough to escape having your hard drive erased as the result of a malware infection, do not assume that you have escaped its grasp. There are inevitable trade-offs when a malware infection takes control of a computer system. On infecting a computer with malware, cyber criminals can literally put a computer to work to accomplish a number of malevolent deeds that financially benefit the malware creator at the victim's expense. The more common types of malware often associated with this type of behavior are malicious adware, spyware, ransomware, backdoors, disable security functionality, and botnets. These types of malicious software usually find their way onto a computer by employing the malware propagation methods discussed previously (e.g., viruses, worms, Trojan horses, or drive-by downloads).

5.4.1 Malicious Adware

Application-based adware, in contrast to web-based adware, is malware applications surreptitiously installed on a computer as the result of a malware infection. This type of malware may generate pop-ups, install unsolicited web browser banners, change the victim's web browser default home page, or redirect the victim's web browser to unrequested websites.

The objective of malicious adware, like legitimate adware, is to make a profit for the adware creator. This can occur when a victim errantly clicks on a pop-up ad, is redirected to view a specific website, or is tricked into buying a fraudulent item, such as fake antivirus software (scareware). Clicking on a malicious ad can also be detrimental to the victim because it can result in a drive-by download and yet another installation of a malware program. Last, but not least, malicious adware can often be less than tasteful in its content—displaying pop-ups or redirecting the victim's web browser to websites that are pornographic or otherwise offensive in nature. This is certainly not content that most users want to appear randomly on their personal, family, or work computers. The one upside of having malicious adware, in comparison to more surreptitious types of malware, is that it makes its presence known and leaves little doubt to the victim of its intentions.

5.4.2 Spyware

The descriptive name *spyware* leaves no question with respect to the function of this type of malware. Spyware, like some types of adware, is a malicious application that is installed on a victim's computer, most likely as the result of a virus, worm, Trojan horse, or drive-by download. Spyware's function is simply to spy on the computer user to accumulate valuable pieces of information from the victim's computing activity. In addition to recording keystrokes typed (i.e., key-logging) on a victim's keyboard, this classification of malware has been known to take screen shots of the victim's monitor, stream video or audio from the victim's computer, and record web browsing habits or even computing habits. The information gathered is then periodically sent over the Internet back to the spyware creator, who then tries to turn that knowledge into money on underground Internet marketplaces. Unlike adware, and like most common types of current malware, the actions of spyware will likely remain unnoticed by the user as it hides in the background, trying to avoid detection. The more information that is obtained and the longer the spyware can persist on a victim's computer, the more profitable it is to the spyware owner. Spyware, and especially key-loggers (Chapter 3), are particularly dangerous as they may be able to steal a user's entire identity, a whole collection of passwords, or financial information and send it across the Internet without the user's knowledge.

To create synergies between different types of malware, some spyware programs are coupled with adware. The spyware observes the browsing or computing habits of the victim and then shares this information with the adware to generate ads that increase the chance of being clicked on or activated by the victim. This kind of spyware basically acts as a malicious form of targeted advertising.

5.4.3 Ransomware

Ransomware, similar in physical appearance to scareware, is a type of malware that will hold data on the victim's computer hostage in return for a ransom payment. On infecting a computer through installation of a virus or Trojan horse, ransomware may either encrypt part of the victim's hard drive (making picture, music, or document files completely unavailable to the computer owner) or may actually lock the user out of his or her computer. The ransomware will then generate a message informing the user of the attack and demand a ransom payment for a decryption or access key. Malware of this nature is troublesome to the victim for two important reasons. First, just like on television or in the movies, paying the ransom fee may not result in obtaining the decryption key. Second, the process of paying the ransom fee may not only result in the loss of money but also risk potential disclosure of personal and financial information to the attacker. Regardless of what the ransomware message states, do not be fooled and fall for this trap. This type of malware is a complete scam and is best prevented with antivirus software, software patches, user education, and most important, performing routine data backups—all topics discussed in Chapter 6. Even if the ransomware encrypts part of a computer's hard drive and renders that particular data unavailable, the victim at least has a data backup copy with which he or she can use to recover from such an attack.

5.4.4 Backdoor

Once malware has a foothold on a computer, the possibilities of its potential malicious actions are endless. To ensure that the victim's computer is accessible at a later time for future updates to the malware or to download additional malware, malware can be equipped with the functionality to essentially create a hidden "backdoor" on the victim's computer. Many times, as was the case with the Love Bug worm, malware used a backdoor to download even more malware onto the infected computer. After the initial infection, the Love Bug worm downloaded a key-logger onto the victim's computer—further compounding the damage that was done. Cyber criminals even go so far as to charge other malware writers a fee to install new malware on a computer on which they have a backdoor established.

5.4.5 Disable Security Functionality

To preserve the malware's functionality and increase its longevity on a victim's computer, on infection some types of malware contain the ability to disable security mechanisms like firewalls, antivirus software, and software update applications. This behavior makes it difficult for the victim to download software to fix vulnerabilities or to remove the malware. The Conficker worm, for example, disabled applications like Windows Automatic Update (i.e., patches) and Windows Security Center (i.e., antivirus software); prevented users from accessing security vendor websites like Symantec.com and McAfee.com; and barred antivirus software programs from updating their virus definitions (Chapter 6). These self-defense techniques are prime examples of the technical capability and cleverness that malware writers possess to preserve the functionality of their malware long after it initially infects the victim's computer.

5.4.6 Botnets

Malware creators also enslave victims' computers into what are known as ro**bot net**works (i.e., botnets). In this case, the function of the malware is to create a backdoor on the victim's computer that allows the malware creator (i.e., a botmaster) not only to access infected computers at a later time but also to instruct the infected computers to perform coordinated and malicious tasks on behalf of the botmaster. These tasks include the brute-force cracking of password hashes, sending spam email, or performing Distributed Denial of Service (DDoS) attacks—attacks in which all bot computers in a botnet request webpages from a single website at a blistering rate, essentially rendering the website useless, hence, denial of service. Another popular application of botnets has been for botnet masters to extort money from online gambling websites by threatening that a botnet will perform a DDoS attack the day before and the day of the Super Bowl, for instance, essentially crippling the website during its most profitable time. To put the size of a botnet into perspective, the Flashback Trojan (2012) is believed to have assembled a 600,000-node botnet, while the Conficker worm (2011) is estimated to have amassed a botnet of as many as 12 million computers. The collective actions of such a large botnet possess enormous capacity to disrupt many services on the Internet and are incredibly difficult to defend against.

5.5 SUMMARY

A critical reader will be quick to point out that, while a plethora of different types of malware have been introduced and their malicious functions have been described, there has been little or no discussion regarding just how to prevent such infections. Methods for protecting one's system against malware are covered in Chapter 6. Now that we have identified different types of malware, learned how malware propagates, and have a basic understanding regarding what malware does once it infects a computer, a context has been established for discussion of preventing, detecting, and responding to malware. We also have a start toward achieving the ability to highlight the strengths and weaknesses of common security mechanisms, such as antivirus software and firewalls.

- Malware is a catchall term used to describe several different categories of potential threats, including viruses, worms, Trojan horses, and many others.

- Malware is malicious computer code that often is executed unintentionally by a user.

- There are a number of ways in which malware can infect a computer. The more popular methods have been through removable media like USB flash drives, documents and executables, Internet downloads, and by means of a network connection, email attachments, webpages, pop-ups, and malvertising ads.

- The simple act of plugging a USB flash drive into a computer is enough to infect a computer with a virus or vice versa.

- A virus is a type of malware that requires a host file and some type of user interaction to spread.

- Documents and executables can also contain viruses. The simple act of opening a document can result in a malware infection.

- A Trojan horse is a type of malware that appears as a legitimate program but contains hidden malware that is executed on a computer when the façade program that masks the malware is installed.

- A worm is a type of malware that can propagate without human interaction and without a host file. Worms typically propagate over networks and have the potential to infect millions of computers in a very short time.

- An email attachment, often coupled with social engineering, is a classic malware distribution method that continues to be highly effective.

- The simple act of viewing a webpage is enough to contract malware by way of a drive-by download.

- Because of the threat of scareware and other types of misleading messages, do not trust or interacted with pop-up ads.

- Even ads on legitimate websites can be malicious and should be treated with caution.

- The predominant function of malware is to generate money for its creator and to avoid detection at all costs.

- The tasks that malware performs once it is installed on a computer include malicious adware, spyware, ransomware, creation of a backdoor, disabling of security functions, and the creation of botnets.

- Malware is best migrated through a defense-in-depth strategy.

BIBLIOGRAPHY

Acohido, B. 2010. Jetliner crash shows dangers of using tainted USB sticks. *USA Today.* http://content.usatoday.com/communities/technologylive/post/2010/08/infected-usb-thumb-drive-implicated-in-deadly-2008-spanair-jetliner-crash/1#.T4RIs46fBGA (accessed April 10, 2012).

Anderson, B., and Anderson, B. 2010. *Seven Deadliest USB Attacks.* Waltham, MA: Syngress.

Andress, J., and Winterfeld, S. 2011. *Cyber Warfare: Techniques, Tactics and Tools for Security Practitioners.* New York: Elsevier.

Baldor, L. 2010. Military relaxes ban on computer flash drives. MSNBC. http://www.msnbc.msn.com/id/35487827/ns/technology_and_science-security/t/military-relaxes-ban-computer-flash-drives/#.T4RJ9Y6fBGA (accessed April 10, 2012).

Bishop, M. 2003. *Computer Security: Art and Science.* Boston: Addison-Wesley Professional.

CBSNews. The Conficker worm. http://www.cbsnews.com/2100-3455_162-4905468.html (accessed April 12, 2012).

DarkReading. 2006. Social engineering, the USB way. http://www.darkreading.com/security/article/208803634/index.html (accessed April 10, 2012).

F-Secure. 2000. Email-Worm:VBS/LoveLetter. http://www.f-secure.com/v-descs/love.shtml (accessed April 12, 2012).

Goodin, D. 2010. It's official: Adobe Reader is world's most-exploited app. *The Register.* http://www.theregister.co.uk/2010/03/09/adobe_reader_attacks/ (Accessed April 10, 2012).

Greenberg, A. 2012. Researchers confirm Flashback Trojan infects 600,000 Macs, used for click fraud. *Forbes.* http://www.forbes.com/sites/andygreenberg/2012/04/06/researchers-confirm-flashback-trojan-infects-600000-macs-being-used-for-clickfraud/ (accessed April 12, 2012).

Hines, M. 2008. Web users in malware crosshairs. *PC World.* http://www.pcworld.com/businesscenter/article/144299/web_users_in_malware_crosshairs.html (accessed April 9, 2012).

Jakobsson, M., and Ramzan, Z. 2008. *Crimeware: Understanding New Attacks and Defenses.* Boston: Addison-Wesley Professional.

Jesdanun, A. 2007. School prank starts 25 years of security woes. MSNBC. http://www.msnbc.msn.com/id/20534084/ns/technology_and_science-security/t/school-prank-starts-years-security-woes/#.T4N-co6fBMo (accessed April 9, 2012).

Lemos, R. 2003. A 20-year plague. CNet. http://news.cnet.com/A-20-year-plague/2009-7349_3-5111410.html?tag=item (accessed April 10, 2012).

List of computer viruses developed in 1980s. 2009. InfoNIAC. http://www.infoniac.com/hi-tech/list-of-computer-viruses-developed-in-1980s.html (accessed April 9, 2012).

Markoff, M. 2009. The Conficker Worm: April fool's joke or unthinkable disaster? *New York Times.* http://bits.blogs.nytimes.com/2009/03/19/the-conficker-worm-april-fools-joke-or-unthinkable-disaster/ (accessed April 12, 2012).

NPR. 2011. The "worm" that could bring down the Internet. NPR. http://www.npr.org/2011/09/27/140704494/the-worm-that-could-bring-down-the-internet (accessed April 12, 2012).

Pfleeger, C., and Pfleeger, S. 2011. *Analyzing Computer Security: A Threat/Vulnerability/Countermeasure Approach.* Indianapolis, IN: Prentice Hall Professional.

Potter, N. 2009. Top 10 computer viruses and worms. ABC News. http://abcnews.go.com/Technology/top-computer-viruses-worms-internet-history/story?id=8480794#.T4bJpo6fBGE (accessed April 12, 2012).

Provos, N., and Holz, T. 2007. *Virtual Honeypots: From Botnet Tracking to Intrusion Detection.* Indianapolis, IN: Pearson Education.

Rajnovic, D., and Caudill, M. 2010. *Computer Incident Response and Product Security.* Indianapolis, IN: Pearson Education.

Rhodes, R. 2011. *Cyber Meltdown.* Eugene, OR: Harvest House.

Salomon, D. 2010. *Elements of Computer Security.* New York: Springer.

Schneier, B. 2011. *Secrets and Lies: Digital Security in a Networked World.* New York: Wiley.

Shactman, N. 2008. Under worm assault, military bans disks, USB drives. *Wired.* http://www.wired.com/dangerroom/2008/11/army-bans-usb-d/ (accessed April 10, 2012).

Skoudis, E., and Zeltser, L. 2004. *Malware: Fighting Malicious Code.* Indianapolis, IN: Prentice Hall Professional.

Szor, P. 2005. *The Art of Computer Virus Research and Defense.* Indianapolis, IN: Pearson Education.

Vance, A. 2009. *Times* Web ads show security breach. *New York Times.* http://www.nytimes.com/2009/09/15/technology/internet/15adco.html?_r=1 (accessed April 12, 2012).

Veiga, J. 2009. *The Myths of Security: What the Computer Security Industry Doesn't Want You to Know.* Sebastopol, CA: O'Reilly Media.

White, S. 2001. When did the term "computer virus" arise? *Scientific American.* http://www.scientificamerican.com/article.cfm?id=when-did-the-term-compute (accessed April 10, 2012).

Wingfield, N. 2009. Microsoft takes aim at "mal-ads." *Wall Street Journal.* http://online.wsj.com/article/SB125323621695721795.html (accessed April 12, 2012).

Zetter, K. 2009. Nov. 10 1983: computer "virus" is born. *Wired.* http://www.wired.com/thisdayintech/2009/11/1110fred-cohen-first-computer-virus/ (accessed April 10, 2012).

CHAPTER 6

Malware: Defense in Depth

6.1 INTRODUCTION

In the context of computers and the Internet, there is no such thing as absolute security. No matter what precautions are taken, computers will always be vulnerable to a certain number of attacks, and there is no single security mechanism that can be purchased or downloaded that will be able to mitigate all potential threats. Although disheartening, this is the current state of computer security, and we must react accordingly. Just as modern medicine cannot always protect one's health against a multitude of diseases, biological viruses, and illnesses, neither can security software vendors protect one's computer and personal data against all occurrences of malware or hacking. As an analogy, consider the common cold. Although it seems likely that the common cold will never be eradicated, one can significantly decrease chances of contacting this illness by washing their hands, avoiding sick people, getting plenty of rest, and keeping their hands out of their nose, eyes, and mouth. This type of multilayer, precautionary, and proactive approach corresponds exactly to the strategy outlined in this chapter to safeguard a computer.

The best defense against the myriad possible malware and hacking events that threaten the confidentiality, integrity, and availability of computing devices and personal information is a defense-in-depth approach to information security. Under this defensive strategy, no single mechanism is responsible for all defensive tasks, and employing a combination of many diverse mechanisms and strategies significantly decreases one's risk of an attack. Like wearing both a belt and suspenders, if one security mechanism fails, we can rely on another to keep our pants up, so to speak.

The five components comprising the defense-in-depth strategy described in this chapter are: (1) data backup, (2) firewalls, (3) software patches, (4) antivirus software, and (5) user education. Each of these components is essential, and the neglect of even one of them increases one's chance of falling victim to malware or of being unable to successfully prevent, detect, or recover from malware attacks.

6.2 DATA BACKUP

If you ask a dentist, "Which teeth should I floss?" the dentist will probably reply, "Only the teeth you want to save." The same principle holds true with respect to data backup—only back up the data that you want to save. We live in a digital world in which personal computers store a vast number of documents, pictures, videos, and financial statements that are, in many respects and to various degrees, invaluable and irreplaceable. Unfortunately, data in its digital form is just as susceptible to destruction as is physical printed data. Data backup is the first technique to be used in the defense-in-depth strategy. It can protect against not only the side effects of malware, but also a number of other computer catastrophes.

Data failures are inevitable, and malware can strike at any time. A hard drive can crash, a glass of water can spill on a laptop keyboard, or malware can delete a hard drive, all without warning. Any one of a good number of such unforeseen events could occur on any given day and result in the destruction of one's most treasured data. Ask yourself this question: If, right now, your laptop hard drive crashes or a piece of ransomware encrypts part of your hard drive, would you be able to successfully recover your data from a backup? This is the ultimate recovery test because failures rarely give warning. If one subscribes to Murphy's law, one knows that failures happen at the most inconvenient of times. If the answer to the question is "no" and you value your data, then it is time to establish a sound backup strategy.

There are a number of both methods and storage mediums that can be used to replicate data for safekeeping. Three of the most common types of backup methods are as follows:

- **File Backup:** Archiving individual files or folders.

- **System Image Backup:** A complete system backup of all system files and personal files. This enables one to completely restore the entire computing environment to a previously saved backup image.

- **System Restore:** Different from a system image backup, a system restore copies only system files and not personal files such as pictures, emails, or other documents. This enables one to restore a computing environment to a previous state without affecting current personal files.

Depending on one's preferred backup method, there are a number of storage media, such as external hard drives, CDs, DVDs, USB (Universal Serial Bus) flash drives, and online backup services that all provide large-volume data storage solutions. Furthermore, any of these options are relatively affordable if one considers their digital data to be priceless, or at least of great value. There is no one-size-fits-all method for backing up data, and each backup solution is dependent on both the method and the storage medium that is chosen. Operating systems (i.e., Windows operating system and Mac OS X) and some external hard drives are equipped with software to perform one or more of the described backup methods. Find the method that works best for you, stick to a normal schedule (e.g., backing up data on a daily or weekly basis), and verify that you can indeed restore your data when needed. In addition to preventing against hardware failures and malware, it is good security practice to keep a backup copy of your most valuable digital items in a secure location separate from the original to guard against threats like fire and theft.

Establishing and using a backup strategy is essential to the preservation and longevity of data with respect to a number of possible threats. Realistically speaking, it is not a matter of planning for *if* your hard drive will fail or your computer will become infected with malware; it is planning for *when* this happens. It is important to note that a computer hard drive (or any computer memory option for that matter) exists in two states: (1) the hard drive is going to fail or (2) the hard drive has failed. Hard drives are not made to last forever, and they will inevitably fail. No matter what ills may befall your computer, having a sound backup strategy will allow you either to recover a previous copy of your data or to transfer it to another computer. For protection against malware such as ransomware, having a backup of data may be the last line of defense. It is necessary to take a proactive approach to data backup because it is likely that you will not have the opportunity to recover data after it has been destroyed or deleted.

6.3 FIREWALLS

Throughout history, many different civilizations have constructed defensive walls or barriers to separate themselves from the dangers of "others." Examples include the Great Wall of China, the French Maginot Line, or Hadrian's Wall in northern England. Each of these structures is an example of a physical barrier that was constructed to fortify a safe zone between an "us" and a "them." It should be no surprise that defenses in cyberspace have employed similar techniques of isolation. Firewalls are the digital equivalent to the previous examples of physical security barriers. They act as defensive mechanisms that protect against dangers that lurk on the Internet. However, just as Hadrian's Wall was not the end-all of defensive structures, and could in fact be circumvented by simply sailing around it in a boat, so can firewalls be defeated. To avoid such a gap in our security defense, we examine exactly what a firewall does and does not protect against and why it is an essential component—but only a component—of the presented defense-in-depth strategy.

6.3.1 Function of a Firewall

A firewall is a security mechanism that provides protection against unwanted and malicious network traffic (e.g., Internet traffic) from reaching a computer. Without a firewall, a computer is essentially a sitting duck and is susceptible to network-based attacks from hackers or malware (i.e., worms) that propagate over a network connection. With a firewall, as conceptually shown in Figure 6.1, a computer is effectively isolated from the Internet. The task of a firewall is to prevent or filter malicious Internet traffic from reaching a computer while permitting legitimate traffic to pass unhindered. Firewalls do not, however, inspect the content of network traffic for malware. As a result, firewalls do not prevent a user from downloading a Trojan horse or a malicious email attachment, and thus other defense-in-depth mechanisms are needed to protect against such threats.

A firewall filters network traffic based on the origin of a request to the Internet, that is, was the action first initiated from the computer behind the firewall? Only replies that were first initiated by Alice's computer behind the firewall are to pass from the Internet back through the firewall. This functionality enables a firewall to protect against worms and hackers

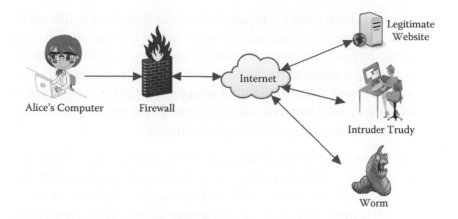

FIGURE 6.1   Conceptual firewall diagram.

like Intruder Trudy, the two predominant network-based threats on the Internet. To better understand why a firewall protects against worms and not against Trojan horses, the basic workings of a firewall are diagrammed in Figure 6.2, which depicts a simplified sequence of events that occurs when Alice's computer, residing behind a firewall, requests a webpage (from CNN, in this example) from a server on the Internet.

(1) To view CNN's website on Alice's computer, Alice issues a request in her web browser by clicking on a hyperlink or bookmark or typing "www.cnn.com" in the web browser address bar and pressing "Enter" on the keyboard. Much like addressing an envelope to be sent by snail mail, this action generates a request message addressed to CNN's web server that will be sent from Alice's computer to CNN's web server via the Internet (Chapter 2).

(2) Before the outgoing request message can be routed from Alice's computer to the Internet and eventually to CNN's web server, it must first pass through Alice's firewall. Because the request message

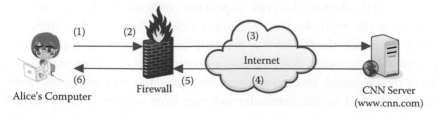

FIGURE 6.2   Functionality of a firewall.

originates from Alice's computer behind the firewall, it is allowed to pass through to the Internet. However, before the request is routed to the Internet, the firewall makes a note that Alice's computer is requesting a webpage from CNN's web server. This action indicates to the firewall that a response message from CNN's web server is to be expected. Therefore, when the anticipated response arrives, it should be allowed to pass through the firewall.

(3) As discussed in Chapter 2, the request message that Alice's computer generated for CNN's homepage is then routed through the Internet and eventually arrives at CNN's web server. In reply to the request, the CNN web server generates a response message that contains the content of their homepage (www.cnn.com), the requested webpage.

(4) The response message from CNN's web server is then routed back through the Internet and ultimately reaches Alice's firewall.

(5) The firewall is tasked with scrutinizing all messages originating from the Internet that wish to pass through to Alice's computer. In this case, because a request was originally initiated for CNN's web server from Alice's computer behind the firewall, the firewall is expecting a response from CNN's web server. Thus, when the expected response arrives, the firewall makes the decision to allow the response message to pass through and routes it to Alice's computer.

(6) When Alice's computer receives the response message from CNN's web server, its contents are interpreted by Alice's web browser, which then displays the homepage for www.cnn.com.

This high-level overview illustrates the simplicity of the firewall's function. The firewall is tasked only with allowing network traffic to reach Alice's computer if a request is first initiated from behind the firewall. Notice that the firewall does not inspect the contents of either the original request or the reply. Such inspection is not the firewall's function, and this is ultimately the reason why firewalls do not prevent us from requesting phishing websites, downloading a Trojan horse or falling victim to a drive-by download. In each of these examples, the user ultimately initiated the request for the particular webpage from within the firewall, and thus the response, whether malicious or not, is routed back to the requesting computer, unhindered by the firewall.

6.3.2 What Types of Malware Does a Firewall Protect Against?

As discussed in Chapter 5, a defining characteristic of a worm is that it is able to spread over a network without human involvement. One of the ways in which worms propagate is by performing an automated process of scanning computers on a network for vulnerabilities that can be exploited. This process is similar to the actions that a hacker performs. However, with a firewall in place, a computer is protected against such network-based activity and resulting attacks. The example in Figure 6.3 illustrates how the functionality of a firewall protects against such threats.

(1) To gain access to a computer, worms and hackers craft malicious messages and send them through the Internet with the hope that the malicious messages are able to exploit one or more vulnerabilities on a target computer.

(2) If a computer is behind a firewall, these malicious messages are not routed to the computer unchecked. As we now know, a firewall inspects all incoming traffic that originates from the Internet.

(3) In this case, because the target computer behind the firewall (i.e., Alice's computer) did not first initiate any requests either to the worm or to Intruder Trudy's computer, the firewall blocks the malicious messages. Only responses to requests that originate from the computer behind the firewall are allowed to travel through the firewall. All unwanted and potentially malicious Internet traffic is thus discarded by the firewall before it ever reaches the target computer.

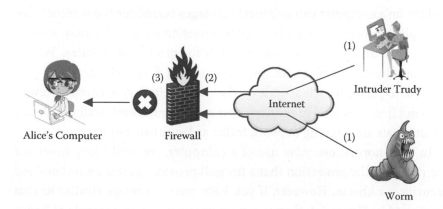

FIGURE 6.3 Malicious requests blocked by a firewall.

6.3.3 Two Types of Firewalls

There are two types of firewalls: (1) software firewalls and (2) hardware firewalls. Software firewalls (also called personal firewalls) are either elements of an operating system or are installed on a computer as a separate application. Hardware firewalls, on the other hand, are built into a router—a device used as a gateway to connect to the Internet. Because both types of firewalls shield computers from the Internet, a question that often arises is: Do I need to be protected behind both a hardware and software firewall? To answer this question, we can apply the defense-in-depth concept to this particular context. At the very least, make sure that the software firewall residing on your computer is turned on. If your computer is a laptop, do not rely on wireless routers at a library or coffee shop to be equipped with a firewall to protect your computer from the Internet. If a coffee shop router does indeed have a firewall, then your computer is protected behind two firewalls. But if the router does not have a firewall, at least your own software firewall is enabled, and your computer will not be susceptible to network-based attacks. A software firewall should always be enabled before connecting to the Internet. Studies have shown that computers without a firewall are probed and attacked within minutes of being connected to the Internet.

In addition to performing the functions already discussed, software firewalls residing on a computer also have more enhanced ability to provide an extra layer of protection against network-based attacks than do hardware firewalls. The advantage that the software firewall has over the hardware firewall is that the software firewall can dictate just which applications on a computer can originate messages bound for the Internet. For example, it is often the case that applications on a computer may, unseen to the user, access the Internet to search for patches or updates. With a software firewall in place, an application must first seek the user's permission to perform such actions on the user's behalf. A hardware firewall does not have this level of scrutiny over outgoing network traffic and, as a result, treats all outgoing network traffic as legitimate requests.

In your normal everyday use of a computer, you will likely never see the results of the protection that a firewall provides as it is an unheralded security workhorse. However, if you have seen a message similar to that illustrated in Figure 6.4, then you have encountered an example of how a software firewall is differentiated from a hardware firewall.

FIGURE 6.4   Firewall request to enable an application to connect to the Internet.

Figure 6.4 illustrates a prime example of a software application request-ing permission from the user to access the Internet through a software firewall. Although these "security alerts" are annoying at times, what they are really asking are questions related to whether you really want a pro-gram such as "Microsoft PowerPoint.app" to be connecting to the Internet (Figure 6.4). The problem is that it is difficult to tell whether the program asking for permission to access the Internet is indeed a necessary applica-tion. As a result, to maintain the functionality of a computer, or for lack of understanding of the messages, many people's default action is often to "Allow." It is also common to be bombarded by so many requests that one quits paying attention to the name of the program and grants access to any requesting program. Although this action will never deny a legitimate program access to the Internet, it becomes problematic when one acci-dentally allows a malicious program to access the Internet. As we know from our discussion regarding spyware, this type of malware will mask itself as a legitimate program and attempt to send collected information back to its creator somewhere on the Internet (Figure 6.5). For malware to exfiltrate data from a computer, the information must first pass through

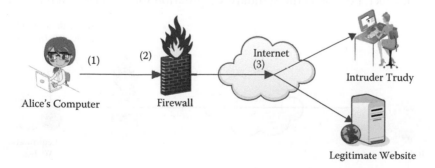

FIGURE 6.5   Firewall blocking a malicious outbound request.

a firewall. Unless one trusts the program asking for permission to access the Internet, it should be blocked. Even if your computer is infected with spyware, if it cannot export your information due to the firewall, a portion of the threat has been successfully mitigated. For the rest of the mitigation, we must turn to our defense-in-depth strategy and rely on antivirus software to identify the malicious program.

6.3.4 Putting a Hole in a Firewall

Thus far, a firewall has been explained to block all messages originating from the Internet that did not first originate from the requesting computer. While this description of a firewall is the predominant use case for personal computers, there are a few exceptions. To better understand what a "hole in a firewall" is and why it is useful, first consider an Internet-facing web server that hosts www.cnn.com, which, for security reasons, surely resides behind a firewall. However, given the current explanation of a firewall, no client requests would ever reach CNN's web server because, by definition of a firewall, all these requests should be blocked by CNN's firewall because they did not first originate from CNN's web server. As shown in Figure 6.6, to enable its millions of clients to be able to request webpages from www.cnn.com via the Internet, a hole is put in CNN's firewall so that clients are able to request web traffic and web traffic only.

When a hole is created in a firewall, it is only done so for a specific type of Internet traffic. In the example shown in Figure 6.6, only web traffic (HTTP, Hypertext Transfer Protocol) is enabled to pass from the Internet through the firewall unhindered. Internet traffic is differentiated by port numbers, which are used to identify the application on the recipient's computer (e.g., CNN's web server) for which the Internet traffic is bound. On the Internet, port 80 is the standard designation for HTTP or web traffic,

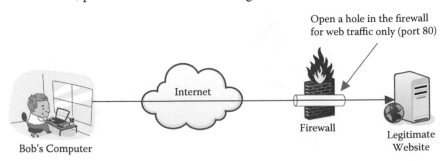

FIGURE 6.6 Creating a hole in a firewall.

port 25 is for SMTP (Simple Mail Transfer Protocol, email), and port 53 is for DNS (Domain Name Service). Because a computer has a single IP (Internet Protocol) address much like an apartment building has a single street address, port addresses can be thought of as apartment numbers for software applications that all reside on the same computer. Therefore, when a web browser issues a request for www.cnn.com, the web browser not only indicates the IP address for www.cnn.com but also indicates the port number (80 for HTTP).

In the context of personal computers (software firewall) or gaming systems (hardware firewall), firewall holes are often required for one to engage in certain types of online games. Much like the example illustrated in Figure 6.6, a hole in a firewall in this context enables online game service providers or other gamers to contact your computer without being hindered by a firewall. While opening a hole in a firewall entails a small security risk, the main point to be taken away from this discussion is that it is much more secure to open a few holes in a firewall than to disable a firewall completely.

6.3.5 Firewalls Are Essential

Now that we have learned that firewalls protect our computers from unauthorized access to and from the Internet, we can also summarize just what firewalls do not protect us against. Just as Hadrian's Wall was not effective against boats that sailed around it, firewalls do not protect against non-network attacks that are not required to pass through a firewall, such as a virus residing on a USB flash drive. Furthermore, firewalls do not prevent people from viewing phishing emails, downloading email attachments that contain viruses, clicking on pop-ups, or downloading Trojan horses from the Internet. A firewall does not differentiate between legitimate and malicious content that is requested by the user and initiated from behind the firewall. Similarly, a virus or worm that propagates via email is able to pass through the firewall. This is possible because, to the firewall, the email transaction appears legitimate as it was initiated from the computer behind the firewall. Not to worry though, the shortcomings of a firewall are compensated for in the defense-in-depth strategy by antivirus software, software patches, data backup, and most important, user education.

To put the functionality of a firewall into perspective, consider the analogy of a lock on the front door of a house or apartment. Like a firewall, the lock prevents untrusted people from entering a home. Although a locked door does not protect against fires, floods, or a criminal breaking in through a window, it represents a basic first step toward security and remains a must-have safety feature for any homeowner. Firewalls function in much the same way by protecting a computer when it is connected to the Internet. Thus, turning off a computer's firewall is equivalent to leaving the front door of a house wide open and then leaving on vacation, in which case one is obviously asking for trouble.

6.4 SOFTWARE PATCHES

Just as fabric patches repair tears in clothing, software patches repair inadequacies in software. Although the term *software patch* can be broadly used to encompass many different kinds of software fixes, such as feature updates, the focus of this section is on patches that are designed to fix security vulnerabilities—the bugs that allow attackers and malware to access computers maliciously.

Software will always have vulnerabilities. It follows that there will always be a race between software vendors who attempt to patch software vulnerabilities and attackers seeking to exploit software vulnerabilities. At the center of this struggle is the computer user, who seeks to minimize the risk of being attacked. In addition to the actions of software vendors and attackers, we, as users, play an important role in this strife by applying software patches as soon as they are available. It should be noted that software patches are not a once-a-month chore, and they are not limited to specific software vendors, but are rather a regular part of secure computing hygiene that concerns all operating systems as well as applications. For this reason, software patches are a vital part of the defense-in-depth strategy.

If a software patch exists for a security vulnerability, then it is logical to assume that there also exists or will soon exist a method of attack to exploit this vulnerability. For this very reason, it is imperative to install software patches when software vendors make them available. Let us use the case of the Conficker worm as an example. Microsoft released a software patch on October 23, 2008, to patch a critical security vulnerability in the Windows operating system. By early November 2008, the first variants of the Conficker worm were detected. This worm exploited the exact vulnerability that Microsoft had sought to patch 1 month earlier. By the end of November 2008, it was estimated that the Conficker worm infected 7 million computers worldwide—many of these infections could have been prevented by the simple installation of a single software patch.

6.4.1 Patch Tuesday and Exploit Wednesday

For the Windows operating system, the predominant operating system on today's market, Microsoft traditionally releases a series of patches on the second Tuesday of every month. Known as "patch Tuesday," this once-a-month event is intended to simplify the patch installation process. However, attackers' awareness of this regular schedule, coupled with the knowledge that large portions of users fail to habitually install these patches in a timely manner, has allowed attackers to take advantage of this monthly cycle. As a result, the day following patch Tuesday is mockingly known as "exploit Wednesday." On the surface, this sequence of events makes logical sense. The public announcement of a new patch is a signal to good guys and bad guys alike that there exists a known vulnerability somewhere in the software. Attackers are able to determine information from the details of announced patches and even reverse-engineer patches to help them create exploits. This phenomenon results in an interesting cause-and-effect relationship between those trying to patch potential vulnerabilities and those trying to exploit them. The user's role in this battle, as evidenced by the Conficker worm example, is to be diligent about information security by patching software as soon as possible. Malware and hackers cannot access your computer if the vulnerability that they are trying to exploit has already been patched.

6.4.2 Patches Are Not Limited to Operating Systems

The discussion of software patches is not limited to the Microsoft Windows operating system alone. It extends to all operating systems, including Apple's Mac OS X and Linux, as well as applications like Adobe Acrobat Reader, Microsoft Office, Chrome, and Mozilla Firefox. Each of these software packages possesses exploitable vulnerabilities that can be regularly identified and patched by their respective vendors. What generally complicates the issue of software patches is that each operating system and application distributes patches using independent and slightly different methods. The most recognizable artifact of these methods is the alert icon on the task bar in the Windows operating system. Other such methods include prompts appearing when an application is started. Many vendors now support automatic updates that install critical patches as soon as they are made available. On some occasions, as a substitution for a patch, software vendors will instead release an upgraded version of their software. Figure 6.7 illustrates an alert message generated by Mozilla Firefox when

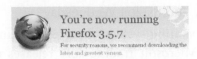

FIGURE 6.7   Mozilla Firefox update notice.

a new and more secure version of the software application is available. Despite the variety of ways in which patches are distributed, it is up to you, the user, to manage and maintain patches for all the software programs that exist on your computer.

6.4.3 Zero-Day Vulnerabilities

Even if a computer's operating system and applications are fully patched, this does not mean that a computer is immune to malware infections. As discussed in Chapter 1, software contains many vulnerabilities, and often these vulnerabilities remain dormant, undiscovered by either good guys or bad guys. When a malware writer discovers and exploits a vulnerability before it is known to exist or before an accompanying patch can be created, such a vulnerability is known as a zero-day vulnerability. Zero-day vulnerabilities are particularly dangerous because computers that possess such vulnerabilities are essentially defenseless. As an example, the Flashback Trojan was able to exploit a zero-day vulnerability by means of a drive-by download and subsequently infected 600,000 computers in a relatively short period of time. While patching a computer is absolutely essential, this security best practice does not remove all vulnerabilities from a computer. This is why user education is such an essential component to the defense-in-depth strategy. Often, the only defense against a zero-day vulnerability is refraining from the action (i.e., clicking on a hyperlink) that triggers the exploit.

6.4.4 Just Patch it

From a user's perspective, one can only eliminate vulnerabilities for which there are available software patches. It is critically important to the defense-in-depth strategy and the security of a personal computer to habitually install software patches as soon as they are made available by software vendors. Malware cannot exploit a vulnerability that has been successfully patched. However, when a vulnerability is left unpatched, as was the case with the Conficker worm, the proverbial door has been left wide open for malware to exploit known vulnerabilities. Just as backing up data is a chore no different in principle from shoveling the driveway or mowing the lawn, so should be updating patches on a computer.

6.5 ANTIVIRUS SOFTWARE

As discussed in Chapter 5, the term *antivirus software* addresses many other types of malware than viruses alone. Depending on the particular security software vendor and product offering, antivirus software often protects against virtually all kinds of malware, including viruses, worms, Trojan horses, spyware, and malicious adware. The function of antivirus software is to prevent, detect, and remove malware from a computer. While this last statement may appear to cast antivirus software as the ultimate computer security defense mechanism, antivirus software, just like firewalls, has limitations to its effectiveness. Nevertheless, antivirus software is a computer security necessity. This section seeks to explain how antivirus software works in practice, its strengths and weaknesses, how malware has adapted to avoid detection, and what we, the users, can do to use this defense mechanism effectively.

6.5.1 Antivirus Signatures

Just as DNA fingerprinting can be used to uniquely identify humans for the purposes of criminal investigations or paternity tests, so can virus signatures be used to identify malware. Each human being has a genetic makeup composed of approximately three billion DNA base pairs constructed from the four essential building blocks of DNA: adenine (A), thymine (T), guanine (G), and cytosine (C). Even though humans share 99.9% of the same genetic makeup, there exists enough uniqueness in the ordering of DNA base pairs from human to human, and modern science can use this uniqueness to accurately identify or fingerprint an individual person. Computer programs and files are very similar to humans in that they can be uniquely identified. In contrast to DNA, software and digital files are composed of combinations of just two essential building blocks: 1s and 0s (Figure 6.8). Similar to DNA, these digital world building blocks can be used to accurately identify different types of computer programs, in particular malware.

Figure 6.8 illustrates that every type of software—malware included— is composed of a sequence of 1s and 0s. The number of these 1s and 0s that it takes to make up a file determines its size. For example, a 2-megabyte computer file is composed of a single string of 16,777,216 1s or 0s. A virus signature is thus comprised of a unique strand or pattern of 1s

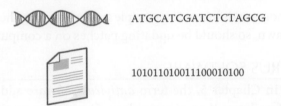

ATGCATCGATCTCTAGCG

1010110100111000010100

FIGURE 6.8   Human and computer file building blocks.

and 0s. Signatures can then be used to identify a program as malicious (Figure 6.9). Antivirus programs installed on a computer contain a large database of virus signatures that can be used to uniquely identify and detect many different types of malware. To determine whether a program or file is malicious, an antivirus program will scan the file, comparing all of the signatures in its database to the file's string of 1s and 0s. If a virus signature is found within a computer file, that particular file will be flagged as malicious.

Antivirus software vendors distribute virus signatures to users through the Internet. Each antivirus program contains the ability to query the antivirus vendor for newly available signatures. Queries can either take place automatically on a predefined schedule or manually if the user initiates a request. If available, these signatures are then downloaded to the user's computer and integrated into the antivirus software's existing database of virus signatures.

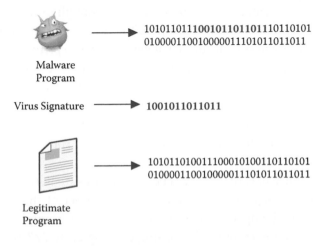

FIGURE 6.9   Virus signatures.

6.5.2 Function of Antivirus Software

Antivirus software prevents, detects, and removes malware by scanning for its presence on a computer system in one of two ways: on-access scanning or on-demand scanning. Before a document is opened or a program is executed, antivirus software will perform an on-access scan of that particular file with its database of known malware signatures to detect whether the file is malicious. This type of scanning prevents viruses and Trojan horses from executing their malicious lines of code by halting the action before it can happen. On-demand scanning, on the other hand, is a broader scanning of all files on a computer during which each file is individually checked for malware regardless of whether it is to be imminently executed. There are two types of common modes for on-demand scanning: quick scan and full scan. A quick scan is tailored to scan in areas of a computer's file system that malware is likely to exist or hide. As the name suggests, a full scan performs an analysis of all computer files that exist on a hard drive. Although full scans are time consuming, they can be useful to detect malware that hides in files or folders not normally analyzed with a quick scan. At the least, a quick scan should be routinely performed on a weekly, if not daily, basis (Chapter 14). Many types of antivirus products allow a user to configure an on-demand (quick or full) scan to begin automatically at a time during which the computer is usually not frequently used, such as at 2 a.m. or during a lunch hour, so that the scan does not disrupt normal usage.

Accompanying each antivirus signature is a series of steps that the antivirus program will follow to remove each individual occurrence of malware. The process of malware removal varies for each antivirus program. Generally, if malware is found, the user is notified and presented with various options for removing the malware from the computer or else is informed that the malware has been removed automatically. Typically, the only action that the user is required to perform during the malware removal process is to confirm that the particular file is malicious and that it should be removed. The technique of using virus signatures to detect malware is generally quite simple and effective—as long as the antivirus software has the signature of the offending malware.

6.5.3 Antivirus Limitations

Antivirus software that utilizes virus signatures cannot detect a malware occurrence if it does not have an accompanying signature for the malware in its signature database. Therefore, antivirus software is only as effective as the collection of signatures that it possesses. This is a significant limitation because malware that does not have a corresponding signature in a computer's database effectively bypasses the antivirus software, one of the defense-in-depth mechanisms. Without other safeguards in place (i.e., patches, data backup, firewalls), it is possible for malware without a known signature to propagate between computers that have antivirus software installed on them. Without regularly updating virus signatures, many types of malicious programs, especially the most recent types of malware, can go about their insidious business undetected.

Antivirus vendors are constantly capturing new occurrences of malware, analyzing them, and creating signatures to distribute to their clients; these signatures are then downloaded as newly available signatures from within antivirus programs. However, this process takes time, and there are often days, weeks, if not months, between the time when a particular piece of malware is released "into the wild" and that when an antivirus software vendor is ready to release an effective signature (Figure 6.10). Furthermore, once a

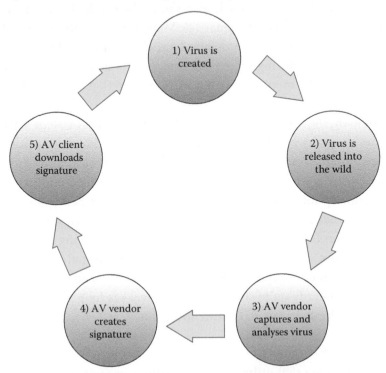

FIGURE 6.10 Virus/antivirus signature life cycle. AV, antivirus.

signature is available, the user must download the signature to his or her computer by means of antivirus software. Just like software patches, each antivirus vendor has its own particular way of distributing antivirus signatures to clients and often makes signatures available on a daily basis. One should determine just how this process works for their particular brand of antivirus software and download signatures routinely on a daily basis.

6.5.4 False Positives and False Negatives

Antivirus software effectiveness depends on a detection mechanism. In the profession of information security, whenever one talks about a detection mechanism, the occurrence of both "false positives" and "false negatives" must be addressed. In the context of antivirus software, a false positive occurs when an antivirus program incorrectly determines that a legitimate piece of software is actually a malware program. Depending on just how the antivirus software reacts to errantly flagging a legitimate program, the results of this phenomenon can be quite devastating. In 2010, a large antivirus vendor inadvertently released a virus signature that detected a critical Windows operating system file as malicious and consequently removed it from all the computer systems on which it was installed. The result of this action sent the affected computers into a constant reboot cycle, effectively rendering them useless. This particular false positive caused thousands of computers, including computers in hospitals, police departments, and multinational corporations all over the world, to crash. A similar false-positive event occurred in 2006 when an antivirus vendor released a virus signature that resulted in the detection and removal of Microsoft Excel from its clients' computer systems. Although antivirus vendors rigorously test their signatures before they are released to their clients, the threat of false positives, although minimal, will always exist.

The opposite of a false positive, errantly detecting a legitimate program as malicious, is a false negative, that is, errantly failing to detect a malicious program as such. This type of error is much more common and often results in a malware infection. False negatives occur when antivirus software does not have an accompanying signature for a specific type of malware. To avoid false negatives, it is imperative that antivirus signatures be frequently updated.

6.5.5 Sneaky Malware

Malware creators are quite aware of the mechanics of antivirus software and the limitations of antivirus signatures. It should be no surprise that malware creators have taken advantage of these limitations to increase malware's effectiveness. Two types of such actions that malware has been known to perform are either to disable the antivirus program on the computer that it infects or to prevent the infected computer from retrieving new antivirus signatures. The Conficker worm followed the latter path. To avoid detection and removal, it prevented infected computers from contacting their antivirus vendors to retrieve the signature needed to remove the worm. Another approach that malware can use to avoid detection is through digital evolution. Malware programs, much like strains of the flu, can have the ability to modify themselves to render the most current defense mechanisms ineffective. This type of malware, known as polymorphic or metamorphic malware, slightly changes its internal sequence of 1s and 0s each time it propagates from computer to computer (Figure 6.11). Although the malware retains the same malicious functionality, a signature that was used to classify the initial version (i.e., v1) of the malware may be ineffective against subsequently altered versions (i.e., v2 and v3). Thus, if a particular malware program is obtained and analyzed, and an antivirus vendor creates a signature for it, the next adaptation of the malware will be unlikely to be flagged by the antivirus program since it is searching for a program with the previous or "original" signature.

To counter morphing malware and the limitations of antivirus signatures, some antivirus products contain a scanning feature known as *heuristic analysis*. In addition to using a signature-based approach, heuristic analysis attempts to monitor the behaviors of software to classify a particular program as malicious. This detection technique is similar to profiling

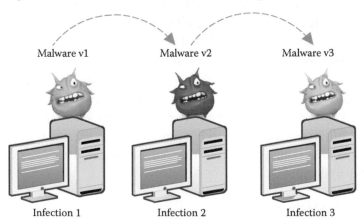

Malware v1   Malware v2   Malware v3

Infection 1   Infection 2   Infection 3

FIGURE 6.11   Metamorphic/polymorphic malware.

of potential criminal behavior by law enforcement officers with the goal of preventing crimes before they happen. While heuristic analysis allows for the detection of malware without an accompanying virus signature, it is also limited in its effectiveness due to accuracy concerns and high numbers of false positives.

6.5.6 Antivirus Is Not a Safety Net

Due to the limitations of antivirus software, it should not be treated as a foolproof safety net. Just because one has antivirus software on their computer does not mean that he or she has carte blanche to click on and download programs at will without risk of a malware infection. When coupled with user education, software patches, and the recommended practices of diligently updating virus signatures and performing routine on-demand scans, antivirus software can represent an effective security mechanism. Without this coupling of multiple defense-in-depth strategies, antivirus software is likely to be only partially effective.

6.6 USER EDUCATION

As a user of information technology, one cannot completely avoid all of the actions and ways in which malware propagates and still be able to utilize the functionality of computers, removable media, and the Internet. One example of common security advice is "do not open email attachments from unknown sources." This advice is not always practical and, as a result, is often discarded in favor of convenience. Apart from being unrealistic in certain scenarios, this statement does not answer the questions of *why* the user should not perform the action, *how* this action could negatively affect the user, and *what* the user should do to protect himself or herself if her or she does indeed need to open an email attachment from an unknown someone. Furthermore, this statement fails to provide the much-needed *context* to understand the limitations of this advice. These are the questions that user education, the subject of this book, seeks to answer. The purpose of user education is to give context to security best practices. Without this context, security advice that stands alone as a single, unsupported statement is vague and not easily understood and as a result is often discounted.

Instead of *never* performing everyday tasks such as opening an email attachment, one can minimize the risk of a malware infection through the defense-in-depth strategy, including user education: the *Why? How?*

What? and the *Context?* For example, in response to "do not open email attachments from unknown sources," one would learn:

1. *Why?* Because email attachments have historically been, and continue to be, a common means by which malware propagates between computers. Attackers use social engineering tactics to increase the likelihood that an unsuspecting user will open an infected attachment.

2. *How?* By simply opening an email attachment, one can infect his or her own computer and, worse yet, may unknowingly enable the malware to subsequently send the same email to everyone in his or her email address book, further compounding the problem.

3. *What?* If you need to open a suspicious email attachment, apply the defense-in-depth techniques. Furthermore, one could scan the document with antivirus software before opening it or even go as far as to contact the sender of the document to verify the origin and intent of its contents.

4. *Context?* Reconsider the advice "do not open email attachments from unknown sources." This statement could lead one to believe that it is then safe to open email attachments from people already known. However, from the example of the Love Bug worm and the knowledge that email addresses can be spoofed to appear as if they were sent from a trusted source, one that has invested in information security user education would possess the context not to make such a false assumption.

If these questions are answered, the user has the know-how and the contextual information to know when to *refrain* from potentially dangerous activities, thus increasing the strength of the defense-in-depth strategy. Much of this chapter and the previous chapters have covered topics of user education in the context of malware. Understanding how malware propagates and what it does once it infects a computer and knowing the functions and limitations of the mechanisms that compose the defense-in-depth strategy are significant components of user education. Although such information does not necessarily prevent an individual from engaging in risky behavior, at least the individual is aware that performing such actions may put both himself or herself and others at increased risk of malware damage and potential loss of personal and private information.

The true test of practical computer security knowledge does not occur when reading a book, sitting in a classroom, taking a quiz, or writing a paper about information security. It happens each and every day as one interacts with computers and the Internet. The threats that we face as users of information technology are constantly evolving, and as a result, user education is not a static body of knowledge. Appendix A contains a list of websites that provide timely and practical articles about a range of computer and Internet security topics, including emerging threats, best practices, recent trends, and current events. This book is not the definitive guide on computer security literacy; instead, it represents a first step enabling you to go forth and read security articles in the popular press; to become more curious about the security settings in your web browser; to begin having conversations about security with family, friends, and coworkers; and to help you understand the practical context surrounding computer security best practices.

6.7 SUMMARY

The first step, which should be common practice of anyone using a computer, is to employ the defense-in-depth strategy: back up your data regularly, enable a software firewall, apply application and OS patches as soon as they become available, diligently update antivirus signatures, and perform routine antivirus scans. These practices, coupled with user education (the how, why, what, and context), will go a long way in protecting you and your computer from the inherent risks of using the Internet.

- Due to the diversity and ever-present threats of malware and hacking, and the fact that no single security mechanism is responsible for all defensive tasks, a defense-and-depth strategy of (1) data backup, (2) firewalls, (3) software patches, (4) antivirus software, and (5) user education provides a multilayer defense strategy.

- Regularly backing up data provides protection and insurance against both malware and a number of types of computer failures. Any data is that is valued should be backed up on a regular basis.

- A computer hard drive or any type of computer storage medium (i.e., USB flash drive, DVD, etc.) exists in two states: either the storage drive is going to fail or the storage drive has failed.

- A firewall is a security mechanism that provides a logical separation between a computer and the Internet and prevents against a number of unwanted and malicious network-based attacks.

- Firewalls do not perform malware detection and thus do not prevent a user from downloading a Trojan horse. Furthermore, firewalls do not prevent against user-initiated actions that lead to phishing attacks or drive-by downloads.

- The main threats that a firewall protects against are network-based attacks carried out by worms and hackers that originate from the Internet.

- A software firewall should always be enabled before connecting to the Internet.

- Although effective at blocking network-based attacks, firewalls do not protect against nonnetwork attacks such as a virus on a USB flash drive.

- Software patches fix software vulnerabilities that malware and hackers seek to exploit.

- It is imperative that software patches for both operating systems and applications are applied and installed as soon as they become available as it is likely that for every patch there also exists a type of malware that is able to exploit the same vulnerability that the patch seeks to fix.

- The function of antivirus software is to prevent, detect, and remove malware from a computer.

- The major limitations of antivirus software are that it can only detect malware for which it has a corresponding signature, the process is completely reactionary to malware threats, and it takes time between when malware is discovered and when antivirus vendors release a signature for a client to download.

- Aware of the techniques of antivirus software, on infection malware has been known to disable antivirus software or prevent a computer from updating virus signatures. Furthermore, some types of malware evolve each time they infect a computer to subsequently change their virus signature.

- Virus detection inevitably can produce false positives (uninfected files that are misidentified as infected) and false negatives (undetected infections). Either situation can be quite troublesome.

- Essential to computer security literacy is user education as it provides the why, how, what, and context for security best practices.

BIBLIOGRAPHY

Baker-Hallam, P. 2008. *The DotCrime Manifesto: How To Stop Internet Crime.* Indianapolis, IN: Pearson Education.

Cheswick, W.R., Bellovin, S.M., and Rubin, A.D. 2003. *Firewalls and Internet Security: Repelling the Wily Hacker.* Boston: Addison-Wesley.

Deal, R. 2004. *Cisco Router Firewall Security.* Indianapolis, IN: Cisco Press.

Doherty, J., and Anderson, N. 2006. *Home Network Security Simplified.* Indianapolis, IN: Cisco Press.

Evers, J. 2006. McAfee update exterminates Excel. http://news.cnet.com/McAfee-update-exterminates-Excel/2100-1002_3-6048709.html (access April 17, 2012).

Filiol, E. 2005. *Computer Viruses: From Theory to Applications.* Berlin: Birkhäuser.

Fitzgerald-Hayes, M., and Reichsman, F. 2009. *DNA and Biotechnology.* New York: Academic Press.

Foster, M. 2007. *The Secure CEO: How to Protect Your Computer Systems, Your Company, and Your Job.* Internet Profit Kit. Wichita, KS: Prime Concepts Group Publishing.

Gibson, D. 2010. *Managing Risk in Information Systems.* Sudbury, MA: Jones & Bartlett.

Groth, D., and Skandier, T. 2005. *Network+ Study Guide.* New York: Wiley.

Leyden, J. 2010. Rogue McAfee update strikes police, hospitals and Intel. http://www.theregister.co.uk/2010/04/22/mcafee_false_positive_analysis/ (accessed April 17, 2012).

McAfee. 2012. McAfee security tips—13 ways to protect your system. http://www.mcafee.com/us/mcafee-labs/resources/security-tips-13-ways-to-protect-system.aspx (accessed April 17, 2012).

McInerney, J. 1999. *Basic Genetics: A Human Approach Teacher Guide.* Dubuque, IA: Kendall Hunt.

Microsoft. 2012. Back up and restore: frequently asked questions. http://windows.microsoft.com/en-US/windows7/Back-up-and-restore-frequently-asked-questions (accessed April 17, 2012).

Nazario, J. 2004. *Defense and Detection Strategies against Internet Worms.* Norwood, MA: Artech House.

Noonan, W.J., and Dubrawsky, I. 2006. *Firewall Fundamentals.* Indianapolis, IN: Pearson Education.

Pfleeger, C.P., and Pfleeger, S.L. 2011. *Analyzing Computer Security: A Threat/Vulnerability/Countermeasure Approach.* Indianapolis, IN: Prentice Hall Professional.

Provos, N., and Holz, T. 2007. *Virtual Honeypots: From Botnet Tracking to Intrusion Detection.* Indianapolis, IN: Pearson Education.

Riley, T., and Goucher, A. 2009. *Beautiful Testing: Leading Professionals Reveal How They Improve Software*. Sebastopol, CA: O'Reilly Media.

Skoudis, E., and Zeltser, L. 2004. *Malware: Fighting Malicious Code*. Indianapolis, IN: Prentice Hall Professional.

Stewart, J.M. 2010. *Network Security, Firewalls, and VPNs*. Sudbury, MA: Jones & Bartlett.

Tilborg, H., and Jajodia, S. 2011. *Encyclopedia of Cryptography and Security*. New York: Springer.

White, C. 2008. *Data Communications and Computer Networks: A Business User's Approach*. Independence, KY: Cengage Learning.

CHAPTER 7

Securely Surfing the World Wide Web

7.1 INTRODUCTION

For most people, the primary method to check their email, shop online, interact with friends via social networking, and access many other aspects of the Internet is through the World Wide Web (WWW or the web). The common application that is used to access such services on the WWW is the web browser. It therefore makes sense that hackers, cyber thieves, and other people intent on doing harm would target peoples' common uses of the WWW and the web browser for their wicked purposes. Surfing the web exposes users to attacks like drive-by downloads, in which the simple act of requesting a webpage can result in a malware infection. Actions on the web can also result in the loss of privacy and personal information. This chapter shows that a typical web browser is a very complex application that provides its user access to data in many different formats. While many of the features that a web browser provides are convenient to its users, these same conveniences can be at odds with security and privacy.

7.2 WEB BROWSER

The WWW was originally designed to enable sharing of data and information among high-energy physicists. As computers became more powerful and graphical user interfaces became more common, the available web content changed. Now, modern web access involves a graphical client

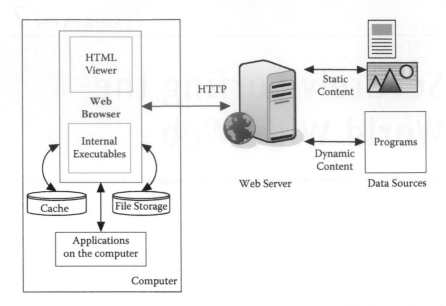

FIGURE 7.1   Web browser and web server interaction.

(the browser) and a web server, as shown in Figure 7.1. The primary form of interaction between a web browser and a web server is to transfer files or data from a web server to a web browser based on requests initiated by the browser. The browser uses a file transfer protocol called Hypertext Transfer Protocol (HTTP) to move data to and from the web server.

7.2.1 Web Browser and Web Server Functions

As seen in Figure 7.1, a web browser consists of several software components that are used to access content stored on a web server, including a viewer that interprets and displays data received from a web server (i.e., webpages). A web browser can also download documents and files from a web server and store them on a user's computer. To decrease webpage load times, web browsers use a storage cache for saving images and other documents received from web servers. Therefore, if you revisit a webpage, your browser might have previously saved some of the images from that website and thus does not need to download the same images again. The browser can also run applications to help interpret the data it receives from the web server. For example, a web browser can launch a media player to play a song or a video player (i.e., Flash Player) to watch a movie. Last, to provide a rich web experience, web browsers can also execute code provided by a web server to support animations, dynamic web content, and other visually appealing yet complex interactions with the server.

The web server, using HTTP, sends data identified by a unique URL (Uniform Resource Locator) that is requested by a web browser. As shown in Figure 7.1, requests are either static or dynamic in nature. The most common example of static web content is seen on websites in which the text and images are the same each time a request for the webpage is made. Static web content and webpages are loosely referred to as Web 1.0. Dynamic web content, on the other hand, typically changes each time a user visits a website or interacts with a website. For example, a web document produced by a search engine (Google, Yahoo!, Bing, etc.) as the result of a user's query is dynamically created from the search results. Other examples include ordering fast food from a website in which the user can simply click on the items wanted on a burrito, for instance, and the webpage dynamically creates the customer's order. This type of rich web experience in which the user interacts with a website or webpage is loosely referred to as Web 2.0.

7.2.2 Web Code

The WWW functions by transferring files from web servers to web browsers that are ultimately to be processed by the web browser's viewer. The primary language used to format web content is called Hypertext Markup Language (HTML). HTML documents contain commands that are interpreted by a web browser and dictate how a webpage's content is to be displayed in a web browser. HTML provides the formatting that one customarily expects when surfing the web, including the fonts, screen locations of images, hyperlinks to other content, and the overall appearance of the webpage. An HTML document also can contain other web programming languages (i.e., JavaScript, Java, Flash)—generally referred to as scripts—that can direct a web browser to execute code or download programs or documents, among other actions. It is not the goal of this section to examine the HTML file format in great detail, but there are certain aspects of the file format that can cause security problems. The next section examines a simple example of an HTML document to uncover some of these security threats.

7.2.3 HTML: Images and Hyperlinks

Figure 7.2 shows a sample webpage that contains text, two images, and two hyperlinks. Figure 7.3 shows the HTML document that the web server

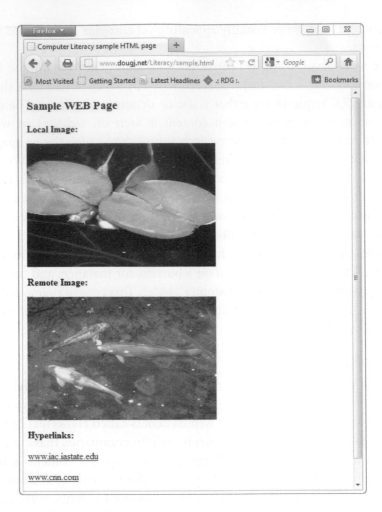

FIGURE 7.2 Example webpage displayed in a web browser.

provided to the web browser to create the webpage shown in Figure 7.2. HTML elements, marked with the "<" and ">," characters are called tags and denote specific types of web content. In Figure 7.3, the first six lines of code are used to provide the browser with formatting information about the webpage. The segment of the HTML document that tells the browser how to create the webpage begins with the tag "<body>". The text displayed on the webpage is bracketed with tags that describe the way the text is to be displayed (i.e., text size <H3></H3>, bold <Strong></Strong>, etc.). The "<img>" tag tells the browser that there is an image to be displayed and tells the browser where to retrieve the image (i.e., src =) and information about how the image should be displayed (i.e., width =, height =). Notice that the

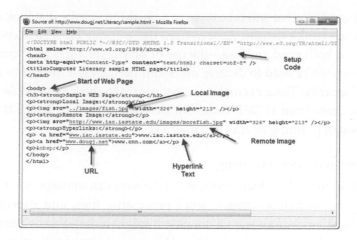

FIGURE 7.3   Sample HTML document.

two image tags have different formats for the source of the image. The first image is identified as "../images/fish.jpg," and since no URL information is provided, it is implied that the image (a JPEG photo) is located on the same web server as the original HTML document. The second image specifies a full URL for the location of the image. To obtain the second image, the web browser must first connect to a different web server and transfer the image from that server to be displayed. By simply viewing the example webpage, one cannot easily tell that the two images originated from two different web servers. Cyber criminals often use the second example of linking a picture from a legitimate website to a phishing webpage to display a bank's actual logos (see Chapter 13 for an example).

The next tag of interest is the "<a>" tag, which is used to indicate a hyperlink. There are two parts to this tag, the text that is displayed by the web browser and the URL that is requested if a user clicks on the hyperlink. Again, there are two different types of examples in Figure 7.3. The first snippet of HTML code shows a hyperlink in which the URL and the displayed text are identical. The second example shows a situation in which the text that describes the hyperlink is different from that of the actual URL. In this case, clicking on the text "www.cnn.com" will take the user to the URL "www.dougj.net." The ability to rename URLs allows the webpage designer to use a more descriptive name for hyperlinks than that of the actual URL, which is often quite obscure and cryptic. This functionality also allows a malicious webpage designer to deceive users and trick them into believing they are clicking on a hyperlink for their bank when they are instead requesting a URL that will take them to a phishing website that looks identical to their bank's website. As seen from these examples, HTML code can be used for both good and bad—the use of linking pictures and renaming hyperlinks can be used to deceive users and perhaps lull them into a false sense of security. These examples are not meant to show all possible issues that can come from HTML code, but they highlight two issues that are often used in phishing attacks (Chapter 11).

7.2.4 File and Code Handling

In addition to HTML documents, web browsers can manage other document types, including images, word-processing files, and executables. Figure 7.4 shows various ways a document might be handled by a browser. As an example, the browser might need to use a helper application (often referred to as a plug-in) to manage various document types. Third parties, either individual programmers or companies, typically write plug-ins for web browsers and make them available for general use. Plug-ins can be classified according to the types of documents or the functions they handle. Executable plug-ins such as Java Applets or ActiveX, for example, handle code that is executed in a browser. Document plug-ins handle different

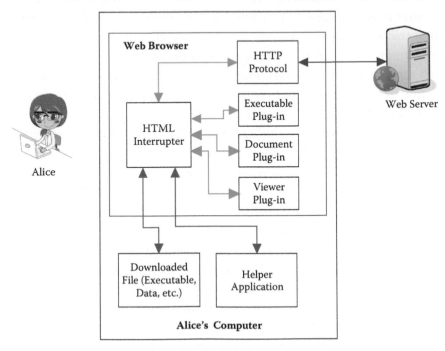

FIGURE 7.4 Web browser plug-ins and document handling.

document types, such as PDFs or word-processing files, and viewing plug-ins handle the displaying of scripts, images, audio, video, or real-time graphics. Sometimes, a document must be viewed using an external application like a word processor program. In addition to viewing various documents, the web browser itself can execute code sent to it by the server. In all of the cases shown in Figure 7.4, the web browser, sometimes with the assistance of a plug-in program, is displaying or executing code sent to it by a web server. Since web browsers often execute and interpret web documents automatically on a user's request, a web server that hosts malicious web content containing attack code poses a significant security threat while browsing the web.

Figure 7.5 shows an example of a few plug-ins used by the Firefox web browser. As highlighted in the figure, PDF documents are to be viewed automatically by an Adobe web browser plug-in. While surfing the web, if a user clicks on a hyperlink for a PDF document, for example, Firefox will open the document and display it without first consulting the user for permission. This type of automatic handling of documents is convenient, but it can also be troublesome if the document that is being opened contains malicious code.

FIGURE 7.5   Web browser plug-ins.

Chapter 5 discussed that webpages, PDFs, and word-processing documents can all contain malicious code that, if executed on a computer, can result in a malware infection. While most people are aware that it is not sound security practice to download and open untrusted programs from the web, the same cannot be said about the simple act of requesting a webpage or allowing a web browser to handle the viewing of files. Referring back to Figure 7.5, by opening such files with a web browser in this manner, whatever code is contained in the PDF file, malicious or not, is automatically executed when a user clicks on a hyperlink for a PDF document. In many ways, the security risk of allowing a web browser to automatically open documents is no different from opening untrusted documents attached to emails. This is why it is important only to click on trusted hyperlinks and to keep a web browser and its accompanying plug-ins up to date and properly patched. Otherwise, with one click of the mouse, a document with malicious code could automatically be allowed to execute on your computer.

A more secure, but less-convenient, alternative to allowing a web browser to handle the automatic viewing of a document can be seen in Figure 7.6. In this example, when a user requests a Microsoft Word document, the

FIGURE 7.6　Examples of helper applications and plug-ins.

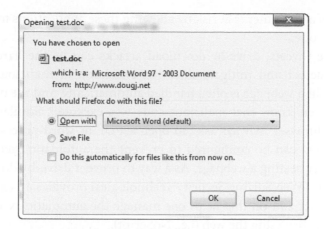

FIGURE 7.7   Open file dialog box.

web browser is instructed to "Always ask." This means that when a hyperlink for a word document is clicked, the user will be presented with the dialog box shown in Figure 7.7. At this point, the user is first provided with the options of opening the document with Microsoft Word, saving the file to the hard drive, or canceling the action. Unlike the PDF example, the file is not automatically opened. The check box in Figure 7.7 labeled "Do this automatically for files like this from now on" correlates to the drop-down menu box highlighted in Figure 7.6. For each type of document to be handled by a web browser, the user can often choose how this is to happen. A Microsoft Word document, for example, can be opened automatically using a helper application [i.e., Use Microsoft Word (default)], saved to the hard drive, or as the setting shows, the user can make such a determination on a file-by-file basis. While allowing a web browser to automatically open a document is convenient, it poses as a significant security risk.

Most webpages, documents, and executables that are downloaded from websites should not be trusted as one does not know what the code contains or who wrote the code. Although this is the case, people are generally not as skeptical about the content they request from the web as they should be. This inherent trust put into the content that is downloaded, viewed, and executed while browsing the web can lead to the execution of malicious code, resulting in malware infections. Referring back to Figure 7.4, one can see that malicious documents might be handled by a plug-in or a helper application or executed by the browser. If any of these programs that execute code contains vulnerabilities, which they likely do, then the integrity of a computer is at risk by allowing these applications to execute untrusted code.

Of these threats, drive-by download attacks can be the hardest web threat to detect and mitigate since the execution of malicious scripts embedded in a webpage is often handled automatically, and the user often does not even know that malicious code was executed. Similar to having a web browser "Always ask" to open a PDF or word-processing file, web browsers can be configured to prevent the automatic execution of scripts on requesting a webpage. As a way to prevent drive-by downloads, Appendix C (Web Surfing Security Technologies) provides an example of a web browser add-on that helps one manage the automatic execution of scripts while browsing the web (i.e., NoScript).

7.2.5 Cookies

A key issue in the early days of the WWW was that websites did not possess the capability to know if two different requests originated from the same user's web browser. Subsequently, websites were not able to track the actions of their users and thus were unable to provide any sense of state or history (i.e., if the user was logged in or not, user identity or preferences, what items the user had in a shopping cart, etc.) to enhance the user's browsing experience. The remedy to this problem was to allow websites to store cookies—small text files—in their users' web browsers. As a result, web browsers now enable websites (i.e., amazon.com, nytimes.com) to read and write information about a user's web browsing behaviors on the user's computer using cookies. Therefore, when a specific user returns to a particular website, the website has the capability to remember who the user is, what the user's past actions were, and the user's preferences. To curtail some privacy concerns, websites are only able to read their own cookies. Thus, amazon.com is not able to directly read cookies created by staples.com in a user's web browser. Because cookies afford both users and websites increased conveniences, it should be expected that this trade-off has associated costs.

Figure 7.8 illustrates the use of cookies. In this example, Alice has visited two websites (i.e., www.amazon.com and www.staples.com), and each of these respective websites has placed cookies on Alice's computer. Generally, cookies are small text files, and thus websites often store many cookies on a user's computer to track the user's actions. Figure 7.9 shows an example of just some of the cookies placed on Alice's computer after she visited a shopping website. One specific cookie in Figure 7.9, indicated by

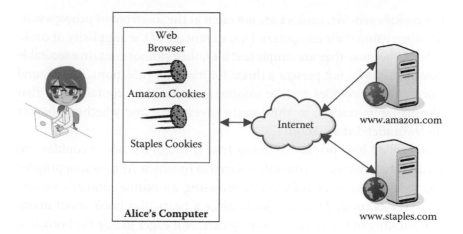

FIGURE 7.8   Web browser cookies.

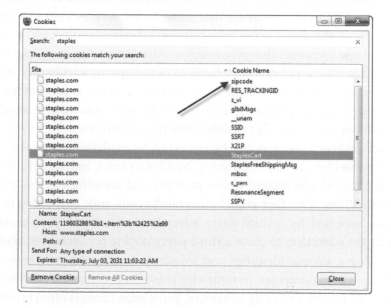

FIGURE 7.9   Cookies in a web browser.

an arrow, contains Alice's zip code. In this case, the zip code was obtained when Alice elected to search for the store nearest to her home. Another common use of cookies is shown in the highlighted cookie, which contains an identifier that points to a shopping cart created by Alice. In this case, Alice did not purchase the item, but the website has tracked this action in a cookie so that if Alice revisits the website, the item can be automatically placed in her shopping cart again. Due to the many beneficial capabilities that cookies provide, cookies are not often at the forefront of people's worries when using their computers. One advantage of the simplicity of cookies is that because they are simple text files, they cannot contain executable code and thus do not present a threat for malware infections. The general concerns with cookies are the information that they contain, how that information is tracked by third-party advertisers, and whether a hacker can learn such information.

To explain how privacy concerns arise through the use of cookies and third-party advertisers, consider a scenario in which Alice is shopping for a birthday present for Bob. While browsing an online retailer's website (ginnybooks.com), Alice decides to place a particular book about marathon running in her virtual shopping cart. Not eager to buy the book that day, Alice knows through the use of cookies that the particular item she selected will remain in her shopping cart when she returns to the website at another time—a convenience that most do not view as a privacy violation. Later in the day, Alice is back browsing the web and decides to visit her local news website. However, much to Alice's surprise, she sees a web-based ad for the very book she placed in her shopping cart earlier in the day on a separate website. Because such an occurrence is too random to happen by chance, Alice feels her privacy has been violated and wonders how another website could possibly know this information.

Alice's privacy concern can be answered by explaining how websites enable advertisers to use third-party cookies to track individuals' habits (i.e., behavioral advertising) across multiple and seemingly unassociated websites. When Alice first visited ginnybooks.com, code embedded in the website, supplied by a third-party advertiser (iknowwhatyoulike.com), enables the advertiser to place a third-party cookie (i.e., tracking cookie) containing a unique identifier and information about Alice's browsing habits on Alice's computer. In return for providing access to its customer's computer and web browsing behaviors, ginnybooks.com is often provided financial compensation. Not only can iknowwhatyoulike.com track Alice on ginnybooks.com, but it can also be used to track Alice when she visits another website that is associated with iknowwhatyoulike.com. Over time, and as Alice browses more and more websites that are in a business agreement with iknowwhatyoulike.com, the third-party advertiser is able to generate a very specific profile of Alice's behaviors and preferred items. This information is then sold by iknowwhatyoudid.com to online advertisers, which are then able to place very carefully crafted ads on websites that Alice visits. All of this is done with the hope this type of behavioral advertising will increase Alice's likelihood to click on the ad and purchase an item. While some see this type of tracking as a convenience, others see it as a privacy violation. How to delete or prevent the use of web browser cookies is discussed further in this chapter.

Another privacy issue concerning the use of cookies occurs when public computers are used to access the Internet. Cookies and other types of remembered browsing actions (i.e., browser history) may be updated during such use, and if another user logs on to the computer later, he or she may be able to determine websites earlier users have visited and some of the actions that were performed on those websites. Similar to the deletion of cookies, this issue is also discussed in more detail further in this chapter.

In addition to privacy concerns, cookies can also present security concerns. As shown in Figure 7.10, some websites have a check box near the username and password fields that is labeled something similar to "Stay signed in." In this case, the website uses cookies—called session cookies—to remember that a user has provided the correct login credentials so that the next time the user visits the website, the user does not have to log in again. This type of password management is distinctly different from allowing a web browser to "remember a password" for a specific website as discussed in Chapter 3 and shown in Figure 3.16. While convenient, this method of password storage is similarly a security risk if another user can at all access the computer; furthermore, there are no "master passwords" to protect access for others to use this feature. If Alice allows her web-based email account to keep her signed in, then Boyfriend Bob or Intruder Trudy is able to access Alice's email account by simply opening Alice's web browser. As a result, having a website remember Alice's login credentials is not a secure option when other people have access to Alice's computer. To read about alternative methods to password management, please see Chapter 3.

Another security concern that deals with the use of session cookies is the credentials stored in the session cookie must be communicated to

FIGURE 7.10   Use of cookies to remember passwords.

the corresponding website before access is granted. For example, if Alice revisits ginnybooks.com while surfing the web over an unsecure wireless network at a local coffee shop (Chapter 9), to authenticate, her session cookie containing her username and password will be sent over the Internet and thus can be observed by Eavesdropper Eve. Known as session hijacking, there exists readily available web browser plug-ins (e.g., Firesheep) that will sniff wireless traffic for unencrypted session cookies and then provide a graphical and automated means to allow the sniffer, in this case Eve, then to log in to Alice's ginnybooks.com account. While some websites encrypt the sending and receiving of session cookies, others do not. Session hijacking is yet another threat to consider when using unsecure wireless networks.

7.3 "HTTP SECURE"

As discussed in Chapter 2, a web browser and a web server engage in a series of back-and-forth communications that are routed through the Internet. When this data transfer takes place without any encryption (i.e., in cleartext), a third-party (i.e., Eavesdropper Eve) has the potential to eavesdrop on such conversations. The most common place for the threat of eavesdropping to materialize is over an unsecure public wireless network, such as typically found in coffee shops, libraries, hotels, and university campuses. Chapter 9 discusses wireless network security in more detail. To prevent against eavesdropping on web traffic, a layer of security was added to HTTP to protect the confidentiality of data as it is being sent between a requesting computer and a web server. This section provides a high-level overview of the functionality of "HTTP Secure" (HTTPS). To find more details about the basics of cryptography, please see Appendix B.

Although not in the original design for the WWW, early architects of the WWW came to realize the significance of eavesdropping and responded by developing the HTTPS protocol to mitigate this threat. Unlike HTTP, which sends messages in cleartext, HTTPS uses cryptography to protect the confidentiality of data that is transferred between a web browser and a web server. To encrypt web traffic during a web browsing session, a unique encryption key is generated each time Alice connects to her bank's website, for example. While HTTPS does not technically prevent against the act of eavesdropping, because the data is encrypted, it mitigates the loss of confidentiality as it is considered mathematically impossible to decrypt such messages. Therefore, even if Eve is able to eavesdrop on Alice's web traffic, Eve will be unable to make sense of the encrypted text and thus Alice's data is safe from Eve.

The factor that determines if a browsing session makes use of HTTPS is whether or not the communicating web server is equipped with a special file called a certificate. In the context of providing confidential communications, a certificate is used to create a unique encryption key whenever Alice begins a web session with her bank. Every website using HTTPS has a unique certificate, and one can think of a certificate as a license to create an encryption key. It turns out there are several types of certificates. One difference among certificates lies in whether the certificate has been signed (i.e., verified) by and purchased from a registered certificate authority—certificates cost approximately a few hundred dollars a year. Web browsers know the identities of certificate authorities, and if the website has a certificate signed by a registered certificate authority, then one knows that the owner of the website purchased the certificate from a trusted source. Websites can also have self-signed certificates that are not purchased but instead created by a website's owner. This allows a web browser to use HTTPS but does not provide the same level of assurance as a signed certificate. Most web browsers will warn the user if the website the user is browsing is attempting to use a self-signed certificate to create an HTTPS connection. Because self-signed certificates are considered to be untrusted, encountering a legitimate website using a self-signed certificate is a rare occurrence. Figure 7.11 shows an example of a certificate, and Figure 7.12 shows the type of message a browser will use to indicate the presence of a self-signed certificate.

Figure 7.11 shows information about a certificate that is owned by Gmail. In this example, Thawte, a trusted registered certificate authority, has verified the certificate. This figure also shows some additional information that, while not part of the certificate, is still interesting. Both the number of times this site was visited and whether cookies were placed on the computer by the website can also be seen. The figure also shows the presence of saved passwords, a topic that was discussed in Chapter 3. Figure 7.12 shows what happens if one visits a website equipped with a self-signed certificate. (Note: The appearance may vary with each browser.) As the message makes it clear, because the website's identity cannot be verified with a signed certificate from a trusted authority, one should not accept the certificate. Unless you absolutely trust the website you are visiting, there are very few reasons to ever accept a self-signed certificate, and

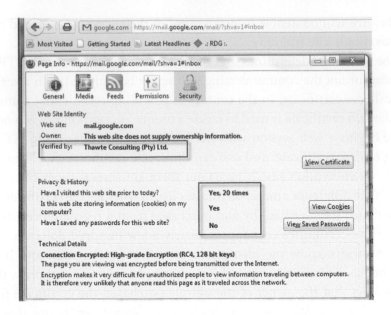

FIGURE 7.11   Certificate information.

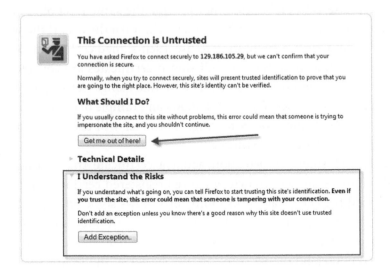

FIGURE 7.12   Self-sign certificate warning.

doing so could lead to the loss of confidential information. Given the basic premise of HTTPS, several questions often arise.

Question 1: If HTTPS mitigates against eavesdropping, then why is it not used by every website? There are two answers to this question; the first is cost related, and the second is that, for many websites, the added security is not warranted. Encrypting web traffic between each individual client and a given web server requires extra computation and thus comes at the cost of time. Because every interaction with the website needs to be encrypted and then decrypted, a client may experience slower loading times and thus a less-favorable experience with a particular website. Furthermore, leading into the answer for the next question, if a website's content does not require encryption, then purchasing a certificate can be an unnecessary cost. This is yet another example of security at odds with convenience.

The second part of the answer to the question of why HTTPS is not used for every website is that many times interactions with a website in cleartext are acceptable because there are no exchanges of confidential information, and the contents of the website are already publically available. Because of this, many websites do not need HTTPS. In addition to providing a layer of security to protect confidential information like passwords and credit card numbers, HTTPS can be used to provide privacy. Even though Alice is not revealing any passwords or financial information while browsing the web in a coffee shop, there are still privacy issues that remain while using standard HTTP. For example, Alice might be searching for information that deals with a specific medical condition. If Alice is using an HTTP connection to search for such information, Eve could gather that information, infer that Alice has some medical issues, and potentially use that information to embarrass Alice. In response to this threat, popular search engines, like Google Search, provide HTTPS to protect their users' security and privacy. To prevent eavesdropping while surfing the web with HTTP, Alice can use the service of a virtual private network (VPN) to encrypt all of her Internet traffic. The details and functionality of VPNs are discussed in Appendix C (Web Surfing Security Technologies).

Question 2: How can one tell if a website is using HTTPS? Web browsers have different ways to indicate that they are using HTTPS. For a long time, web browsers displayed the HTTPS protocol in the web address bar in addition to a closed padlock image in the lower corner of the web browser window. More recently, web browsers have adopted a color-based scheme to indicate the security level of HTTPS connections by controlling the color of the area next to the URL in the web address bar—often called the favicon area, with the favicon being the small picture displayed in the web address bar (Figure 7.13). Due to a lack of standards, some web browsers still use padlocks as a visual indicator of an HTTPS connection, and some use both padlocks and a color-based indicator in the favicon area to denote when HTTPS is being used.

Figures 7.13–7.15 show examples of web address bars for three different security levels of HTTP/HTTPS for both the Firefox and IE (Internet Explorer) web browsers. Figure 7.13 provides an illustration of web address bars that use HTTP and thus do not provide any level of encryption. In addition to the HTTP protocol in the URL, an unencrypted web connection can further be confirmed by the absence of a color indicator in the favicon area and lack of a closed padlock. The next set of examples in Figure 7.14 shows the web address bar for a HTTPS connection when the respective web browsers are connected to a web server that has a standard signed certificate. It can be seen that the favicon area in the Firefox web browser is blue, while the IE web address bar does not use a similar color as an indication. Unlike Firefox, IE also displays a closed padlock to denote

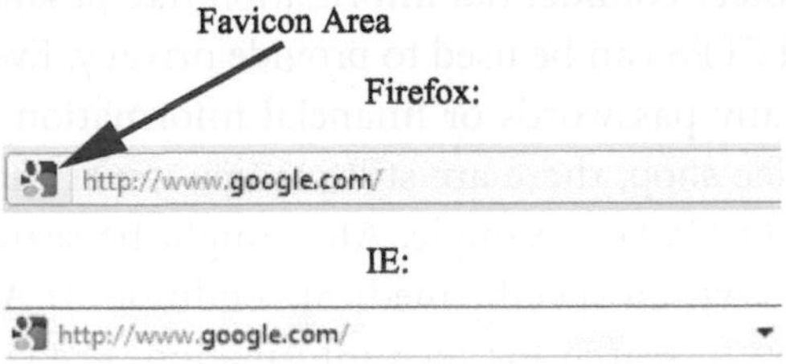

FIGURE 7.13 HTTP (No color + No padlock = No HTTPS).

FIGURE 7.14 Standard HTTPS (Blue or closed padlock = Standard HTTPS).

FIGURE 7.15 Extended validation HTTPS (Green = EV HTTPS).

an HTTPS connection. In the third example, Figure 7.15 illustrates two HTTPS connections that have a green favicon area (IE also has a padlock), which indicates that an HTTPS connection has been established using an Extended Validation (EV) certificate. In comparison to a website with a standard certificate (i.e., blue favicon area or padlock), a website that has an EV certificate (i.e., green favicon area) has fulfilled an additional identity verification process and has also paid a premium cost to obtain such a certificate. The motivation behind the EV certificate is to instill more trust into the web. Therefore, when Alice visits a website with an EV certificate, she can have more confidence that she is indeed communicating with a reputable website.

Question 3: What threats does HTTPS protect against? There is a misconception that if a website makes use of HTTPS it is secure and therefore can be trusted. Question 3 can best be answered by reviewing just what HTTPS means in practice. First, it means that web communications between a web browser and a web server are encrypted and therefore cannot be read by an eavesdropper. Furthermore, HTTPS and its associated certificate provide an additional level of trust in that it identifies the owner of a website domain. If a certificate authority has signed a certificate, then you can trust that the website you are visiting via HTTPS is what it says it is. For example, if you visit the URL https://www.gmail.com/ and the HTTPS indicator appears in the web address bar (see Figure 7.15), then you can be confident that the website is indeed gmail.com. However, if you are tricked into visiting a website that uses HTTPS and cosmetically looks like gmail.com (as the result of clicking on a misleading hyperlink, for example) but the domain name of the website is not that of gmail.com (Chapter 11), then you are on a phishing website. Because many people have been coached to blindly trust websites that make use of HTTPS, phishing websites actually spend money to buy a legitimate signed certificate for their website to enable HTTPS—something anyone can do using a credit card. As discussed in Chapter 11, one cannot use the presence of HTTPS alone to evaluate the legitimacy of a website; one must consider other factors as well. Last, HTTPS does not protect a web server from malware infections or hacking incidents and similarly does not prevent against spyware or any type of key-logging device on the user's computer. To reiterate, HTTPS prevents against eavesdropping and verifies that the owner of a website is who they say they are, whether legitimate or malicious.

Why do websites use both HTTP and HTTPS? Through your web browsing experiences, you may have noticed that some websites use both

HTTP and HTTPS during a single browsing session. For performance reasons, some websites only use HTTPS to authenticate the user (i.e., to encrypt the exchange of a username and password) and then default back to HTTP for the remainder of the user's interactions with the website. As previously discussed, encrypting and decrypting each web request takes added time and thus decreases webpage load times. In the past, many web-based email providers exhibited this very practice. The website would securely authenticate the user using HTTPS, but once logged in, the website would resort back to HTTP. The use of HTTP in this context was both a security and a privacy risk as it allowed for the sniffing of all email correspondences—often information people consider private and confidential. In response, many web-based email providers now provide HTTPS encryption by default for their clients' entire email sessions and thus prevent the threat of eavesdropping. Often, web-based email accounts allow their users to select an option in their preference settings to "Always use HTTPS." When browsing the web, HTTPS should be used whenever possible to prevent the disclosure of private and confidential information.

7.4 WEB BROWSER HISTORY

Cookies and passwords are not the only types of information that are stored by web browsers. To provide a more convenient web browsing experience, web browsers store many other types of information. Depending on your own personal views, the storing of such information can be invasive to one's privacy. One such type of information, as previously described in Section 7.2.1, is that web browsers typically store elements of webpages like text and pictures so that on revisiting the same website, the web browser does not have to download the same content again. This feature is referred to as *browser cache* and is intended to speed up the use of the web. Figure 7.16 shows an example of the number of items stored in a web browser's cache.

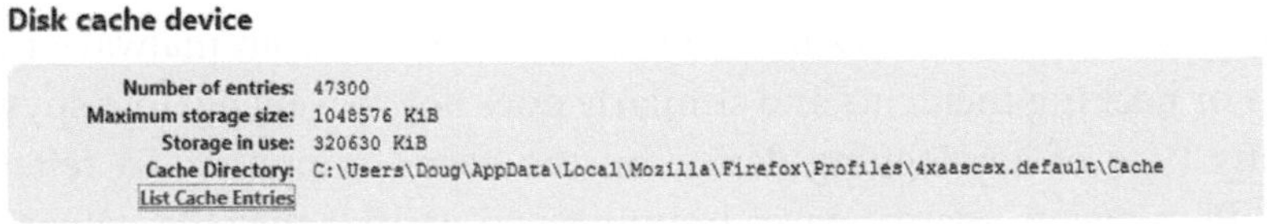

Disk cache device

```
        Number of entries:  47300
    Maximum storage size:  1048576 KiB
         Storage in use:  320630 KiB
        Cache Directory:  C:\Users\Doug\AppData\Local\Mozilla\Firefox\Profiles\4xaascax.default\Cache
        List Cache Entries
```

FIGURE 7.16 Cache example.

Figure 7.16 indicates that the web browser cache (i.e., disk cache device) has 47,300 entries, and Figure 7.17 shows two entries from the cache indicating the two images from the example shown in Figure 7.2. As one can see, the cache has saved the images along with the date and time the image was downloaded and further indicates the time remaining before the image will be removed from the cache. From a user's standpoint, these saved files can present a privacy problem if someone gains access to your computer. The simple act of visiting a webpage leaves trails behind in a web browser that can last much longer than one often expects.

In addition to cache, web browsers possess the capability to remember the URLs of the websites that one has visited. Often referred to as autocomplete, an illustration of this feature can be seen in Figure 7.18. In this example, the user has typed "www.esp" in the web address bar, and the web browser responds by enumerating a list of previously visited URLs that match the inputted text.

Another function a browser will provide is to "autofill" text fields within a webpage. Similar to the autocomplete feature for the web address bar, autofill provides the service of populating text fields on a website by providing a list of items that one has already typed (Figure 7.19). Each of these types of information is saved by the web browser and is designed to speed up or simplify your web browsing experience.

http://www.dougj.net/images/fish.jpg	180860 bytes	2	2011-07-21 08:35:59	2011-07-26 00:46:48
http://www.iac.iastate.edu/images/morefish.jpg	231961 bytes	1	2011-07-21 08:35:59	2011-07-30 22:29:38

FIGURE 7.17   Cache images stored on a computer.

FIGURE 7.18   Web address bar autocomplete.

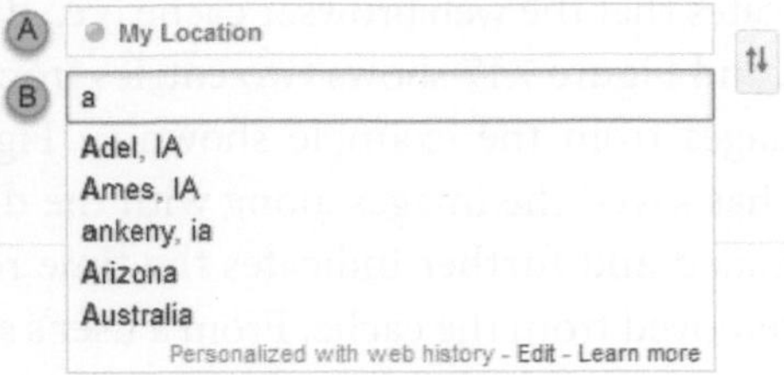

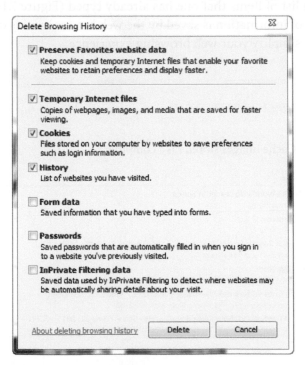

FIGURE 7.19 Text field autofill.

Aside from privacy concerns when using a web browser on a private computer, there are many related issues with using a web browser on a public computer. Situations arise when you do not want the next person using the shared computer to learn your activities by the digital breadcrumbs that web browsers accumulate about their users' actions. There are two predominant ways to prevent the next users of a private or shared computer from learning your actions; the same means can also be used to prevent or delete tracking cookies. First, web browsers allow you to "Clear All History" after using a web browser. As shown in Figure 7.20, performing this action will

FIGURE 7.20 Clear all web browser history.

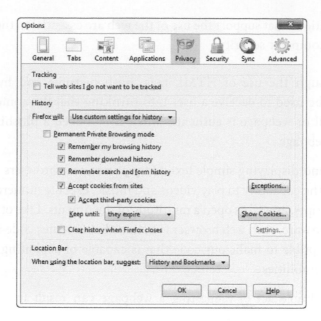

FIGURE 7.21   Limiting browser history.

delete all of the web browser's history, including cookies, cache, and form and search history. The second option is to limit or prevent what the web browser is capable of remembering about your actions as you browse the web. For example, in Figure 7.21, one can prevent the Firefox web browser from remembering any personal information by checking the "Permanent Private Browsing mode" check-box or one can select a custom setting to prevent the use of individual components like cookies or download history. In addition to these controls, many popular web browsers also enable the user to browse the web while in "private browsing mode." As discussed in more detail in Appendix C (Web Surfing Security Technologies), private browsing mode prevents the web browser from remembering the actions of the user.

7.5 SUMMARY

Due to the almost ubiquitous use and reliance on the WWW among computer users, attackers have spent a great deal of time attempting to exploit both human and technical vulnerabilities that coincide with the use of the web. The central focus of these attacks is the web browser and the functionalities that a web browser affords to make one's web experience richer, convenient, interactive, and timely. Many of these qualities have serious security and privacy implications. Understanding how a web browser functions, security and privacy trade-offs, and both the security features and limitations that support the use of the web are essential to the goals of practical computer security.

- Through the use of HTML tags, both pictures and hyperlinks can be used to deceive a user into thinking that the content in an email or webpage is authentic when it is indeed a phishing email or webpage.

- Beyond displaying simple text and pictures, web browsers also possess the capability to play videos and music, execute numerous types of scripts, as well as open a multitude of documents. Like other types of software, each web browser function that executes code is equally susceptible to malicious code that is capable of exploiting software vulnerabilities.

- The simple act of requesting a webpage can result in a drive-by download of malware.

- Web browser cookies enable websites to track users' actions and thus provide a sense of state or history to web browser interactions.

- In addition to the information stored in web browser cookies, how that information is recorded, shared, and transmitted over the Internet presents many security and privacy concerns.

- The use of web browser cookies epitomizes the trade-offs between security/privacy and convenience.

- HTTPS mitigates against the threat of eavesdropping and the loss of confidentiality by encrypting web traffic between a requesting computer and corresponding web server.

- Although not all web transactions require the use of HTTPS, any private or confidential information submitted over the Internet should be done so using HTTPS whenever possible.

- Just because a website uses HTTPS does not guarantee that the website is legitimate or secure. Cyber criminals can just as easily buy certificates that enable them also to create HTTPS websites.

- HTTPS does not prevent against key-loggers, malware, or hacking incidents.

- Cookies, cached images, form and search history, browsing history, and remembered passwords all provide conveniences but also present security and privacy risks.

BIBLIOGRAPHY

Andrews, M., and Whittaker, J.A. 2006. *How to Break Web Software: Functional and Security Testing of Web Applications and Web Services*. Boston: Addison-Wesley Professional.

Angwin, J. 2010. The web's new gold mine: your secrets. *Wall Street Journal*. http://online.wsj.com/article/SB10001424052748703940904575395073512989404.html (accessed April 30, 2012).

AWPG. 2012. Consumer advice: how to avoid phishing scams. http://www.anti-phishing.org/consumer_recs.html (accessed April 30, 2012).

Ceruzzia, P.E. 2003. *A History of Modern Computing*. Cambridge, MA: MIT Press.

Deans, P.C. 2009. *Social Software And Web 2.0 Technology Trends*. Idea Group Inc.

Garfinkel, S., and Spafford, G. 2001. *Web Security, Privacy and Commerce*. Sebastopol, CA: O'Reilly Media.

Gobel, J.G., and Dewald, A. 2010. *Client-Honeypots: Exploring Malicious Websites*. Munich, Germany: Oldenbourg Verlag.

Gourley, D., and Totty, B. 2002. *HTTP: The Definitive Guide*. Sebastopol, CA: O'Reilly Media.

Governor, J., Nickull, D., and Hinchcliffe, D. 2009. *Web 2.0 Architectures*. Sebastopol, CA: O'Reilly Media.

Howard, R. 2010. *Cyber Security Essentials*. Boca Raton, FL: CRC Press.

Jones, R. 2005. *Internet Forensics*. Sebastopol, CA: O'Reilly Media.

Morley, D., and Parker, C.S. 2010. *Understanding Computers: Today and Tomorrow, Introductory*. Independence, KY: Cengage Learning.

Oppliger, R. 2009. *Ssl and Tls: Theory and Practice*. Norwood, MA: Artech House.

Parsons, J.J., and Oja, D. 2010. *Practical PC*. Independence, KY: Cengage Learning.

Pfleeger, C.P., and Pfleeger, S.L. 2011. *Analyzing Computer Security: A Threat/Vulnerability/Countermeasure Approach*. Indianapolis, IN: Prentice Hall Professional.

Realtimepublishers.com, and Sullivan, D. 2005. *The Definitive Guide to Controlling Malware, Spyware, Phishing, and Spam*. San Francisco, CA: Realtimepublishers.com.

Schafer, S.M. 2011. *HTML, XHTML, and CSS Bible*. New York: Wiley, Inc.

Shelly, G.B., Woods, D.M. and Dorin, W.J. 2010. *HTML, XHTML, and CSS: Comprehensive*. Independence, KY: Cengage Learning.

Sydell, L. 2010. Smart cookies put targeted online ads on the rise. National Public Radio. http://www.npr.org/templates/story/story.php?storyId=130349989 (accessed April 30, 2012).

Zimmer, M.T. 2007. *The Quest for the Perfect Search Engine: Values, Technical Design, and the Flow of Personal Information in Spheres of Mobility*. Ann Arbor, MI: ProQuest.

CHAPTER 8

Online Shopping

8.1 INTRODUCTION

When the infamous bank robber Willie Sutton was asked why he robbed banks, he replied, "That's where the money is." The online equivalent to the bank robber is the cyber criminal. Unlike the bank robber, however, the objective of the cyber criminal's heist is to steal personal, confidential, and financial information (for the sake of brevity, all such information is referred to as "financial information" in this chapter). This financial information is then turned into a profit for the cyber criminal either by using the information directly or by selling it in an underground market.

When online shopping first emerged, people were—and still are—reluctant to partake due to the uncertainty of sending their financial information across the Internet and the threat of cyber criminals. This initial hesitancy has gradually dissipated over time as consumer confidence has grown. Many people have accepted the risks of online shopping in return for the conveniences it affords, and this collective action has catapulted online shopping into a multibillion-dollar industry. During the fourth quarter of 2011, U.S. consumers spent more than $50 billion online—more than $1.25 billion on Cyber Monday alone. Cyber criminals, aware that online financial exchanges are "where the money is," have also cashed in on this cyber phenomenon to the tune of an estimated $10 million during the 2011 holiday season alone. While online shopping is convenient for the consumer, it is accompanied by a number of threats and attacks that attempt to trick the consumer into buying false

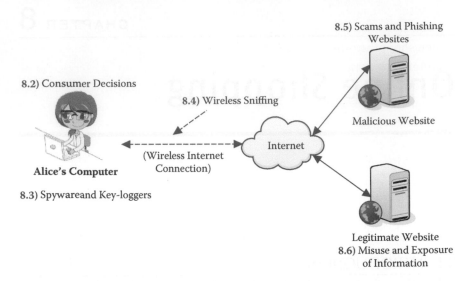

FIGURE 8.1 Sources of financial information disclosure. (Numbers in the figure refer to section numbers in the text.)

products, disclosing financial information, and performing actions that may result in a malware infection (i.e., spyware) leading to the disclosure of financial information.

This chapter explores the common threats and attacks that a consumer would most likely face when shopping online and the corresponding mitigation techniques and best security practices. Figure 8.1 illustrates the five principal means through which financial information is errantly disclosed or stolen when one is shopping online. Although the topics discussed in this chapter are presented in the context of computers and the Internet, many of the security best practices discussed can be abstracted and applied to shopping in the physical world as well.

8.2 CONSUMER DECISIONS

By most accounts, shopping online is a voluntary activity. This means that consumers make decisions about where they are going to shop, what information they are going to disclose, and how they are going to pay for the items that they desire to purchase. While it is true that not all that can go wrong when shopping online is the fault of the consumer (sometimes the disclosure of financial information is the fault of the online retailer), there are a number of decisions that a consumer can make that will decrease the risk of accidentally disclosing financial information.

8.2.1 Defense in Depth

When shopping online, or performing any activity online for that matter, maintain the defense-in-depth strategy outlined in Chapter 6. Make sure that you have recently performed a backup of your data, apply the most current web browser and operating system patches, enable your firewall, and ensure that your antivirus software is enabled and that its signatures are up to date. If you take these steps, the risk and potential impact of a malware infection has been decreased, even if you get tricked into visiting a malicious website as the consequence of an online shopping activity.

8.2.2 Credit Card versus Debit Card

When purchasing items online, a consumer is afforded the most protection under U.S. federal law and in the payment procedure when using a credit card as opposed to a debit card. Although credit and debit cards look similar in appearance, they differ in payment procedures—the financial steps taken to transfer money from the card owner to the online retailer. A credit card allows consumers to buy items on credit, operating on the concept of buy now, pay later. When a purchase with a credit card is made, the credit card issuer (e.g., Visa) initially pays for the item. Every 30 days or so, the credit card issuer assesses the credit card owner a bill for the month's transactions. This payment procedure is advantageous to the consumer because if a credit card number is compromised and fraudulent charges are made, the initial money used to pay for such purchases has been supplied by the credit card issuer and not by the consumer's bank account. This payment procedure also affords the credit card owner the ability to dispute fraudulent charges and withhold payments until fraudulent charges have been investigated.

Debit cards, unlike credit cards, are not afforded the same protection due to the fundamental differences in payment procedures. A debit card is similar to an electronic check. If a fraudulent purchase or withdrawal is made with a debit card, the money is directly withdrawn from the card owner's checking account, and the financial transaction is made immediately. Due to the speed of such transactions, the ability to issue a stop payment to thwart a fraudulent purchase is highly unlikely.

Two separate laws protect credit cards and debit cards, and each of these laws affects the card owner's liability for fraudulent charges. Credit cards are protected under the Fair Credit Billing Act (FCBA). Under the FCBA, if a credit card owner reports that a card or card number has been

Fraud Reported	Credit Card	Debit Card
Before use	$0	$0
Within 2 business days	$50	$50
Between 2 and 60 business days	$50	$500
After 60 business days	Unlimited	Unlimited

FIGURE 8.2   U.S. maximum liability for credit and debit card owners.

stolen before a fraudulent act occurs, the credit card owner is not liable for any of the fraudulent charges that ensue (Figure 8.2). If a credit card owner notices a fraudulent charge on his or her monthly bill, he or she has up to 60 days from the bill issue date to send the creditor a written dispute regarding the fraudulent charges. Within this 60-day time period, the credit card owner is liable for a maximum of $50 for the fraudulent charges. If a fraudulent charge has not been identified before the 60 days have elapsed, the credit card owner becomes liable for any and all damages. In reality, though, credit card companies or banks will often waive such fees or liability costs for the credit card owner.

Debit cards, on the other hand, are protected under the Electronic Funds Transfer Act (EFTA). Under the EFTA, debit card owners have only two business days to dispute a fraudulent charge, following which their maximum liability increases from $50 to $500 (Figure 8.2). After 60 days, just like for credit card owners, the maximum liability for debit card owners becomes unlimited. The real question is not whether one should use a credit card or a debit card when shopping online, but why one would use any method of payment other than a credit card given the protection in payment procedure that is afforded under law to the credit card owner.

8.2.3 Single-Use Credit Cards

To provide enhanced security and to reduce the anxiety people feel when disclosing a credit card number online, many credit card issuers provide a free service for their customers that allows them to use virtual credit card numbers for online transactions. A virtual credit card number is a temporary credit card number randomly generated by the credit card issuer on behalf of the card owner. The user of the virtual credit card service does not actually receive a physical card but instead receives a virtual number for temporary use. Users of virtual credit cards are able to set the virtual card's purchase limit, expiration date, and number of uses. They can also limit the use of the card to specific online merchants if they so choose.

When an online purchase is made, the user presents the virtual credit card number to the online retailer, and the subsequent transaction appears on the user's normal credit card bill with the virtual number listed next to the purchase. If the transaction details are compromised, or if an online retailer's credit card database is hacked, the use of a virtual credit card decreases the amount of damage that an attacker can inflict. While the benefits of a virtual credit card are quite obvious, taking the added steps needed to increase security when shopping online is at odds with user convenience. Because of this, virtual credit card numbers are not widely utilized even though this service has been available for quite some time.

8.2.4 Passwords

Many online retailers either require or give consumers the option to create password-protected online accounts to make purchases. For the customer's convenience, these online accounts contain financial information such as names, shipping addresses, and credit card numbers. This information is not stored on your computer but on the online retailer's server. To prevent unauthorized access to such accounts, one should employ the password security best practices outlined in Chapter 3.

8.2.5 Do Your Homework

Just as the Internet provides numerous options to choose online retailers, it also provides the means for researching these same retailers. Generally, the safest choice is to shop with merchants that you know and trust and that have well-established reputations. If you are faced with the decision of whether to purchase an item from an unknown online retailer, be sure to do some research about the company before making a purchase. A reputable company will list at least one phone number that can be used to inquire about the company's business practices as well as a physical address. Before making a purchase, carefully examine the physical location of the retailer. Consumers who shop with companies located outside the United States might not be afforded the same consumer protections that are granted under U.S. federal and state law when one is shopping with a U.S.-based company. Other useful pieces of information to understand before disclosing financial information are the company's privacy policy, shipping details, and cancellation and return policies. Because collecting and analyzing such information may be tedious at times, an alternative is to consult the Better Business Bureau's website (www.bbb.org) to learn more about a particular online retailer, its business practices, and any potential frauds linked to that retailer. The broad number of online retail options that are available to the consumer can make online shopping both convenient and overwhelming at the same time. Be sure to take the time to perform some basic research before making a purchase, especially when dealing with lesser-known retailers, to ensure the security of your financial information.

8.3 SPYWARE AND KEY-LOGGERS

Never make a purchase online or divulge any financial information on a computer that you do not trust. The list of untrusted computers should include computers at a library, retail store, coffee shop, friend's house, and so on. Key-loggers and spyware are constant threats on untrusted computers. Entering any financial information on such a computer could be the equivalent of handing your name, credit card number, and home address directly to a cyber criminal. If you believe that your computer has a malware infection, you should treat it as an untrusted machine. Online purchases should not be made until all malware has been removed from the computer. It is imperative to consistently follow the defense-in-depth strategy so that, when one does want to make an online purchase, he or she has confidence in the security of his or her computing environment.

8.4 WIRELESS SNIFFING

Due to the threat of an attacker sniffing wireless traffic (Chapter 9), one should refrain from purchasing items online when a computer is connected to an unsecure wireless network. Although using HTTPS (Hypertext Transfer Protocol Secure) may mitigate the risk of sniffing, there are websites that do not use HTTPS for entire browsing sessions; as a result, financial information may be sent in cleartext over the Internet. This information can subsequently be sniffed on an unsecure wireless network.

8.5 SCAMS AND PHISHING WEBSITES

When making decisions about shopping online, ask yourself, Would I do this in the real world? Apply the same scrutiny that you would use to assess a door-to-door salesman to the emails that you receive about so-called super deals or factory closeouts. If you would not give your credit card to a salesman on the street selling an "Amazon Kindle3 for $8.76," then do not provide your credit card number to a website claiming to sell the same item (Figure 8.3). Furthermore, if you would not choose to be led down a suspect alleyway in a foreign country in search of a good deal,

FIGURE 8.3   Phishing email touting great deals.

then do not click on a hyperlink or pop-up message offering similar savings. Let common sense and shopper's intuition prevail. Do not settle into a false sense of security just because you are shopping while sitting in the comfort of your own home.

Figure 8.3 provides a classic example of a malicious email message enticing the reader to click on a hyperlink in hopes of being able to purchase mainstream products at a 90% discount. When confronted with a similar email or pop-up ad, remember that if something is too good to be true, it usually is. To avoid falling victim to online scams such as phishing websites, never click on a link in an email to begin your online shopping activities. It is a better security practice to travel to the specific website from which you are trying to make a purchase by typing in the correct URL (Uniform Resource Locator) and locating the deal yourself. In addition, never click on a pop-up ad and strongly refrain from clicking on web-based advertisements. These are all known means of leading an online shopper to phishing websites or webpages that attempt drive-by downloads. Furthermore, as seen in Figure 4.8, other types of malicious emails attempt to deceive the reader into thinking they made an expensive purchase. The objective of these emails is to trick the user into opening the "invoice" or "statement" attached to the email. Opening any type of file attached to such an email is likely to result in the execution of malicious lines of code and potentially a malware infection.

While it is always good security practice to take caution when shopping online, be particularly alert during holiday shopping seasons. Cyber criminals are well aware of consumer behaviors and, like retailers, also ramp up their efforts during such times. The same can be said about releases of new or highly sought products such as cell phones or tablet devices.

8.5.1 Indicators of Trust

To prevent falling victim to online scams and phishing websites, there are a few "indicators of trust" that one can search for on a retailer's website or in one's own personal web browser. The presence of these indicators provides a higher degree of confidence that one is indeed shopping at a reputable and secure website.

- **URL:** Ensure you have traveled to the webpage yourself by typing the correct URL, using a bookmark, or by the coupling of a search engine and a link scanner (Appendix C: Web Surfing Security Technologies). Before submitting any financial information, verify that the URL conforms to the website on which you expect to be shopping (Chapter 11).

- **Link Scanner:** Check a link scanner indicator to ensure that the webpage or domain name has not been flagged as malicious (Appendix C: Web Surfing Security Technologies).

- **HTTPS:** Any time you enter financial information online, make sure that the webpage you are viewing is encrypting the web traffic with HTTPS. Confirm that the web address bar is blue or green and make sure that the lock icon in the web browser is closed (see Chapter 7). Remember that the use of HTTPS only verifies that data is encrypted as it travels between your computer and the online shopping web server, and that the website is indeed who it says it is, whether malicious or not. On its own, HTTPS does not guarantee that a website is secure or is not a phishing website, as many computer security tip websites and articles coach people to believe.

If a website accepts financial information but does not make use of HTTPS, take your business elsewhere. HTTPS is a fundamental security mechanism, and if a company is unable to implement this security best practice properly, then it is likely that the company does not place a high value on the security of consumers' information. It is quite possible that such a website will also follow other suspect security practices.

8.6 MISUSE AND EXPOSURE OF INFORMATION

Misuse of information or large-scale data breaches of information from online retailers occur with enough frequency that this topic warrants our concern. Even when one is shopping online with a trusted computer over a trusted wired Internet connection on the website of a well-known company that utilizes HTTPS, financial information is still at risk. As discussed in Chapter 3, the well-known online retailer Zappos, which is owned by Amazon, was hacked, exposing the names, email addresses, addresses, phone numbers, password hashes, and last four digits of credit card numbers of more than 24 million customers. As presented in Chapter 1, *there is no such thing as absolute security*. Data breaches of this nature are simply an intrinsic risk of shopping online and should motivate us to limit the amount of information disclosed to an online retailer and to monitor all credit card activity diligently.

8.6.1 Disclosing Information

When shopping online, provide only the minimal amount of information necessary to make a purchase. Some online retailers will attempt to solicit additional information about a customer's lifestyle for the purposes of target advertising, spam emails, and even snail mail. Sometimes, online merchants will present information fields garnered with an asterisk, indicating that the consumer must fill in the marked field to complete the purchase (Figure 8.4). If a "required" field attempts to request information not related to the purchase details, such as your birthday or your mother's maiden name, strongly consider taking your business elsewhere as there are plenty of online retailers that do not force consumers to disclose non-related personal information. Information such as a Social Security number is never required to make a purchase. If you find yourself on a website that requests this information, cease all interactions as it is highly likely that the website is part of a scam.

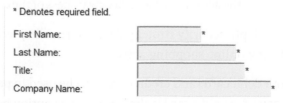

FIGURE 8.4   Required text fields.

8.6.2 Audit Credit Card Activity

At a minimum, monitor your credit card activity for suspicious charges on a weekly basis. Diligence is the key to thwarting cyber criminals and stopping fraudulent charges before they become the consumer's burden to pay. Attackers are well aware that making a fraudulent purchase or withdrawing large sums of money (i.e., $4000 at a time) will appear as highly suspicious activities to the credit or debit card owner. As a result, cyber criminals have been known to employ more subtle techniques to avoid detection by buying items such as designer purses at reputable stores. To audit your own purchases, keep a record of receipts or confirmation statements you receive after purchases and cross-check your monthly credit card or bank account statements with those records to ensure that they are consistent. Be aware that fraudulent purchases may not appear on your statement for hours, days, or even months after a credit card number is compromised since it takes time for cyber criminals to sell and abuse such information.

8.7 SUMMARY

Along with the convenience of online shopping comes the added risk of falling victim to an online scam. Cyber criminals have built a million-dollar industry based on the fact that many people do not exhibit such caution when shopping online. Although not all of the risks of online shopping can be avoided, a great deal of them can by the choices the consumer does or does not make. To shop safely online, use common sense and apply the best practices discussed in this chapter.

- As online shopping has evolved into a billion-dollar industry, it has also become a prime target for cyber criminals looking to steal financial information.

- Online shopping is largely a voluntary activity in which many threats can be mitigated by the actions and security awareness of the consumer.

- The defense-in-depth security strategy described in Chapter 6 should be applied during online shopping activities.

- Although both debit cards and credit cards can be used to pay online shopping expenses, a credit card is the more secure option because of favorable consumer protection laws and payment procedures.

- Single-use credit cards with virtual account numbers offer increased security over conventional credit cards.

- The careful online shopper will take advantage of the Internet's power for researching potential shopping websites before making a purchase.

- Due to the threat of spyware, online purchases should only be made from trusted and secure computers.

- Avoid using wireless networks, especially in public places, when shopping online to prevent against the threat of eavesdropping. At the very least, ensure that an online retailer makes use of HTTPS before financial information is disclosed.

- When shopping online, one should maintain a commonsense attitude and not be lulled into a false sense of security. If the deal seems "too good to be true," it usually is, even if the deal was forwarded from a trusted friend.

- There are certain indicators, such as a valid URL, link scanner, and the use of HTTPS, that can be used to examine the trustworthiness of an online retailer.

- Provide only the minimum information necessary to make a purchase, and if a website requires information not related to the purchase, strongly consider taking your business elsewhere.

- One should frequently monitor credit card statements for fraudulent or mistaken charges. Credit card laws are usually quite protective to card users as long as protests are filed in a timely manner.

BIBLIOGRAPHY

Barrett, J. 2009. Credit and debit cards: what you need to know. http://www.nytimes.com/2009/01/06/your-money/credit-and-debit-cards/primercards.html?_r=1 (accessed April 22, 2012).

Better Business Bureau. 2012. Home page. http://www.bbb.org/us/Find-Business-Reviews/ (Accessed April 22, 2012).

Biegelman, M. 2009. *Identity Theft Handbook: Detection, Prevention, and Security.* New York: Wiley.

Identity Theft Response Center. 2010. ITRC fact sheet 131. http://www.idtheftcenter.org/artman2/publish/c_guide/Fact_Sheet_131.shtml (accessed April 22, 2012).

Kelly, M. 2011. Consumers will lose $10M to cyber crime this holiday season. *VentureBeat.* http://venturebeat.com/2011/12/18/holiday-shopping-cyber-crime/(accessed April 22, 2012).

Larkin, E. 2009. Go virtual for safer online shopping. *PCWorld*. http://www. pcworld.com/article/171865/go_virtual_for_safer_online_shopping.html (accessed April 22, 2012).

Mitic, S. 2009. *Stopping Identity Theft:10 Easy Steps to Security*. Berkeley, CA: Nolo.

Newton, M., and French, J. L. 2008. *Bank Robbery*. New York: Infobase.

Oram, A., and Viega, J. 2009. *Beautiful Security*. Sebastopol, CA: O'Reilly Media.

Poulsen, K. 2012. *Kingpin: How One Hacker Took Over the Billion-Dollar Cybercrime Underground*. New York: Random House Digital.

Privacy Rights Clearinghouse. 2011. http://www.privacyrights.org/fs/fs23-shopping.htm (accessed April 22, 2012).

Sherman, E. 2012. Zappos hacked: 24 million accounts at risk. CBSNews. http://www.cbsnews.com/8301-505124_162-57359700/zappos-hacked-24-million-accounts-at-risk/ (accessed April 22, 2012).

Whitney, L. 2012. U.S. online spending hit $50 billion last quarter. CNet. http://news.cnet.com/8301-1023_3-57372567-93/u.s-online-spending-hit-$50-billion-last-quarter/ (accessed April 22, 2012).

CHAPTER 9

Wireless Internet Security

9.1 INTRODUCTION

Wireless networks are literally all around us as we move through our everyday lives. No longer just found in private residences, airports, and coffee shops, wireless networks are now present in buses, airplanes, restaurants, and city parks, just to name a few places. Coupled with the abundance of Wi-Fi-enabled mobile devices (i.e., smart phones, laptops, tablets) able to connect to wireless Internet networks, we are immersed in a culture of technology that enables effortless and seamless connection to the Internet. While wireless networks provide the convenience of untethered access to the Internet, they also present a number of security threats that must be recognized and accounted for in order to use these networks safely. Such threats and corresponding wireless security best practices are the focus of this chapter.

The topic of wireless security can be broken down into two parts. First is a description of how wireless networks work, providing the necessary context to describe the common types of threats and attacks that occur while using wireless networks. The second is a discussion of security best practices from two perspectives. First is that of accessing a public wireless network as a user, perhaps in an airport or coffee shop. The second is from the viewpoint of an administrator of a private wireless network, such as one that might be found in a home or apartment. Examining wireless security from the perspectives of both a user and an administrator will shed light on the security threats that you will most likely face when using wireless networks and reveal how wireless security best practices can mitigate against such threats.

9.2 HOW WIRELESS NETWORKS WORK

Often referred to as a wireless Internet network, Wi-Fi, Wireless Ethernet, or IEEE (Institute of Electrical and Electronics Engineers) 802.11 a/b/g/n, these terms are all synonyms for technology that allows computers and mobile devices to connect to the Internet over a network without need for interconnecting wires (i.e., Ethernet cables). As illustrated in Figure 9.1, the topic of wireless networks only considers the first hop to the Internet or, in other words, the wireless network created by a wireless router that serves as a gateway to access the Internet. The communications that take place between the wireless router and the Internet (i.e., wired network) are not generally considered to be a practical security concern. The focus of this chapter is the immediate threats one encounters when connecting a computer to a wireless router.

Figure 9.2 shows the most common wireless protocol names, their accompanying frequencies, data rates, and typical indoor transmission distances. Unlike a wired network that is confined to the actual wire, a wireless network's maximum transmission distance is its only restriction. Wireless signals can pass through objects, walls, and floors; into the apartments or houses of neighbors; and even into the outside street or parking lot. This wide-ranging transmission capability is convenient but also presents serious security implications.

To provide the context for further discussions of security, it is first necessary to understand how wireless routers work and how they communicate with wireless devices. Although this discussion is focused on

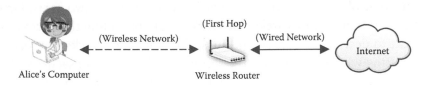

FIGURE 9.1   Wireless network diagram.

Protocol Name	Frequency	Data Rate	Typical indoor transmission distance
802.11a	5 GHz	54 Mbps	115 Feet
802.11b	2.4 GHz	11 Mbps	125 Feet
802.11g	2.4 GHz	11–54 Mbps	125 Feet
802.11n	2.4/5 GHz	200 Mbps	230 Feet

FIGURE 9.2   Common wireless Ethernet protocols.

using a laptop computer to access a wireless network, the same principles hold true for any type of Wi-Fi-enabled device, including smart phones, tablets, and PDA-type devices. It should be noted that the technologies used to access the Internet over a Wi-Fi network are fundamentally different from those used to access the Internet over a cellular network with a smart phone. Because of these differences, the threats faced when using a wireless network are not generally considered to be practical threats when accessing the Internet over a cellular network.

To better understand how wireless networks work in practice, imagine that Bob is in a coffee shop, and he opens his laptop with the intention of casually browsing the Internet. To be able to access the Internet, Bob must first connect to a wireless router—presumably one owned by the coffee shop. The first step in this process is for Bob to open his laptop's wireless network connection manager. This action typically produces a list of wireless routers within the immediate vicinity of Bob's laptop or, in other words, within the transmission radius of the wireless router (Figure 9.3).

Bob's computer knows that there are wireless networks in the area because public wireless routers purposefully broadcast their existence with a beacon signal much like a lighthouse announces the presence of a harbor or a navigational danger. Contained within this beacon signal is the wireless router's Service Set Identifier (SSID), more commonly known as the wireless router or network name (e.g., IASTATE in Figure 9.3). The security indicator of the wireless network (a yellow exclamation mark denotes an unsecure network in Figure 9.3) and the strength of the connection signal typically accompany the SSID name inside the wireless

FIGURE 9.3   Wireless connection manager for Bob's computer.

connection manager. As shown in Figure 9.3, in the Windows 7 operating system, the absence of a yellow exclamation mark next to an SSID name indicates that a particular wireless network requires an access password and encryption of the Internet traffic between the wireless router and the connecting Wi-Fi device. Such a network is referred to as a *secure wireless network*. A wireless network with a yellow exclamation mark does not require a password, and it does not encrypt wireless traffic; as a result, it is referred to as an *unsecure wireless network*.

To connect to a wireless network, Bob clicks on a particular SSID listing in the network connection manager and his computer does the rest of the work behind the scenes to establish a connection. If the wireless network is a secure network, then Bob must first authenticate to the router by providing the correct password (Section 9.5.3).

Once Bob's computer is connected to a wireless router, he can begin browsing the web, engage in instant messenger chats, and check his email. To do this, Bob's computer and the wireless router engage in a series of message exchanges that are broadcast wirelessly, hence the term *wireless network*. Because Bob's laptop does not know the physical location of the router in the coffee shop, it broadcasts Internet transactions in an omnidirectional manner so that the wireless router, somewhere within the radius of a city block (i.e., a New York north-south city block or approximately 264 feet) from the computer (Figure 9.2), will be able to "hear" the messages. Depending on the router and a number of other factors, the maximum transmission distance of a router will vary. The wireless broadcasting of Internet transactions has security implications and is one of the main risks that one faces when connecting to a wireless network.

9.3 WIRELESS SECURITY THREATS

While wireless networks afford the convenience of untethered wireless access to the Internet, they are also accompanied by the threats of sniffing (Section 9.3.1), unauthorized connections (Section 9.3.2), rogue routers (Section 9.3.3), and evil twin routers (Section 9.3.4). Before discussing the security best practices when using and administering wireless networks, we first build on our knowledge of how wireless networks work and discuss these threats.

9.3.1 Sniffing

Similar to eavesdropping on phone conversations, a threat faced when using a wireless network is that another computer is able to "sniff" one's wireless traffic (i.e., digital eavesdropping). For wireless sniffing to be possible, the attacker's computer must first be connected to the same wireless router as the victim's computer. As previously discussed, when computers communicate with a wireless router, they transmit their communications for all to be heard in the nearby vicinity. This means that all computers connected to the same Wi-Fi network are able to hear each other's conversations. Because there is no beneficial or legitimate functional objective for capturing and processing other computers' network traffic, the normal action of a computer is simply to ignore all other wireless traffic other than the traffic that is specifically addressed to the given computer (Figure 9.4).

To reverse this default behavior of a computer and listen to others' Internet traffic, there are a number of free, legal, and readily available software programs (e.g., Wireshark or TCPDUMP) that can put any normal computer into what is called "promiscuous mode"—requiring no special attacking hardware. Promiscuous mode enables a computer connected to a wireless router to receive and capture (i.e., sniff) all wireless Internet traffic to and from the router and from all computers connected to the router (Figure 9.5). Because the attacker's computer passively listens, there is no way for one to determine if traffic is being sniffed or not. The utility of sniffing software programs even goes so far as to let the sniffer filter specific Internet traffic such as AOL IM (instant messaging) conversations

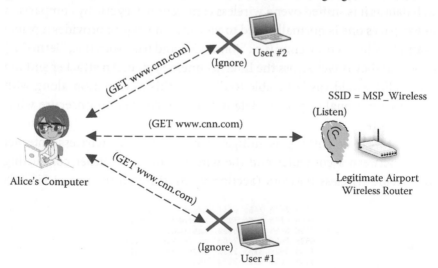

FIGURE 9.4   Default computer behavior.

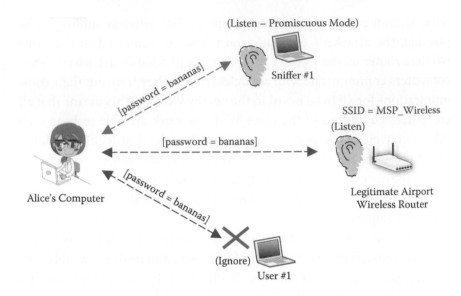

FIGURE 9.5   Sniffing computer put in promiscuous mode.

or even display webpages simultaneously as they are seen on the victim's computer. The main threat of sniffing is the attacker's ability to sniff passwords, credit card numbers, session cookies (Chapter 7), and other forms of sensitive or confidential information broadcast in clear text over an unsecure wireless connection.

Figure 9.6 provides an actual screen capture of the representation of web data as it is sniffed over a wireless connection. Cryptic by comparison to webpages one is normally used to viewing, this figure provides a prime example of how a username (i.e., "johnny5") and password (i.e., "letmein") appear as they travel across the Internet unencrypted. An attacker sniffing this traffic would easily be able to discover this information along with any other personal or private data not encrypted over an unsecure wireless network.

The threat of sniffing is mitigated by encrypting wireless Internet traffic between a computer and the wireless router by either connecting to a secure wireless network (Section 9.5.3), through the use of HTTPS

```
7264 2e68 746d 6c3f   k/password.html?
3d6a 6f68 6e6e 7935   username=johnny5
643d 6c65 746d 6569   &password=letmei
653a 205f 5f75 746d   n..Cookie:.__utm
3338 362e 3133 3131   z=208037386.1311
3138 2e37 372e 7574   163910.318.77.ut
```

FIGURE 9.6   Sniffed wireless Internet traffic.

(Hypertext Transfer Protocol Secure) (Chapter 7), or by utilizing a virtual private network (VPN) (Appendix C). Using any of these methods, even if web traffic is sniffed, it will be unreadable to the attacker because it is encrypted. To encrypt all Internet traffic, including that of a desktop email client, then using a secure wireless network or a VPN provides the most protection. If any of these options are not available, choosing not to send confidential information like passwords or credit card numbers can further mitigate the threat of sniffing over unsecure wireless networks.

9.3.2 Unauthorized Connections

When connecting to a wireless router at a coffee shop or public library, there should be an expectation that many unknown, and thus untrusted, people are connected to the same wireless router. Because of this, one must assume that his or her traffic will be sniffed and therefore should act accordingly (Section 9.4). This same communal sharing of a wireless network, however, should not occur with a wireless router that you own and use in your private residence. The term *piggybacking* refers to a user connecting to a private wireless network not intended to be available for general public use. An attacker who piggybacks connects to a wireless router without permission and often even without knowledge of the router's owner; thus, it is an unauthorized connection. Many times, piggybacking is enabled because the owner of the wireless router failed to activate the router's security mechanisms that require all users to know a password before being granted access to the network (Section 9.5.3). For example, if a person in an apartment building fails to secure access to his or her wireless network with a password, neighbors would then be able to piggyback on to this wireless network because wireless networks easily pass through the walls of an apartment. Think back to the initial discussion on your router's typical transmission distance and imagine a sphere the distance of a city block around your wireless router. How many untrusted people have the ability to access your wireless network?

The risk that piggybackers pose ranges from a simple nuisance to downright illegal and harmful activity. The least-concerning action of a piggybacker is the needless sharing, by the owner, of a limited amount of bandwidth with one or more piggybackers. A more significant threat is that, once a piggybacker is connected to a wireless network, he or she may have the capability for accessing the admin controls for the wireless router (Section 9.5.1), sniff wireless traffic, and gain unrestricted access to the Internet. Once connected to a wireless network, a perpetrator has the ability to commit crimes like downloading and uploading illegal content such as pirated music, software, or pornography or using the wireless network as a staging point from which to attack other computers or send threatening messages. If any such occurrences do happen, they will be traced back to the offending wireless router and ultimately to the router's owner. A Buffalo, New York, man found this lesson out the hard way, having his house raided by FBI (Federal Bureau of Investigation) agents, who accused him of downloading child pornography. Only later did the man learn that the perpetrator was his 25-year-old neighbor piggybacking on his unsecure wireless network. Needless to say, not only do you want to prevent piggybackers from eavesdropping on your wireless traffic, but also you want to defeat those who seek to use your wireless Internet connection to mask their illegal activities.

Some piggybackers will even go as far as posting the locations of unsecure wireless networks online so that others can exploit them. Known as "war driving," an attacker will drive through a neighborhood or city street with an open laptop, searching for unsecure wireless networks. Once found, the attacker records the SSID, address, or the GPS location of the unsecure wireless network and then posts the information on the web for all to see. Based on this information, cyber criminals can then use these unsecure networks to perform their dirty deeds. Australia and some European countries have gone so far as to make unsecure wireless networks illegal and will punish offenders with a monetary fine.

9.3.3 Rogue Router

When one connects to a public wireless network such as one found in a coffee shop or airport, often the only information known about the wireless network is the network's SSID. Most often, it is not possible to see the physical router that a computer is communicating with or learn any information about the router, such as its owner or the router's security settings. Thus, in many ways, many people blindly connect to public wireless routers. This tendency to connect to unsecure wireless networks without concern for security can be problematic as attackers are often able to exploit this blind trust.

Attackers have been known to create rogue wireless access points in public places such as an airport terminal, for example, with an enticing SSID similar to "Free_Airport_WIFI." Establishing an unsecure and inviting wireless network in the presence of a busy and laptop-toting crowd creates a trap for potential victims (Figure 9.7). When airport commuters

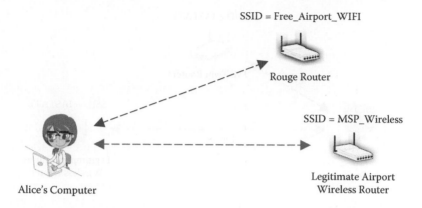

SSID = Free_Airport_WIFI

Rouge Router

SSID = MSP_Wireless

Legitimate Airport
Wireless Router

Alice's Computer

FIGURE 9.7   Rogue router attack.

connect to the "free" wireless network, the attacker is then able to sniff all of the wireless traffic of its victims. After a few hours of sniffing traffic, the attacker boards his or her next flight with victim's data in hand, never to be seen again. In addition to just sniffing wireless traffic, some rogue networks will even require their victim to establish an account (to steal a username and password combination from the user) and charge for service (costing the victim real money to use the Internet and simultaneously stealing the victim's financial information).

Rogue routers are not unique to airports and can also be found in apartment buildings, hotels, coffee shops, and other places where people frequently connect to the Internet. Under the assumption that every public network is insecure or rogue, in the next section we discuss how to act appropriately when connecting to public networks.

9.3.4 Evil Twin Router

To provide wireless connectivity for large areas such as an airport terminal, hotel, or college campus, many wireless routers are often installed in strategic locations to provide broad coverage and are typically assigned the same SSID. As a result, depending on the location of the user, one may be within the range of several wireless routers at one time. To simplify the process of connecting to a wireless network, network connection managers will often only display the SSID of the wireless network that has the strongest signal (for all routers with the same SSID). That way, the user is provided with presumably the best connection available. While helpful in most contexts, such a convenience can and has been exploited by attackers.

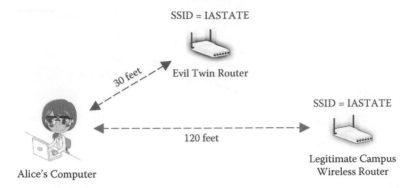

FIGURE 9.8   Evil twin router attack.

Known as the "evil twin" router attack, Eavesdropper Eve can establish a wireless network connection with the same SSID as a college campus, for example, and position her evil twin router near a victim (i.e., Alice). That way, when Alice attempts to connect to the normal SSID of her college campus (IASTATE in Figure 9.8), Alice's wireless connection manager will choose the evil twin router due to its proximity and presumably strong signal connection instead of the legitimate campus router. Eavesdropper Eve is then connected to the same router as Alice and therefore can sniff Alice's Internet traffic. Due to the difficultly of discovering an evil twin router attack, this threat presents yet another risk one must consider when engaging in any confidential actions over an unsecure wireless router.

The four threats discussed in this section take advantage of the capabilities of wireless routers either to steal confidential information or to use a wireless network as a staging point from which to commit other crimes. In the following section, we discuss wireless security best practices, first from the perspective of a user accessing a public Wi-Fi network and then from the perspective of a wireless network administrator.

9.4 PUBLIC WI-FI SECURITY

When connecting to a wireless router in a public space (secure or not), users beware. It is best to assume that a public wireless network is not secure, and that an attacker will be able to sniff all of your wireless traffic. It follows that wireless networks in public places should primarily be used to surf the web recreationally. Even though interacting with websites that make use of HTTPS mitigates the threat of sniffing web traffic by means of data encryption, as discussed in Chapter 7, other threats like session hijacking remain a concern. Apart from refraining to use public wireless networks, the best security defense to prevent against the many threats wireless networks present is to use a VPN to encrypt not only web traffic but also all Internet traffic (Appendix C). Furthermore, one should also assume that a public wireless network is not protected behind a firewall, and people should ensure that their software firewall is enabled before connecting to any such wireless network. In addition to technical security mechanisms, user education, including the understanding of the limits of security mechanisms and the specifics threats that accompany wireless networks, is a key defense.

Using laptop computers in public places presents threats that are not only digital but also physical in nature. Engaging in activities on your computer in a crowded place increases the threat of someone nearby purposely observing your actions. Known as "shoulder surfing," this is the act of observing information while glancing over the shoulder of a victim. Some shoulder surfers are quite adept at reading keystrokes as they are typed, words off a screen, or even numbers on a credit card. When in a public place, it is best to leave confidential transactions for a later time when you can be connected to a secure and trusted network and have privacy from those around you. For avid travelers, privacy filters for computer screens can be purchased to help mitigate the threat of shoulder surfing.

Also, when using a computer in a public space, beware of leaving your computer at a table when using the restrooms, buying an item, or stepping outside to take a call. Criminals are thieves of opportunity, and many computers are stolen when they are left unattended even for short periods of time.

9.5 WIRELESS NETWORK ADMINISTRATION

As illustrated in Figure 9.9, there are many cost-effective technologies and easily deployable methods that one can use to receive an Internet connection into their home. To create a wireless Internet network, one typically attaches a wireless router to the device in the house that receives the Internet connection (e.g., cable modem), or the receiving device serves a dual purpose as a receiver and a wireless router. The resulting Wi-Fi network that the wireless router creates is virtually the same for each method and independent of how the Internet connection originates in the house. As a result, and despite the fact that each type or brand of wireless router may be slightly different, the security concerns and administrative security controls for Wi-Fi networks remain largely consistent.

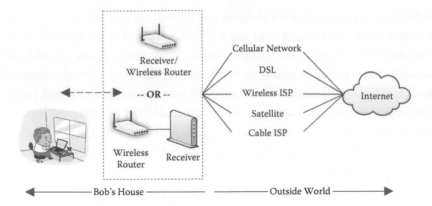

FIGURE 9.9   Wireless Internet network. DSL, digital subscriber line; ISP, Internet service provider.

As the owner and thus the administrator of a wireless router, there are a number of safeguards and precautions that one must take to mitigate the previously described threats. This section provides the security best practices for administrating a wireless network in your private residence.

9.5.1 Default Admin Password

To access the configuration and security controls for a wireless router, one must access the wireless router's administrative (admin) webpage. To do this, first connect a computer to your wireless network and then enter an IP (Internet Protocol) address, such as 192.168.1.1, into the address bar of a web browser. Each brand of router has a slightly different IP address that is used to access the admin page, and this information can be found in the router's documentation. This action displays the router's admin control webpage that allows the router admin (i.e., you) to change the router's security settings.

Many wireless routers are sold and configured with the same preestablished admin password or with no password at all. Furthermore, the default admin passwords for many different brands of routers are no secret and are posted on publicly available websites. Because of this, it is best to change a router's admin password during initial router setup (Figure 9.10). Failing to change the default admin password would enable anyone connected to your wireless router to access the router's same admin controls, which could result in numerous devious deeds, including locking you out of your own wireless router. If it is suspected that such an action has occurred,

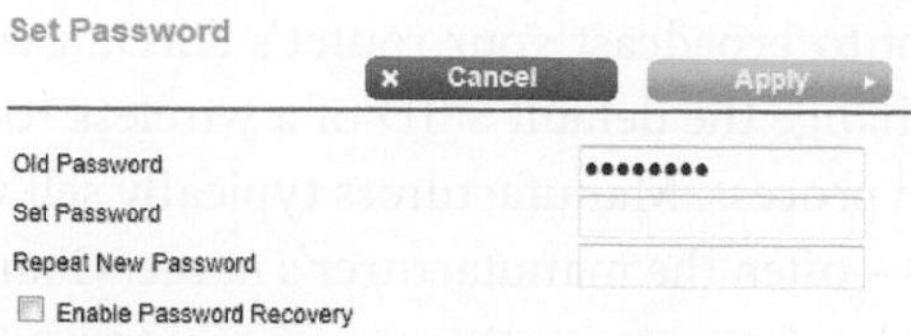

Set Password

| x Cancel | Apply ▶ |

Old Password ●●●●●●●●
Set Password
Repeat New Password
☐ Enable Password Recovery

FIGURE 9.10   Router administrator password.

reset the router by pressing the physical restart button on the back of the router and then immediately change the default admin password.

9.5.2 Service Set Identifier

As previously described, most wireless routers broadcast their SSID so that any Wi-Fi device within the nearby vicinity of the router will be able to detect, and thus connect to, the wireless network. While it makes sense for a public Wi-Fi hot spot, such as one found in a coffee shop or library, to broadcast its SSID to make the router's existence known to its patrons, the same cannot be said for a home wireless network. From a security perspective, you do not want to broadcast your SSID and make your network known to your neighbors or to a war driver cruising by on the street. Remember that a wireless network is not confined by a wall or door, but instead by the maximum transmission distance of the wireless router. When a wireless network is used in a private residence, its users who access the wireless network should already know the SSID, much like one remembers a username. Furthermore, many wireless network managers enable a user to save and automatically connect to previously known wireless networks. Therefore, the only real reason to broadcast an SSID for a home wireless router is for the convenience of not needing to remember the wireless network's name. Once again, security is at odds with convenience. As shown in Figure 9.11, many wireless routers allow the admin to disable the broadcasting of the SSID.

Wireless Network
☑ Enable SSID Broadcast
☐ Enable Wireless Isolation
Name (SSID):   Bob's House
Region: North America ▼
Channel: Auto ▼
Mode: Up to 150 Mbps ▼

FIGURE 9.11   Disable broadcast SSID.

If you choose not to broadcast your router's SSID, a wise choice, it is also important to change the default SSID of a wireless router during the router's initial setup process. Manufacturers typically sell wireless routers with the same SSID—often the manufacturer's name. Changing this SSID will prevent an attacker from attempting to connect to your network, even if the SSID is not being broadcast, by simply guessing well-known default router names. If you do choose to broadcast your router's SSID, consider your privacy when doing so. Do not change your router's name to something personal such as your family's name (i.e., Bob's House) or other information that can be used to identify you or provide an attacker with a hint regarding what your password might be.

9.5.3 Wireless Security Mode

To create a secure wireless network, one must first enable the router's security mode (illustrated in Figure 9.12). Enabling the security mode on a wireless router provides two distinct security benefits. First, it requires that a user wishing to access the wireless network must first authenticate to the router with a password. Authentication prevents unwanted users (i.e., piggybackers) who do not know the password from connecting to your wireless network. To prevent attackers from guessing your password, it is important to exhibit the same password best practices discussed in Chapter 3 when choosing the password that controls access to your wireless router.

The second security benefit of enabling wireless security is that it encrypts wireless traffic that travels between your computer and the wireless router. The use of encryption mitigates the threat of eavesdropping. Just as HTTPS encrypts data between your computer and a corresponding web server, wireless security encrypts data over the wireless connection. Even if an attacker were able to piggyback on your network, the attacker would not be able to readily view your wireless traffic in plaintext.

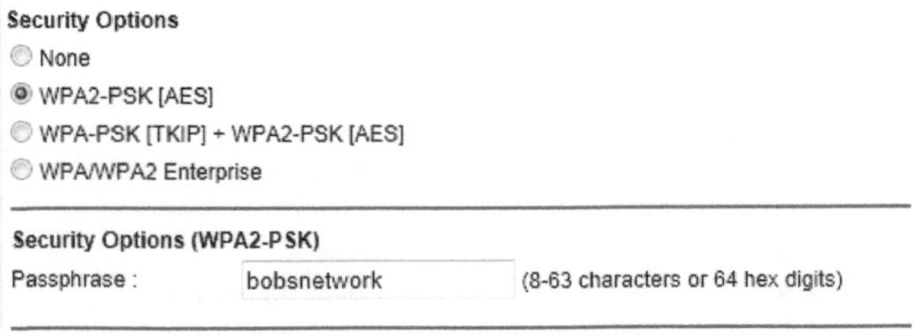

Security Options
○ None
◉ WPA2-PSK [AES]
○ WPA-PSK [TKIP] + WPA2-PSK [AES]
○ WPA/WPA2 Enterprise

Security Options (WPA2-PSK)
Passphrase :   bobsnetwork   (8-63 characters or 64 hex digits)

FIGURE 9.12 Enable wireless security mode.

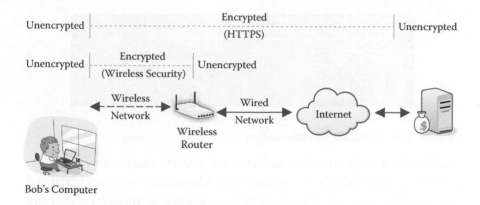

FIGURE 9.13   Wireless encryption versus HTTPS.

Figure 9.13 illustrates the difference between encrypting data when using a secure wireless network and when using an HTTPS connection.

When enabling the wireless security mode on a wireless router, not all security options are created equal. Although it is outside the scope of this chapter to go into much detail with respect to popular security options, here is a simple set of rules to follow:

1. WPA2 (Wi-Fi Protected Access 2) is the newest and most secure option and should be selected if available.

2. WPA (Wi-Fi Protected Access) is older and less effective than WPA2 but certainly better than WEP (Wired Equivalent Privacy). If WPA2 is not available, then WPA should be chosen over WEP.

3. WEP is the least-secure option but still better than no security at all (i.e., disabling the security mode).

In summary, enabling the security mode on a wireless router provides two security benefits that together create a secure wireless network. Authentication prevents unwanted piggybackers from connecting to your wireless network; encrypting the wireless data prevents against eavesdroppers. It should be noted that these two security benefits come hand in hand, meaning that one cannot be enabled without the other.

9.5.4 MAC Address Filtering

In addition to knowing the SSID of a wireless router (i.e., SSID is not broadcast) and knowing a password to access a wireless network, wireless routers

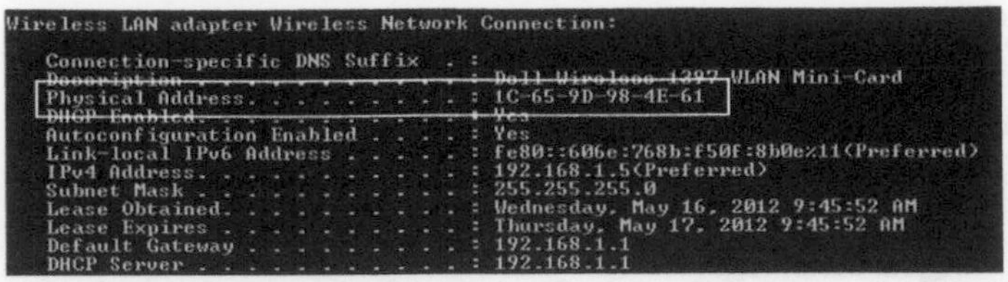

FIGURE 9.14   MAC address screenshot.

enable a third authentication mechanism to prevent against unwanted pig-gybackers: MAC (Media Access Control) address filtering. Every wired and wireless network card in a computer has a unique MAC address that can be used as a unique identifier. In addition to an IP address, a MAC address is used by a computer to communicate with a wireless router. Unlike IP addresses that can change each time a computer connects to a particular network (by means of DHCP, Dynamic Host Configuration Protocol), a MAC address is a more permanent hardware address that accompanies a network card. Similar to finding an IP address of a computer, one can find the MAC addresses of wired and wireless network cards in a Windows computer by opening up a command window (via Start > Run > cmd) and typing "ipconfig/all." Illustrated in Figure 9.14 is the MAC address (six groups of two hexadecimal characters) for a given computer.

A MAC address is a useful identifier for wireless networks because it can be used by a wireless router as an additional form of authentication to either permit or deny access to a particular wireless network. Many wireless routers possess the ability to provide MAC address filtering or, in other words, only allow computers to connect to the given network that have specific MAC addresses that have been identified and configured in the wireless router's controls. Shown in Figure 9.15 is a typical security menu for administering MAC address filtering for a wireless router. This security control denotes that only computers with MAC addresses that are populated on the provided page are allowed to access the wireless

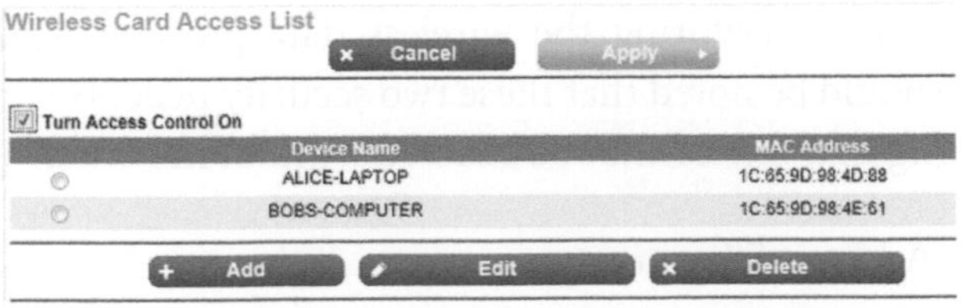

FIGURE 9.15   Wireless router MAC address filtering control.

network. This way, a wireless network administrator can exclude all other computers from connecting to their wireless network, even if the SSID and wireless network password are known or leaked. In the example shown in Figure 9.15, only Alice's laptop and Bob's computer with the MAC addresses of 1C:65:9D:98:4D:88 and 1C:65:9D:98:4E:61, respectively, would be able to connect to the given wireless network. As the administrator of a wireless network, one can add and delete MAC addresses of different computing devices as needed. The use of a MAC address filter provides an added layer of defense to protect unwanted piggybackers or hackers from accessing a home wireless network.

9.5.5 Firewall

Enabling a wireless router's firewall protects a wireless network and the computers connected to it from the dangers and unwanted traffic originating from the Internet (Figure 9.12). As discussed in Chapter 6, even if a computer already has a software firewall enabled, it is still strongly advised to turn on the router's firewall as an added security measure. Doing so protects a computer connected to your wireless network that does not have a firewall. It also provides defense in depth for those computers that are firewall protected.

9.5.6 Power Off Router

When your wireless router is not going to be used for an extended period of time, simply turn the device off. Just like powering off a computer, attackers cannot attempt to access your wireless network if the device is turned off. As an added benefit, this action also saves energy.

9.6 SUMMARY

The conveniences afforded by wireless networks are accompanied by a slew of security threats. By examining how wireless networks work, understanding their common security threats, and learning how these threats are mitigated, both as a user of a public wireless network and as an administrator of a private wireless network, a practical overview of wireless network security has been provided.

- Although the default action of a computer is to ignore all other Internet traffic communicated over a wireless network, a computer can be put into promiscuous mode, enabling a computer to sniff all Internet traffic on a wireless network.

- An SSID is a beacon signal broadcast by a wireless router to announce the presence of a wireless network nearby.

- A secure wireless network requires user authentication in addition to encrypting Internet traffic between the wireless router and connected wireless devices.

- An unsecure wireless network does not require authentication and does not afford the protection of data encryption.

- The predominant threat of using wireless networks is an attacker is able to sniff wireless network traffic passively and observe confidential and private information.

- To trick users into connecting to a phony wireless network, attackers employ both rogue router and evil twin router attacks.

- Piggybacking is the act of connecting to a wireless network without the permission or authorization of the network owner. Piggybackers can be annoying if they consume a significant amount of bandwidth and can be a security concern if they perform criminal acts like downloading illegal content or using the wireless network to attack other computers.

- Public wireless networks, whether secure or not, should be used with the upmost caution. Due to the many threats that wireless networks present, one should refrain from engaging in confidential or private actions while using a public wireless network.

- In addition to sniffing, using a public wireless network carries with it the physical threats of shoulder surfing and theft if one leaves a wireless device unattended.

- As an administrator of a wireless network, it is essential to change the router's default password during the initial setup and enable the wireless router's security mode.

- To provide defense in depth when administering a wireless network, one can disable the router's SSID, require user authentication, and perform MAC filtering.

- Enabling a wireless router's firewall protects all devices connected to the wireless router and is a security best practice.

BIBLIOGRAPHY

Barken, L. 2004. *How Secure Is Your Wireless Network? Safeguarding Your Wi-Fi LAN*. Indianapolis, IN: Prentice Hall Professional.

Challener, D., Yoder, K., Chatherman, R., Safford, D., and Van Doorn, L. 2007. *A Practical Guide to Trusted Computing*. Indianapolis, IN: Pearson Education.

Cisco Networking Academy. 2010. *IT Essentials: PC Hardware and Software Companion Guide*. Indianapolis, IN: Cisco Press.

Danchev, D. 2010. Wardriving police: password protect your wireless, or face a fine. ZDNet. http://www.zdnet.com/blog/security/wardriving-police-password-protect-your-wireless-or-face-a-fine/6438 (accessed May 1, 2012).

Earle, A.E. 2005. *Wireless Security Handbook*. Boca Raton, FL: CRC Press.

Gast, M. 2011. *802.11 Wireless Networks: The Definitive Guide*. Sebastopol, CA: O'Reilly Media.

Gupta, M., and Sharman, R. 2009. *Social and Human Elements of Information Security: Emerging Trends and Countermeasures*. Hershey, PA: Idea Group.

Hadnagy, C. 2010. *Social Engineering: The Art of Human Hacking*. New York: Wiley.

Harrington, J.L. 2005. *Network Security: A Practical Approach*. New York: Academic Press.

Holt, A., and Huang, C.Y. 2010. *802.11 Wireless Networks: Security and Analysis*. New York: Springer.

Hurley, C., Rogers, R., Thorton, F., and Baker, B. 2007. *WarDriving and Wireless Penetration Testing*. Waltham, MA: Syngress.

Jielin, D. 2007. *Network Dictionary*. San Jose, CA: Javvin Technologies.

Kanellis, P. 2006. *Digital Crime and Forensic Science in Cyberspace*. Hershey, PA: Idea Group.

Kirk, J. 2012. In Australia, secure your Wi-Fi—or face a visit from the police. *Network World*. http://www.networkworld.com/news/2012/032312-in-australia-secure-your-wi-fi-257580.html?source=nww_rss (accessed May 1, 2012).

Mueller, S., Soper, M.E., and Sosinsky, B. 2006. *Upgrading and Repairing Servers*. Indianapolis, IN: Pearson Education.

Parsons, J.J., and Oja, D. 2012. *New Perspectives on Computer Concepts 2013: Comprehensive*. Independence, KY: Cengage Learning.

Solomon, M.G., and Kim, D. 2011. *Fundamentals of Communications and Networking*. Sudbury, MA: Jones & Bartlett.

Thompson, C. 2011. False porn accusations underscore Wi-Fi privacy dangers. *Seattle Times*. http://o.seattletimes.nwsource.com/html/nationworld/2014867387_wifi25.html (accessed May 1, 2012).

Vacca, J.R. 2010. *Network and System Security*. Waltham, MA: Syngress.

Vladimirov, A.A., Gavrilenko, K., and Mikhailovsky, A. 2005. *Hacking Exposed Cisco Networks: Cisco Security Secrets and Solutions*. New York: McGraw-Hill Professional Medical/Technical.

Wong, D. 2011. *Fundamentals of Wireless Communication Engineering Technologies*. New York: Wiley.

CHAPTER 10

Social Networking

10.1 INTRODUCTION

Flash forward to 30 years from now and envision a presidential race in which both candidates have actively participated in social networking throughout their entire lives. Imagine that they not only have Facebook accounts, but also have used other services, such as MySpace, Flickr, Tumblr, Pinterest, YouTube, Twitter, LinkedIn, Orkut, blogging, or even other services yet to be invented. The digital footprints amassed by such candidates will undoubtedly be substantial, and if history is a reliable indicator, every wall post, blog entry, picture, and tweet will be examined under the finest microscope—likely needing to be explained, apologized for, or defended.

Just like these future presidential candidates, as a user of social networking you also will accumulate an online digital footprint, and it will inevitably be tied to you as you progress through your life. It is unlikely that you will face the level of scrutiny expected to be faced by a presidential candidate, but you also will be held accountable for your digital persona—and not only the online content you generate but also the content posted about you by others. Today, such long-term consequences of sharing information in the virtual world are difficult to predict since this social phenomenon is still in its infancy. What we do understand today are the short-term security and privacy consequences of social networking and public information sharing. In the context of social networking, this chapter focuses on how malware is distributed on social networking sites, what type of information is shared, with whom this information is shared (i.e., "friends"), and how such information could potentially be used to one's detriment.

10.2 CHOOSE YOUR FRIENDS WISELY

In the physical world, friends are people to whom we are attached by feelings, affection, or personal regard. In the world of social networking, however, the definition and application of the term *friend* is much more vague and loosely applied. For example, an individual who you have just met for the first time at a social gathering might not pass the test of being a friend in the physical world, but increasingly this type of casual connection is more than enough to pass the friendship test in the virtual world. Simply knowing a person's face, name, or possible association to another "friend" is usually enough for many to enter into an online friendship with an individual. At other times, a simple friend request is sufficient, regardless of familiarity with the individual or any previous personal connection. In respect to online security and privacy, the choices made when befriending people in the digital world and the content (i.e., profile information, pictures, status updates, etc.) shared with them should not be taken lightly as such choices can have negative consequences in the real world.

10.2.1 Access Control

To understand the concept of a friend in the context of social networking, Facebook is used as a case study. The designator *friend* on Facebook in many ways represents the amount of information people are willing to share with that individual. Thus, the designation of a friend represents a form of access control to private information, much like a password protects access to an online account.

The structure of Facebook's privacy controls is determined by a user's association with other Facebook users (i.e., friends or "friends of friends") or more broadly to everyone on the Internet. These designations are then used to provide access control to information such as "your status, photos, and posts" or "photos and videos you're tagged in." On Facebook, the most granular level of privacy control is the ability to restrict one's own content to that of one's friends (custom settings and "lists" can further refine the number of friends able to view specific content). While this designation may appear to provide a high degree of privacy, there are a number of factors, including friend gluttony, relative privacy, and nonchalant befriending habits, that can dilute this sense of privacy. Each of these topics is explored in this section.

The next level of access control is to label information viewable to friends of friends. On average, each Facebook user has approximately 245 friends. If each of those friends has 245 friends, then by labeling information as private to friends of friends, you are essentially sharing information with thousands of people. Needless to say, that group contains many people that you may not know. Under this privacy setting, you should consider not only the security and privacy implications of sharing this content with the friends that you have, but also the implications of sharing it with the friends of each of your friends.

The least-private setting is to label information as accessible to "everyone." In this context, everyone means more than just Facebook users—it means literally everyone on the Internet, including search engines and those not logged in to Facebook. To discover what personal information is available about you online via Facebook, try performing a Google search with your own name and the term *Facebook*. What you find may surprise you.

10.2.2 Friend Gluttony

If the average Facebook user has 245 friends, how many of these people are truly friends in the physical sense of the word? Despite appearances, social networking is not a popularity contest, and there are no awards for having the most friends. In reality, stockpiling friends can actually be harmful. Adding more people with whom you choose to share your information increases your chances of having that information used against you (i.e., physical theft, cyber bullying, identity theft, spear phishing, stalking). If you have been nonchalant with your acceptance of friend requests in the past, know that entering into an online friendship with an individual does not bind you to that relationship forever. Clean out your friend list from time to time just as you would remove contacts you no longer call from your cell phone. Doing so will correct possible befriending mistakes of the past and minimize access to your private information. To determine whether to remove a friend, use a friend's birthday notice as a barometer. If you do not wish that person a happy birthday, then simply remove the person from your friend list.

10.2.3 Relative Privacy

When online content is designated as private to friends on a social networking site, what does the term *private* really mean in this context? When taken at face value, the term *private* would lead one to believe that such information is only viewable by users of a particular social networking site with whom one grants a certain status (i.e., friend or friend of friends), and the extent of those who have access to this information ends with these friends. The reality of privacy in the context of social networking, however, is quite different. Digital information is incredibly difficult to keep private. If digital content can be seen or heard, it can be easily copied, reproduced, and redistributed. The same principle holds true for digital content generated in the world of social networking.

For example, imagine that one day after a long stressful week at work you update your Facebook profile with a short rant about your displeasure with your work environment. There is nothing that would prevent a coworker who is also a friend from taking a screen shot of your profile and emailing that information to your boss. It is true that your wall posts are private to your friends—which prevents others from directly viewing your information—but there are no controls in place to stop your friends from sharing this information with whomever they please. In this context, information is only relatively private as friends have unrestricted access to your information.

It is safe to assume that whatever content you disclose on a social networking site has the potential to be viewed by all, whether they are a friend or a friend of a friend or not involved in social networking at all. Furthermore, you must be willing to be held accountable for that content now and in the future. A Georgia high school teacher learned this lesson the hard way after an anonymous person (claiming to be one of her student's parents) emailed her school district Facebook pictures of her holding alcoholic drinks while on a European vacation. As a result of the email, the Georgia teacher ultimately resigned over the pictures that were taken 2 years prior to when they became the center of controversy. Given the ease at which photos can be viewed on social networking platforms, even if they are marked private, one can imagine that this is not an isolated incident. Although the Georgia teacher claims that the photos were marked as private and that she was not "Facebook friends" with her students or their parents, the mystery remains on how a supposed parent got a hold of the pictures. Perhaps one of her friends, such as a coworker, was not a friend after all. Just as a song can be ripped from a CD and sent to a friend as an email attachment or shared on a peer-to-peer network, so can the pictures and content that you post online be copied, saved, and redistributed to whomever a friend desires.

10.2.4 Why Do You Want to Be My Friend?

It is a fallacy to believe that just because someone went through the trouble of attempting to befriend you on a social networking site that not

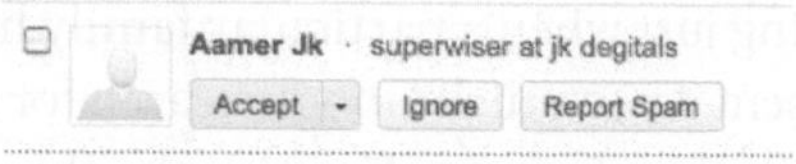

FIGURE 10.1   Suspicious friend request.

befriending them would be rude. The Internet is full of bad people with ill-intentioned motives for befriending people online, including spam, malware distribution, identity theft, stalking, cyber bullying, and phishing. Figure 10.1 illustrates an example of a befriending attempt from a potential cyber bad guy—note the obvious misspelling. Accepting a stranger's friend request might seem harmless at first, but it may be difficult to determine his or her true intentions. Befriending strangers can be a poor and lasting decision since many people tend to retain online friends over time.

As social networking increases in popularity, more and more cases of friend-related incidents are emerging. For example, a Florida man was arrested for cyber stalking and sexually harassing female sorority pledges of five universities by posing under a false name on Facebook as a sorority alumnus. Under the pretext that pledges would not be accepted into their respective sororities if they did not comply, the man under the names of "Marissa" and "Lexie" made several inappropriate and illegal demands. When you are faced with the decision of adding a friend on a social networking site, consider the privacy implications of the personal information and photos you are about to share with that individual now and in the future. If you do not immediately recognize the person, have a direct association to the person, or feel comfortable sharing personal and private content with the person, simply do not accept their friend request.

10.3 INFORMATION SHARING

For honest, respectful, and law-abiding people, it might be difficult to understand how information sharing on social networking sites can be unsafe. Cyber criminals, however, have made their living exploiting the casual manner in which people disclose information. This section explores the types of information that are shared on social networking sites and how such information can be detrimental to both one's security and one's privacy.

10.3.1 Location, Location, Location

Publicly provided information has been used against unsuspecting victims since long before the advent of social networking. For decades, newspaper obituaries and wedding announcements have supplied burglars with information indicating just when a particular family household is likely to be empty. In the present day, a quick Google search for an address can even provide a burglar with turn-by-turn directions to the next vacant target.

Social networking sites allow their users to share their current location information via a multitude of methods, including status updates, tweets, check-ins, and photos accompanied with geolocation (i.e., GPS) information. Although it is potentially fun, convenient, or trendy to let your friends on a social networking site know that you are on vacation or that you have just "checked in" to a local restaurant, what these services also do is provide a real-time alert to everyone who has access to your social networking page about where you are not—namely, your house or apartment. One website, PleaseRobMe.com, went as far as to compile location-sharing data from multiple social networks to provide real-time lists of empty homes. The website creators sought to bring awareness to the dangers of posting publicly available location information. As one can imagine, even without the help of PleaseRobMe.com, burglars have already taken notice and have used such information to their advantage. The following are news headlines regarding robberies attributed to social networking and publicly posted information:

- "Burglars Said to Have Picked Houses Based on Facebook Updates"

- "Facebook 'Friend' Suspected in Burglary—Couple Believes Childhood Friend Stole $10,000 Worth of Valuables When Couple Said Online They Would Be Out of Town"

- "How Facebook Can Ruin Your Vacation—A Florida Couple Vacationing in New York Returned Home to Find Their Home Ransacked and $30,000 of Jewelry and Electronics Missing"

- "Man Robbed after Posting His Vacation on Twitter"

- "Thieves Plunder Apartment for Facebook Booty"

In addition to supplying the information that you are not home, and potentially even the exact GPS coordinates of your residence, social networking sites with photo-sharing capabilities can also provide a would-be burglar with the layout of the inside of your residence, including the inventory and location of your most expensive possessions. With all of this information in one location, all a burglar needs to do to case a house is log in to their Facebook account. This is yet another reason why privacy settings, what you share, and the control of access to your online profile is so important. By posting your real-time location online, you are potentially telling someone you barely know (among your group of friends) that you are not home—information that few people would share with a stranger in the real world.

10.3.2 What Should I Not Share?

When interacting with social networking sites, and even in a more general context, it is beneficial to your security and privacy to reveal as little information about your identity as possible. To answer the question, "What information should not be made public?," think of the information that you use to authenticate yourself when filling out a government form, credit card application, or tax return or when purchasing an item over the phone: your full name, home address, phone number, date of birth, place of birth, Social Security number (or last four digits), driver's license number, credit card, CCV (card code verification) number, and so on. Different combinations of these pieces of information can uniquely identify you in certain contexts and thus should not be shared on social networking sites. Some social networking users even go so far as to use a semipseudonym to mask their full name and allow their social network (i.e., association to friends) to establish their true identity. Just as an attacker can assume your identity in the digital world by learning your username and password, an attacker can assume your identity in the real world by learning your private information (i.e., identity theft).

For an attacker to be successful in stealing your identity, it is not necessary for the attacker to discover your identity information in a single place (i.e., Facebook profile). If an attacker comes by your Social Security number on an underground auction site or gains your credit card number by way of a data breach, then revealing your full name, address, and date of birth on a social networking site is enough for an attacker to patch together enough details to steal your identity. Do you ever wonder how some spammers, phishers, and telemarketers come across personal contact information? In some cases, people give it to them directly.

In addition to not sharing identity information, it is advantageous not to reveal information on a social networking site that can be used to guess one's passwords or security questions. Hackers use software programs— called password profilers—that are able to read and parse the text from a Facebook profile and, based on known password semantics, construct a list of likely passwords to guess. Similarly, when you choose the answer to a security question such as, "What is the name of your pet?" do not provide the name of the pet that appears in numerous pictures on your social networking profile.

10.3.3 Opt In versus Opt Out

A discussion of privacy controls for any specific social networking platform will likely be outdated before this book even goes to print. To learn about the most current social networking security and privacy best practices, please see the suggested reading list in Appendix A (Reading List). Instead of addressing specific measures, the following discussion focuses on the terms *opt in* and *opt out* as they apply to privacy settings.

It is quite possible that a social networking site's default privacy settings do not align with your personal privacy interests. In the study of computer security, there is a well-established principle that holds that the default state of a computer system should be the most secure state (e.g., a firewall should be enabled by default). If this principle were translated into the realm of social networking, it would assert that the default state of privacy controls should be their most restrictive setting. In this case, a user would need to consciously opt out of the most private setting instead of having to opt in to the most private setting, as is typically the case with social networking sites today. It is in the best financial interest and philosophic belief of social networking sites for their users to share as much content as possible. As a result, by simply creating a social networking account, you may be sharing more information simply by default than you are comfortable in sharing.

Social networking sites are constantly evolving. Because of this, the term *privacy fatigue* has been coined to describe the confusion and declining attention paid by users to frequent changes to privacy controls. Regardless of the actions taken by social networking sites, by voluntarily using such services (read the terms of service agreement), the responsibility of monitoring and understanding privacy settings ultimately falls squarely on your, the user's, shoulders. To aid in user understanding of privacy controls, many social networking sites provide thorough and informative privacy guides. Just as you would regularly monitor your credit card activity, it is good security and privacy practice to review your privacy settings regularly and to make sure that you fully understand what information and with whom you are sharing. Realize that privacy settings are not static, and to preserve your own comfort level of privacy, new controls or changes to existing privacy controls may require you to opt out of the default settings. For example, when Facebook released a facial recognition feature that automatically suggests the tagging of friends in pictures, this service was enabled by default. Therefore, if a Facebook user was not comfortable with the service or felt it violated his or her privacy, the user was required to opt out of this feature.

10.3.4 Job Market

Internet search engines and social networking sites are together becoming the de facto clearinghouse for the assessment of one's digital persona—the evaluation of the content you post and that others post in relation to you. In a fraction of a second, a search of a name can unearth details of a person's life that a decade ago would have taken a private investigator weeks or months to uncover. Although the Internet and social networking can be used in this way for a number of purposes (i.e., date screening, neighbor evaluation, etc.), understanding how a digital persona affects the job hiring process provides a relevant case study to help better understand the implications that sharing information online can have on one's personal and professional life.

In 2010, Microsoft commissioned Cross-Tab—an online market research firm—to perform a survey regarding the ways in which viewing a digital persona has an effect on the decisions made by hiring professionals and, conversely, how consumers perceive the use of their digital persona in the hiring process. The results of the survey were eye opening. Of the U.S. companies surveyed, 75% stated that hiring professionals are required by corporate policy to conduct online research about candidates. For the same companies surveyed, 70% claimed that they had rejected candidates based on information that they discovered online, while only 7% of consumers interviewed believed that their digital persona affected their chances of being hired. For the consumers surveyed, these findings represent a significant gap between perception and reality. The following types of information most heavily influenced candidate rejections:

- Concerns about the candidate's lifestyle

- Inappropriate comments and text written by the candidate

- Unsuitable photos, videos, and information

- Inappropriate comments or text written by friends and relatives

- Comments criticizing previous employers, coworkers, or clients

- Inappropriate comments or text written by colleagues or work acquaintances

- Membership in certain groups or networks

The old adage of "show me who your friends are, and I'll tell you who you are" applies in the virtual world as well. As a job candidate, not only are you responsible for the content that you generate, but also you are liable for the content generated by your online friends. This is yet another reason to choose your friends wisely.

It is likely that either now or in the future your digital persona will be evaluated alongside your resume when you are being considered for a job. This begs the question: "Should I delete my social networking accounts?" Of the U.S. companies surveyed, 85% said that a positive reputation influenced hiring decisions, and 50% said that it had a strong influence. If done tastefully and managed proactively, social networking and the digital persona it portrays can be beneficial to a job candidate. However, if maintaining such a persona is not a task that one is willing (or able) to perform routinely, it can also lead to rejection.

Whether you have just landed a new job or have been with the same company for over 30 years, do not become careless with the management of your digital persona. There are numerous accounts of people being fired from their jobs for content that they posted online. This happens so often that such an occurrence has been termed *Facebook fired*. The moral of the story is always to manage your digital persona as if you are on the job market—otherwise, the lack of doing so may unwillingly put you there.

Apart from discovering information about one's social networking life by means of the public Internet, employers have taken the use of candidate screening and social networking to a whole new level. Some employers have actually requested that job candidates disclose their username and password during an interview so that interviewers can log in to the candidate's Facebook account and browse through posts, pictures, friends, and other types of private information. In addition to the legal concerns and the clear violation of Facebook's terms-of-service agreement, this type of password solicitation presents troubling security and privacy concerns that one must consider before revealing a password to an interviewer. First, it is never a good security practice to disclose a password to anyone, let alone a stranger. If you do decide to disclose your password, change your password immediately after the interview. This is yet another reason why it is vital not to use the same username and password across multiple accounts. Second, in respect to privacy, remember that you have the option to say "no thank you." Although it may unfortunately cost you a job, perhaps working for an employer with such invasive privacy practices was not the right fit anyway. Furthermore, when one sequesters access to their Facebook account, they are potentially violating not only their own privacy, but also the privacy and trust of their friends. In addition to requesting passwords, corporations are requiring that job candidates befriend a human resource (HR) employee, thus giving the HR employee access to content intended to be private. Given these trends in interview practices, one should be prepared to respond to such requests and understand the full impact of their decision before an interview begins.

10.4 MALWARE AND PHISHING

As social networking has increased in popularity, it has garnered much attention from scammers, phishers, and malware distributors. This is due to the very principles that have made social networking so popular: People want to be social online. In this context, *social* means generating content and interacting with content generated by others by clicking on almost anything and everything. Unfortunately, not all content on social networking sites is what it appears to be, and errant clicks can result in malware infections and identity theft. This section discusses the methods that cyber criminals use to exploit the common uses of social networking and why these methods have been successful.

10.4.1 Koobface

First appearing in 2008, the Koobface worm (anagram for Facebook) has become the most notorious malware spread via social networking to date. Koobface targets users on Facebook, Myspace, and Twitter, among other services, and it infects both Macs and PCs. Although the threat of Koobface has subsided as of late—a trend that could be reversed at any time—it provides an apt case study as it epitomizes how malware can spread via social networking sites.

To a potential victim, the threat of the Koobface worm first appears as a message, tweet, or wall post from a friend (someone who the victim already knows), similar to what is shown in Figure 10.2. Malicious messages of this nature are effective because they use social engineering tactics to directly target the human vulnerability of curiosity by purposefully crafting enticing messages related to recent events or scandalous pictures.

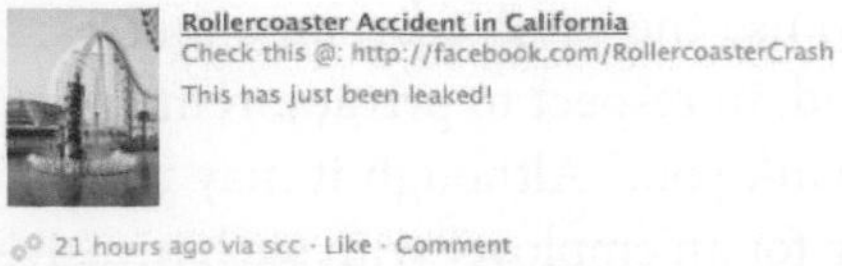

Rollercoaster Accident in California
Check this @: http://facebook.com/RollercoasterCrash
This has just been leaked!

⚙ 21 hours ago via scc · Like · Comment

FIGURE 10.2   Malware message with hyperlink.

They also target the implicit trust that social networking users place in the content generated by their friends. Just as is the case with malicious emails (e.g., the Love Bug worm), just because a friend posts content online, it does not mean that the content is free of danger even if that person is your parent, boss, or tech-savvy little brother.

When curiosity triumphs over good judgment, a victim clicking on a hyperlink with the hopes of viewing a video about a "Rollercoaster Accident in California" is often redirected to a third-party website (outside the social networking platform). The victim's computer is then either subjected to a drive-by download or the malicious website presents the victim with a pop-up message requiring the download of an update for Adobe Flash Player (or similar program) to view the video. In the latter scenario, such an update is a complete scam and is actually a Trojan horse that installs the Koobface malware. By either of these two methods, if the Koobface worm is downloaded and installed on the victim's computer, the social networking friends of the victim become the next targets of the malware, and the cycle continues.

The Koobface worm resides on the victim's computer (not within a social networking platform) and utilizes the victim's social networking accounts to propagate. To do this, the Koobface malware downloads a number of software components onto the victim's computer, including a key-logger that steals the victim's social networking usernames and passwords. Using the victim's social networking accounts, the Koobface worm then takes the action of posting similar messages on the walls of each of the victim's friends. In addition to propagating and gaining access to a victim's computer, Koobface has also been known to install other forms of malicious software, including fake antivirus programs and malicious adware.

Malware propagation on social networking sites relies heavily on the intense desire of people to know or see eye-catching webpages, pictures, or videos and their misplaced trust in the content that their friends generate and share. The next time that you see a wall post claiming to be a video of a "WHALE Smashing Into A Building!" (Figure 10.3), you can

FIGURE 10.3   Malware message with hyperlink.

FIGURE 10.4   Malware message with hyperlink.

be quite confident that such a video is likely a ruse to install malware on your computer. Moreover, just because your best friend from high school posts a message on your wall enticing you to win a free iPad (Figure 10.4), it does not mean that such claims can be trusted. It is highly likely that your friend has fallen victim to malware such as Koobface that uses social networking sites to propagate.

10.4.2 Applications

Social networking has expanded beyond simply social networking services and now includes third-party applications and plug-ins that interact directly with a social networking platform. Because of the enormous popularity of social networking applications like FarmVille and Mafia Wars, malware distributors have created similarly appealing fronts for gadgets or games that are nothing more than applications to trick you into installing malware on your computer. Common scams for malicious Facebook applications include the "Dislike" button and "who's stalking my profile"—an application claiming to allow you to see who has viewed your photos. Twitter has its equal share of rogue applications that claim to show a user who has "unfollowed" them or "TimeSpentHere"—an application that supposedly reports the collective hours that one has spent on Twitter. When a malicious application is installed, it is able to gain access to your profile information and friend list—a privilege also shared with legitimate applications. Malicious applications then use this information to spread the scam to your friends' walls or inboxes and can potentially make you vulnerable to spear phishing attacks and identity theft. Just as it is important to be skeptical about the software programs you download from a webpage, be equally vigilant about the applications you download through a social networking site.

10.4.3 Hyperlinks

If a hyperlink can be a phishing- or malware-laden mine, then social networking sites are some of the most dense and dangerous minefields on the Internet. Malicious hyperlinks are found not only on sites like Facebook and Twitter but also as posted comments on other social networking sites like YouTube and Flickr. As discussed in Chapter 5, hyperlinks are a threat because of the potential for drive-by downloads and phishing sites. Without a careful eye, these hyperlinks can be difficult to read and decipher (Chapter 11). Services that shorten URLs (Uniform Resource Locators) that condense standard URLs into a more compact form can further complicate the task of determining the legitimacy of a web address (Figure 10.5).

Made popular on the microblogging site Twitter, which limits tweets to 140 characters, URL-shortening services enable the efficient sharing of linked web content. Unfortunately, cyber criminals have also found URL-shortening services handy for the task of masking the URL of the webpage that they want their victims to visit (Figure 10.6). When one first views a shortened URL, all of the lessons learned in Chapter 11 are

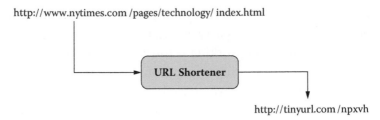

FIGURE 10.5 URL shortening.

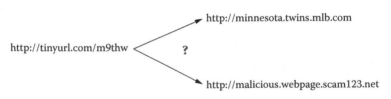

FIGURE 10.6 Shortened URL obfuscation.

rendered useless. There are no indications regarding whether the shortened URL will redirect you to a news website or a malware-infested website (Figure 10.6).

To avoid the obfuscation of URL shorteners, one can utilize a number of web browser plug-ins and preview services that enable the user to first view the shortened URL in its full form before clicking on it. Such services will allow you to apply the lessons learned in Chapter 11. If you are not able to expand a shortened URL to confirm its true origin, then be aware that clicking on such a hyperlink is a roll of the dice that could end in a malware infection, a phishing webpage, or both.

10.4.4 Phishing

Phishing attacks are not limited to personal or business email and represent a very real threat on social networking sites. Spear-phishing attacks are particularly potent on social networks due to the disclosure of personal information, associations to entities, and relationships to friends— all information that can be used to craft a compelling spear-phishing message. Like email-based phishing attacks, social networking phishing threats also appear as messages in your inbox. However, phishing attacks can present themselves in other forms as well. Figure 10.7 provides an example of a potential phishing scam. On clicking on the link to claim a "Free Southwest Ticket…Only 19 left!" the victim is taken to a webpage and asked to provide personal information to claim the "free" prize, leading to the theft of identity information. Such scams also prompt victims to establish a password-protected account with the fake website because scammers know that victims tend to use the same username and password at many different sites.

Social networking sites are rife with similar phishing schemes, all of which end in the same way. It should be further noted that financial institutions will never solicit personal or confidential information via social networking sites.

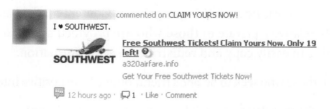

FIGURE 10.7 Social networking scam.

10.5 SUMMARY

When generating content on a social networking site, it is safest to assume that any text, pictures, or video that you post will exist online forever. Removing such information from the Internet or a social networking site is much like removing a tattoo. It takes a lot of time, money, and pain, and it may not be possible to remove all remnants of past decisions made. Online sites will remove information if it is incorrect or slanderous, but not because it is embarrassing or detrimental to your career.

A handful of social networking sites have together accumulated billions of users. As of May 2012, Facebook alone had over 901 million users and continues to grow. If you were in the business of malware distribution or phishing, you would also spend your time targeting social networking users. Social networking has countless upsides, but like most things in life, with the good comes the bad. Defeating the perils of social networking is chiefly done through user education and the defense-in-depth techniques discussed in Chapter 6.

- Those who have actively engaged in social networking will inevitably amass a digital footprint of online content associated to their name.

- The word *friend* has taken on new meaning with the advent of social networking.

- Designating an individual as a friend is a form of access control that often enables that person to view information considered personal and private.

- Engaging in online friendships and associations with people who would not be considered friends in the real world can have negative consequences.

- Just as there is no such thing as absolute security on social networking sites, there is no such thing as privacy. Content marked as private is only relatively private to those who are provided access, and such friends can easily copy and redistribute such information.

- Not all those who seek to be one's friend online have positive intentions.

- The inviting nature of social networking makes it easy for one to overshare personal and confidential information.

- When one's location is shared online, it provides evidence that one is not at home, and sharing such information can have unexpected consequences.

- Only minimal personal information should be shared online. When engaging in social networking, people often omit their birth year and operate under a semipseudonym (first and middle name).

- The default privacy settings of a social networking site do not likely align with the practices of more private users. As a result, this may cause people to have to opt out of the default settings and select more private controls and restrictions on personal data.

- Reviewing social networking sites has become a common practice for employers considering job candidates. The information that is posted on one's social networking site, whether by the owner or the owner's acquaintances, can have both positive and negative effects on one's chance of getting a job.

- Employers have even gone as far as asking job applicants for their Facebook account username and password during an interview or asking the job applicant to befriend an HR representative.

- Malware distribution and phishing attacks are potent threats on social networking sites due to people's curiosity, willingness to interact with links and content, and the unfounded trust that they place in content posted by friends.

- Like applications that run on an operating system (Chapter 2), social networking platforms also enable the use and execution of applications. Just like downloading a Trojan horse from the Internet, similar malware threats exist for social networking applications and plug-ins.

REFERENCES

Baltazar, J., Costoya, J., and Flores, R. 2009. The real face of KOOBFACE: the largest web 2.0 botnet explained. Trend Micro. http://www.trendmicro.com/cloud-content/us/pdfs/security-intelligence/white-papers/wp_the-real-face-of-koobface.pdf (accessed May 3, 2012).

Bilton, N. 2010. Burglars said to have picked houses based on Facebook updates. *New York Times*. http://bits.blogs.nytimes.com/2010/09/12/burglars-picked-houses-based-on-facebook-updates/ (accessed May 2, 2012).

Bishop, M. 2003. *Computer Security: Art and Science*. Boston: Addison-Wesley Professional.

Borzo, J. 2011. Employers tread a minefield. *Wall Street Journal*. http://online. wsj.com/article/SB10001424052748703954004576089850685724570.html (accessed May 2, 2012).

Boutin, P. 2011. Facebook's new friend-sorting features. *New York Times*. http:// gadgetwise.blogs.nytimes.com/2011/09/14/facebooks-new-friend-sorting-features/ (accessed May 2, 2012).

Calongne, K. 2010. LSU PD solves high-profile cyber-stalking case. LSU Media Center. http://www.lsu.edu/ur/ocur/lsunews/MediaCenter/News/2010/12/item23064.html (accessed May 2, 2012).

CBSNews. 2010. Facebook "friend" suspected in burglary. CBSNews. http://www. cbsnews.com/2100-500202_162-6331796.html (accessed May 2, 2012).

Cluley, G. 2012. Facebook profile viewer rogue application spreads on social network. Sophos. http://nakedsecurity.sophos.com/2012/03/27/facebook-profile-viewer-rogue-application/ (accessed May 3, 2012).

Colon, A.D. 2012. *Social Media Marketing Risk Management for Safety and Profit: How to Make More Money, Cut Costs and Mitigate Your Social Media Marketing Risks Now Before It's Too Late!* Charleston, SC: Createspace Independent Publishing Platform.

Coursey, D. 2009. Facebook privacy changes go live; beware of "everyone". PC World. http://www.pcworld.com/businesscenter/article/184090/facebook_privacy_changes_go_live_beware_of_everyone.html (accessed May 2, 2012).

Cross-Tab. 2010. Online reputation in a connected world. Cross-Tab. http:// go.microsoft.com/?linkid=9709510 (accessed May 3, 2012).

Downey, M. 2009. Get schooled Barrow teacher done in by anonymous "parent" e-mail about her Facebook page. *Atlanta Journal-Constitution*. http://blogs. ajc.com/get-schooled-blog/2009/11/13/barrow-teacher-done-in-by-anony-mous-e-mail-with-perfect-punctuation/ (accessed May 2, 2012).

Facebook. 2012. Data use policy. http://www.facebook.com/about/privacy/ (accessed May 3, 2012).

Facebook. 2012. Key facts. http://newsroom.fb.com/content/default.aspx?News AreaId=22 (accessed May 2, 2012).

Hacker, P. 2012. What to do if your Twitter account is hacked. Chronicle of Higher Education. http://chronicle.com/blogs/profhacker/what-to-do-if-your-twitter-account-is-hacked/38414 (accessed May 3, 2012).

Hadnagy, C. 2010. *Social Engineering: The Art of Human Hacking*. New York: Wiley.

Haines, L. 2011. Thieves plunder apartment for Facebook booty. The Register. http:// www.theregister.co.uk/2011/12/07/facebook_booty/ (accessed May 3, 2012).

Hough, A. 2010. Please Rob Me website causes fury for "telling burglars when Twitter users are not home." *The Telegraph*. http://www.telegraph.co.uk/technology/twitter/7266120/Please-Rob-Me-website-tells-burglars-when-Twitter-users-are-not-home.html (accessed May 2, 2012).

Ibata, D. 2011. Ruling goes against Barrow teacher who lost job over Facebook posting. *Atlanta Journal-Constitution*. http://www.ajc.com/news/ruling-goes-against-barrow-1198216.html (accessed May 2, 2012).

Ionescu, D. 2010. Geolocation 101: how it works, the apps, and your privacy. *PCWorld*. http://www.pcworld.com/article/192803/geolocation_101_how_it_works_the_apps_and_your_privacy.html (accessed May 2, 2012).

Keizer, G. 2010. Koobface worm targets Mac users on Facebook, Twitter. *Computer World*. http://www.computerworld.com/s/article/9193720/Koobface_worm_targets_Mac_users_on_Facebook_Twitter (accessed May 3, 2012).

McCarthy, C. 2010. The dark side of geo: PleaseRobMe.com. CNET. http://news.cnet.com/8301-13577_3-10454981-36.html (accessed May 2, 2012).

Mello, J.P. 2010. Gang uses Facebook to rob houses. *PCWorld*. http://www.pcworld.com/article/205295/gang_uses_facebook_to_rob_houses.html (accessed May 2, 2012).

Millian, M. 2011. Facebook lets users opt out of facial recognition. CNN. http://articles.cnn.com/2011-06-07/tech/facebook.facial.recognition_1_facebook-ceo-mark-zuckerberg-facial-recognition-face-recognition?_s=PM:TECH (accessed May 3, 2012).

Mills, E. 2011. Beware the bogus "TimeSpentHere" Twitter App. CNet. http://news.cnet.com/8301-27080_3-20067919-245.html (accessed May 3, 2012).

Mulholland, A. 2011. How Facebook can ruin your vacation. AOL. http://news.travel.aol.com/2011/01/07/how-facebook-can-ruin-your-vacation/ (accessed May 3, 2012).

Press Association. 2011. Facebook users experience privacy fatigue. Huffington Post. http://www.huffingtonpost.co.uk/2011/11/03/facebook-users-privacy-fatigue_n_1073131.html (accessed May 3, 2012).

Salomon, D. 2010. *Elements of Computer Security*. New York: Springer.

Schroeder, S. 2010. Beware of fake dislike button on Facebook. *USA Today*. http://www.usatoday.com/tech/news/2010-08-16-facebook-dislike-fake_N.htm (accessed May 3, 2012).

Springer, J. 2010. Today "instrumental" in Facebook predator arrest. MSNBC. http://today.msnbc.msn.com/id/40603486/ns/today-today_tech/t/today-instrumental-facebook-predator-arrest/#.T6GN578sFi4 (accessed May 2, 2012).

Sullivan, B. 2012. Govt. agencies, colleges demand applicants' Facebook passwords. MSNBC. http://redtape.msnbc.msn.com/_news/2012/03/06/10585353-govt-agencies-colleges-demand-applicants-facebook-passwords?lite (accessed May 3, 2012).

Tsukayama, H. 2012. Your Facebook friends have more friends than you. *Washington Post*. http://www.washingtonpost.com/business/technology/your-facebook-friends-have-more-friends-than-you/2012/02/03/gIQAuNUlmQ_story.html (accessed May 2, 2012).

Valdes, M., and McFarland, S. 2012. Employers ask job seekers for Facebook passwords. *Seattle Times*. http://seattletimes.nwsource.com/html/nationworld/2017794577_apusjobapplicantsfacebook.html (accessed May 3, 2012).

Whitney, L. 2012. Facebook: don't reveal your password to snooping employers. CNET. http://news.cnet.com/8301-1009_3-57403259-83/facebook-dont-reveal-your-password-to-snooping-employers/ (accessed May 3, 2012).

WPXI. 2009. Man robbed after posting his vacation on Twitter. WPXI. http://
www.wpxi.com/news/news/man-robbed-after-posting-his-vacation-on-
twitter/nGgbC/ (accessed May 3, 2012).

CHAPTER 11

Social Engineering: Phishing for Suckers

11.1 INTRODUCTION

Just as malware exploits software vulnerabilities, social engineers exploit human vulnerabilities to accomplish their goals. Social engineering is the art of manipulating people to reveal information or perform actions that are not in their best interest. In many ways, it is much easier for a social engineer to trick you into giving him or her your credit card number or password or to install malware on your computer than it is for an attacker to accomplish the same goal through other more technical means. This is why many current malware propagation methods include some sort of social engineering trickery (e.g., Love Bug worm, fake antivirus) to accomplish their goals.

Social engineers are essentially con artists who use confidence tricks, among many other cunning techniques, to carry out their attacks. As discussed in Chapter 5, instead of hacking into a corporation from the Internet, one group of would-be attackers scattered malware-infested USB (Universal Serial Bus) flash drives in the target corporation's parking lot. By exploiting the human vulnerabilities of curiosity and goodwill, the attackers were able to get unsuspecting employees to pick up the USB flash drives on their way into work and unknowingly install malware on their computers.

Social engineering is a broad term that encompasses many types of scams—in both the virtual and the real worlds—including the more commonly known term *phishing*. While the predominant focus of this chapter is on identifying and avoiding common phishing scams, this chapter also examines how social engineering techniques are used to distribute malware—two scenarios that often end in identity theft. When applying the defense-in-depth strategy to the mitigation of social engineering tactics, user education is often key and sometimes the only defense. The goal of this chapter is to provide basic awareness of common social engineering tactics to enable you to identify social engineering attacks and to demonstrate how to read and analyze URLs (Uniform Resource Locators).

11.2 SOCIAL ENGINEERING: MALWARE DISTRIBUTION

With an ever-increasing focus on computer security and the ubiquitous use of firewalls, malware distributors can no longer rely on the uncontested exploitation of computers via the Internet. In many cases, hackers now must fool their victims into performing an action, like opening an email attachment or clicking on a hyperlink, to bypass a firewall. To do this, malware distributors use a number of social engineering techniques and introduce these attacks into common activities (i.e., opening emails, browsing the web, social networking) that people already perform on a daily basis. This section explores ways in which malware is distributed under the disguise of social engineering—enabling you to recognize and prevent such attacks before you become a victim.

11.2.1 Instant Messages

Like email, instant message programs such as AOL instant messenger, Skype, and Facebook Chat all provide the means for an attacker to send a malicious message with the goal of installing malware on your computer. Coupled with a hyperlink, such malicious messages will appear on your computer promising, for example, to show you an embarrassing picture of a popular celebrity. If you click on the hyperlink, it is likely that your computer will be subjected to a drive-by download of malware or another similar attack. Instead of appealing to the human vulnerability of curiosity, malware distributors will alternatively use instant messaging programs to attack the human vulnerabilities of urgency and insecurity, as seen in Figure 11.1.

Claiming to be from "Update Support," the malicious message in Figure 11.1 provides a prime example of how social engineering techniques are used to fool a victim into performing an action that is not in his or her best interest. This malicious message uses numerous—perhaps suspiciously

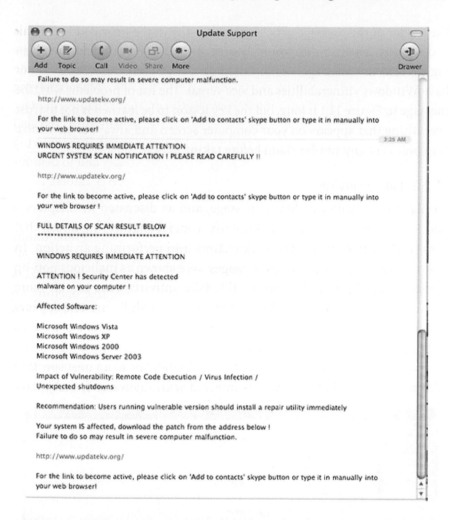

FIGURE 11.1 Malicious Skype message.

so—attempts to convince the victim that clicking on the provided hyperlink is a positive thing to do. Knowing that it is good security hygiene to keep one's computer free of malware and for your system to be properly patched, this social engineering attempt claims that "Security Center has detected malware on your computer!" and, "Your system IS affected, download the patch from the address below!" Despite the numerous action words and perceived threats issued by this chat message, both the wording and the context of the message should raise red flags. First, neither Microsoft nor any other software vendor for that matter will ever send you an update via an instant messaging program. Second, the wording, grammar, and punctuation used in the message are poor, a dead giveaway that the sender of the message is not legitimate. Third, the provided hyperlink is obviously not from Microsoft. Fourth, although it is difficult to tell in Figure 11.1, this message was captured on a Mac computer (Macs do not have Windows vulnerabilities and vice versa). The list of problems with the message in Figure 11.1 is long, but the key lesson to be learned is not to trust everything that appears on your computer screen and always to scrutinize the context of any similar claim before taking action.

11.2.2 Fake Antivirus

Similar to the malicious Skype message, and as discussed in Chapters 5 and 8, fake antivirus pop-ups exemplify a social engineering attack that uses scare tactics intended to trick victims into performing an action. In past discussions, fake antivirus messages were shown as malicious pop-up messages. In Figure 11.2, however, this fake antivirus ruse is a bit more sophisticated than a pop-up. Notice that even though Figure 11.2 appears to show a common view of Windows Explorer, it is in fact a malicious webpage displayed in a web browser.

The display is full of visual cues that would indicate to an unsuspecting victim that his or her computer is infected with malware. The objective

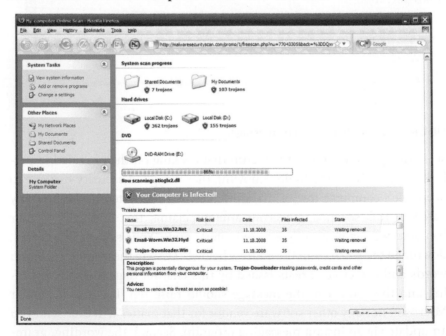

FIGURE 11.2   Fake antivirus webpage.

of this ploy is to convince the victim into believing that there is malware installed on his or her computer, and that the fake antivirus will be able to remove the newly detected malware by downloading a specific program or the victim paying for a malware removal service. Note that a legitimate antivirus software company will never prompt you to install software on your computer as the result of simply viewing a webpage. The only antivirus scans that should occur on your computer should originate from the legitimate antivirus software that you have installed, and on-demand scans should appear only at times when you have scheduled an antivirus scan to occur. Anything else should be considered highly suspect and probably malicious.

11.2.3 Emails

For years, emails have been on top of the list of methods that attackers have used to distribute malware. Emails are quick and effective and can be sent in incredible volume to many potential victims. Furthermore, attackers need not send malicious emails from their own accounts, but often do so from accounts of people they have victimized. For an attacker to be successful, it is not critical that all the victims fall for the trap—only a small percentage.

As was discussed with the Love Bug worm in Chapter 5, email attachments coupled with a touch of social engineering have been a highly potent combination for malware distribution. Although the email attachment for "patch-8559.zip" is not nearly as compelling to open as is a love letter attachment, the attachment in Figure 11.3 provides a more recent example

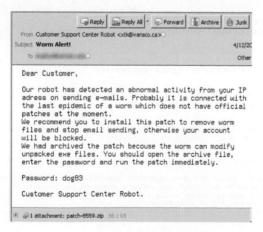

FIGURE 11.3   Malware distribution via email attachment.

of social engineering. In this case, the attacker hopes that the victim will believe that his or her computer is acting abnormally, and such behavior requires a patch, thus taking the bait and opening the ZIP file. This action would likely result in malicious code embedded in the ZIP document attempting to install a malicious program on the victim's computer. Do not be fooled by emails that attempt to invoke a sense of urgency or insecurity. If you do not know who the email is from, or even if you do know the sender but are not expecting a "patch," certainly do not open either the email or the attachment. Furthermore, a legitimate software vendor will never send a software patch by means of an email.

Drive-by downloads do not require a victim to open a suspicious email attachment; instead, all that one needs to do to become a victim is simply to request a malware-laden webpage by clicking on a hyperlink. Computer users are often unaware that they can contract malware from this action, and all the attacker needs to do to be successful is use social engineering tricks to intrigue their victims into clicking on a hyperlink in an email. In the example shown in Figure 11.4, a malicious email provides enticing hyperlinks to see the photos from Dr. Gregory's vacation. The goal of this email is to get the victim to click on the http://plurx.com/?photo. asp=5&asn=99819 hyperlink to view the alleged photos. In reality, however, no such photos exist, and if a user clicks on the hyperlinks, it is likely that the user's computer will be subjected to a drive-by download. Other similar types of messages are concocted to pique the interest of a victim and range from "making all your dreams come true" to "discounts on

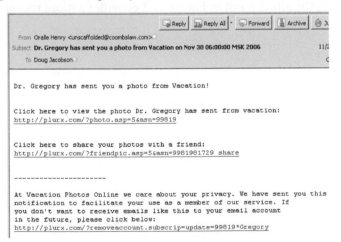

FIGURE 11.4 Malware distribution via email hyperlink.

pharmacy drugs" and everything in between. As a computer user seeking to keep your computer free of malware, the last thing you want to do is believe these claims and click on hyperlinks in suspicious emails.

11.2.4 Phone Calls

Social engineering scams are not restricted to only the digital world but also exist in the real world. Based on the life of a real person, the character of Frank Abagnale in the movie *Catch Me if You Can* is a prime example of a social engineer at work. With keen observation skills, confidence tricks, and insight into human psychology, Frank impersonates the roles of a teacher, doctor, lawyer, and pilot—in the process deceiving a number of people into divulging sensitive information.

In a manner reminiscent of Franks Abagnale's exploits, malicious social engineers have used conventional phones, often posing as computer security experts. Offering a "free computer security checkup," these smooth-talking social engineers attempt to dupe their victims into allowing the attacker to gain remote access to their computer. This enables the attacker to install spyware or a backdoor to the victim's computer, leading to theft of personal and financial information. Just as you would avoid pop-up ads and suspicious emails, do not act on unsolicited phone calls from so-called computer security experts and certainly do not give a stranger any passwords or your credit card number. A legitimate company will never initiate a phone call asking you to give them remote access to your computer, and it will not walk you through steps of installing software on your computer from the web.

11.3 PHISHING

While the previously described attacks use social engineering tactics to distribute malware, ultimately leading to the theft of personal information, phishing attacks seek to accomplish the same goal, taking a slightly different approach to doing so. Phishing attacks try to steal personal information directly by using social engineering tactics to mimic trustworthy sources. If trust is gained, the victim haphazardly discloses personal information directly to the attacker. This section provides examples of ways in which phishing attacks are typically carried out.

11.3.1 Phishing Emails

Perhaps the most well-known and prevalent form of phishing occurs through the use of email. Phishing emails, which are different from spam emails (legitimate, but annoying), seek to obtain your personal and private information by tricking you into replying to an email message, visiting a website that is a malicious façade of a legitimate website, installing spyware on your computer (i.e., drive-by download), or a combination of these techniques.

Figure 11.5 is a phishing email that relies heavily on social engineering tactics to fool its victim into reacting to a "desperate situation." Although emails of this type appear to be sent by someone already known to the receiver, such as a son or granddaughter, rest assured that this is most likely not the case. What this type of phishing email is relying on is that the victim falls hook, line, and sinker for the desperate plea, takes immediate action, and replies to the email. An attacker receiving a reply often sends instructions to the victim describing the procedure to wire transfer of money to a designated account.

One of the best defenses against this type of attack is to be aware that they exist and that you should not trust everything you read and receive on the Internet. If an email is suspicious, copy part of the text from the email into a search engine. Popular email attacks will return results indicating that you are not the first person to receive such an email. Also, you should double-check with a trusted source concerning the contents of such an email. A call to a family member or friend could easily verify whether the email request is bogus. Furthermore, if one does reply to such an email, ask the requesting person to authenticate themself by asking a question that only the alleged person in trouble would be able to answer. When presented with such emails or scams, take the time to scrutinze the message, especially before wiring money to a nondescript number.

FIGURE 11.5   Dramatic phishing email.

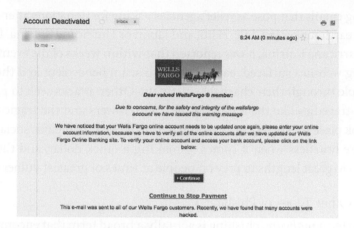

FIGURE 11.6 Bank phishing email.

Other forms of phishing emails present themselves as emails from legitimate corporations (e.g., banks, PayPal) and use scare tactics to entice victims into clicking on a hyperlink to perform some action concerning their banking account, as was seen in Figure 11.4. On clicking on the ">Continue" button or the "Continue to Stop Payment" hyperlink in Figure 11.6, the victim will not be taken to the correct bank's actual website but instead to a website showing a login portal similar in appearance to that bank's login webpage. At this point, if the user enters his or her username and password or any other information into what is assumed to be the correct bank's website, it will be sent directly to the attacker. Compounding the problem for the victim is that, despite entering the correct username and password for the victim's actual bank account, the login attempt to the fake site will be denied. Unaware that this is an attack, this often prompts victims to try other frequently used username and password combinations and thus gives the attacker not only their bank's login credentials but also other online account credentials.

Phishing emails are not restricted to only those types described but also can exist in many different forms. The best way to defeat phishing attacks is to be critical of all emails, regardless of origin, and never click on hyperlinks in an email that promise to take you to a website. The best security practice is always to type the URL of the site that you wish to visit yourself or use a trusted bookmark.

11.3.2 No Shame Game

Social engineers are tactless predators often seeking to take advantage of people's emotions and sympathy after tragic events. Examples include phishing emails that pose as relief agencies asking for donations after events like the earthquakes in Chile, Haiti, and Japan or Hurricane Katrina. In fact, after Hurricane Katrina, it was reported that within weeks of the event, 4000 phishing websites surfaced, each looking to scam benevolent and thoughtful people through their charitable instincts. Other attacks seek to prey on human tragedies like the attack on the Twin Towers and the tragic events that took place in Norway in 2011. Whatever the case, malicious social engineers are heartless when it comes to making a quick dollar, and they will often go to great lengths to prey on people at times of greatest vulnerability.

11.3.4 Other Types of Phishing

Like the term *malware*, phishing is actually a broad term that encompasses many different varieties of social engineering-type attacks. The following explanations are used to better describe the nuances that differentiate some of the more common phishing attacks:

Spear phishing: Unlike phishing, which is analogous to broadcasting a net for any sucker, spear phishing is a more targeted attack. For example, a phishing email might address the victim with a general greeting like "Dear valued customer." A spear-phishing email, on the other hand, would use the victim's actual name, as seen in Figure 11.7. This touch of personalization increases the likelihood that the victim would click on the hyperlink to view the "report," especially if the victim appears to have received the email from someone they already know.

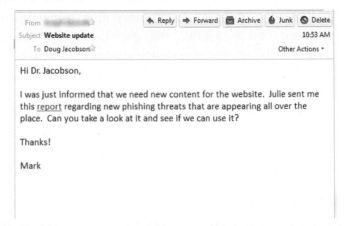

FIGURE 11.7 Spear phishing email.

Targeting a specific victim in a spear-phishing email can go beyond simply using the victim's name, and this is one reason why public information sharing can be at odds with security. Public information provides a social engineer with ammunition for crafting a compelling spear-phishing message. For instance, if your Facebook profile is public and it can be seen that you clearly like fantasy baseball and the Minnesota Twins, then a spear-phishing email addressed to your name on the topic of fantasy baseball and the Minnesota Twins might seem innocent, thus making it more likely for you to take action, such as clicking on a malicious hyperlink. Such an attack, for example, may ask you to set up a new account to receive special and free insider statistics. In this case, the attacker is hoping that you establish the "new account" with the same username and password that you use for your email account or bank account. This is a prime example of why you do not want to use the same username and password combination on multiple websites.

SMiShing: Similar to phishing, SMiShing is the act of phishing through Short Message Services (SMSs), more commonly known as texting. The tactics employed by those who SMiSh are very similar to those of phishers (i.e., URLs or phrases like "act immediately"), and the same defense mechanisms of not replying to any such messages also apply to SMiShing attacks. Popular SMiShing attacks include a text message that claims one has won a Walmart gift card. To claim the prize, the victim is led to a website and asked to submit private information.

Whale phishing: When an attacker targets high-ranking corporate officials, executives, and chief executive officers (CEOs) (i.e., big fish), this type of phishing is known as whaling.

Vishing: Vishing is nothing more than a voice phishing (i.e., vishing) attack that occurs over a landline phone, cell phone, or voice call over the Internet (e.g., Skype).

11.4 DETECTING A PHISHING URL

A fundamental skill in thwarting phishing attacks is to be able to read, dissect, and understand all of the components comprising a URL. In the presence of a phishing attack, one generally has two opportunities to read a URL before accidentally disclosing personal information. The first opportunity occurs when one decides whether to request a webpage by either clicking on a hyperlink or typing a specific URL into the web browser address bar and hitting "Enter." Reading a URL as it is typed in a web address bar is straightforward, while hyperlinks are another story. In a web browser, placing the mouse directly over a hyperlink reveals the true URL that a hyperlink leads to on the web (Figure 11.8). Depending on the web browser used, this actual URL will appear in either the bottom left- or in the right-hand corner of the web browser window. Notice in the phishing email shown in Figure 11.8 that, although the hyperlink claims to point to YouTube (i.e., http://youtube.com/inbox?feature=mhsn), the true URL, shown in the bottom left-hand corner of the window, in fact points to a completely different URL—a phishing website. The text label on a hyperlink does not need to be the same as the URL for the hyperlinks (Chapter 7), and phishers often use this technique of misdirection to fool their victims into errantly clicking on a hyperlink.

The second opportunity for reading a URL before entering or submitting any private information on a given website is provided in the web address bar (Figure 11.9). At this point, if a user has already requested a phishing webpage, then the act of typing or submitting any information

FIGURE 11.8   Hyperlinks misdirection.

FIGURE 11.9   Web address bar.

on the webpage will send it directly to the phisher. If one cannot tell from the looks of a website that it is a phony, reading the URL in the web address bar is often the last defense before one becomes a phishing victim. In any of these cases, being able to read a URL successfully will go a long way in preventing phishing attacks and guarding against malware infections.

11.4.1 Reading a URL

Just as a mailing address represents a unique and specific location in the physical world, a URL denotes a unique and specific web document address in the cyber world. A URL (i.e., http://www.google.com/) is nothing more than a cryptic set of instructions that enables your computer—with the help of the Internet—to send and receive web documents and information to and from other computers and servers connected to the Internet.

Unlike webpages of the early 1990s, many webpages today are no longer passive documents from which one simply reads text or views pictures. Today's web (Web 2.0) represents an interactive experience in which one is frequently submitting information (i.e., passwords, credit card numbers, etc.) into webpages that are then routed through the Internet to other computers and servers. In this context, the URL is the location on the Internet to which you are sending your personal and private information. Tricking you into entering your private information into a phony website designed to look like a legitimate website is at the heart of what phishing attacks are all about. Being able to read a URL successfully can be either a first line of defense when one determines whether to click on a URL or a last line of defense before one reveals confidential information to a phony website.

Figure 11.10 provides an example used in the next sections to demonstrate how to break down and better understand the purpose and significance of each part of a URL.

11.4.2 Protocol

When browsing the web, there are two predominant protocols (Hypertext Transfer Protocol [HTTP] and Hypertext Transfer Protocol Secure [HTTPS])

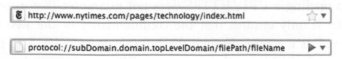

FIGURE 11.10   URL breakdown.

Protocol

http://www.nytimes.com/pages/technology/index.html

FIGURE 11.11   URL protocol.

that determine how information is sent between your computer (i.e., point A) and the website you are visiting (i.e., point B). The location of the protocol in a URL is, as seen in Figure 11.11, always the leftmost part of the URL and trailed by the characters ://.

To better understand the significance of the protocol with respect to security and privacy, consider the following analogy. Browsing the web with the HTTP is similar to mailing a letter in a clear envelope: Any postal worker, mail carrier, or anyone with access to the sender's or receiver's mailbox would be able to read the letter's content. Needless to say, if this were the case, one would not want to write confidential information in such a letter. Browsing the web with HTTPS, on the other hand, is similar to sending a letter in an unbreakable and opaque envelope locked with a key that can only be unlocked by the receiver. In this case, a postal carrier or anyone else possessing the letter would be unable to determine the letter's contents, and they would not be able to pick its lock. It follows that, to prevent against eavesdropping, all confidential information (i.e., passwords, credit card numbers, etc.) should be sent over the Internet using HTTPS. Many websites that accept confidential information will already make use of HTTPS without requiring the user to perform any other actions. Other websites, like Google Search, give users an option. The typical URL for Google Search is http://www.google.com/. However, by typing https://www.google.com/ in a web browser address bar and pressing "Enter," one can still make use of Google Search, but with the added confidentiality of HTTPS. Some websites provide the added security of HTTPS, while others do not—entering "https" for the protocol of a URL is an easy way to check. When browsing the web, both a secure mail carrier (i.e., HTTPS) and an insecure carrier (i.e., HTTP) will get your letter (i.e., web traffic) to its destination, but only HTTPS provides the added service of confidentiality while data is in transit.

When reading a URL, HTTPS does not guarantee that a website is legitimate; it only ensures that the confidentiality of the web content is preserved as it moves through the Internet from point A to point B. In fact, some phishing websites purposefully use HTTPS because the attacker knows that security tip websites coach people to believe that the

FIGURE 11.12   Phishing URL with HTTPS.

presence of HTTPS in the URL indicates a safe website. Consider the URL in Figure 11.12. Although the URL shows HTTPS as the protocol, it is not a legitimate banking website and thus should not be trusted.

Conversely, the absence of the HTTPS protocol for any website that accepts personal or financial information is an indication of a phishing website. When viewing a webpage, if you are asked to provide a username, password, or credit card number and you see HTTP instead of HTTPS in the web address bar, be aware that the website you are visiting is likely to be a phishing website. At the very least, this is an indication that the website has very little regard for its users' security and privacy. In either case, do not enter confidential information on such a webpage.

11.4.3 Top-Level Domain Name

A top-level domain (TLD) can be thought of as a URL's association—by country (.cn, .tk, .ru, .uk, .us) or more generally (.com, .net, .biz)—on the Internet, similar to that of a country code or business sector. Just as an email address belongs to a specific service provider (i.e., @gmail.com or @hotmail.com), each website belongs to a TLD (i.e., .edu, .net, .info). To locate the TLD in Figure 11.13, start to the right of the protocol (e.g., http://) and read from left to right until you reach the first single backslash in the URL; mark this spot. Now, from this spot, read from right to left until you encounter the first period; mark this spot. Between the two marked spots is the TLD (i.e., .com in this case). Note that these instructions for reading a URL are independent of this example and can be applied to any URL.

By themselves, TLDs are not definitive indicators of whether a website is legitimate. For example, even though .com is perhaps the most recognized TLD, a website that has the .com TLD is not necessarily safe. In fact, 60% of phishing websites have one of the following four TLDs: .com, .net, .tk, and .cc. To determine the legitimacy of a TLD, it must be examined in context with the other components of the URL and, more specifically, the domain name.

FIGURE 11.13   Top-level domain name.

11.4.4 Domain Name

The domain name of a website is its unique identity on the Internet and is similar in its uniqueness to your email address—no two email addresses can be exactly the same. Just like an email address, the domain name reflects the identity of the website with which one expects to communicate. Domain names are purchased from Internet domain registrars (e.g., Bluehost or GoDaddy) and are exclusive to the purchaser. To locate the domain name in Figure 11.14, start at the TLD (i.e., .com) and read from left to right until you reach the next period. The domain name is the combination of the next period-delimited text to the left of the TLD (i.e., nytimes) and the TLD (i.e., .com).

In Figure 11.14, the domain name of this URL is nytimes.com, and thus one should expect to be viewing the NYTimes website. Because no two domain names can be the same, a phishing website cannot masquerade under the same domain name as nytimes.com. A phishing website must use a different domain name. For example, if you expect to be viewing your bank's website (i.e., Bank of America), the displayed domain name should be consistent with this expectation. In Figure 11.15, it is clear that the domain name is webportallogin.com and clearly not bankofamerica.com; thus, this URL is that of a phishing website.

A common trick that phishers play is to register websites with names that are similar to, but not quite the same as, domain names of legitimate websites. This is known as cyber-squatting or typo-squatting. In the following example, can you determine which of the following domain names is the correct one for Microsoft?

a. micrsoft.com

b. micosoft.com

c. microsoft.info

d. microsoft.com

e. microsoft-verify.com

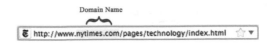

Domain Name

http://www.nytimes.com/pages/technology/index.html

FIGURE 11.14   Domain name.

`http://www.bankofamerica.com.us.webportallogin.com/signin.html` ▶ ▼

FIGURE 11.15   Phishing example using subdomain trickery.

The answer is d. There is only one true domain name for Microsoft (microsoft.com), and the others are simply phonies. Attackers are successful in using typo-squatting to fool victims because, at first glance, a slightly misspelled domain name looks close enough to one's expectation of the correct domain name that it may not raise an immediate red flag.

11.4.5 Subdomain Name

If a domain name is a unique identifier like a city name in a given state (not always the case, but let us assume so), then a subdomain can be thought of as a suburb of a domain name. In the context of the Internet, subdomains are often used to name and organize servers under a single domain name. Some websites have many subdomains, while others have none. The subdomain name is located in between the protocol (i.e., http://) and the domain name (i.e., nytimes.com). In Figure 11.16, the subdomain name is www—a common subdomain name that is an abbreviation for the World Wide Web.

Unlike domain names, subdomains are not unique, and the owner of a domain name can choose to have as many subdomains as desired and subsequently give each subdomain any name. Although many websites have adopted the naming convention of labeling their subdomain as www, this is not always the case. Consider, for example, Wikipedia's website shown in Figure 11.17. The URL for Wikipedia's English language webpage has a subdomain name of en—most likely standing for "English."

The flexibility given in the selection and naming of subdomains is used by phishers to fool you into thinking that you are on a legitimate website. As illustrated in Figure 11.15, the subdomain of this URL might lead users to believe that they are on Bank of America's website. However, on closer examination, it can be seen that the domain name for this URL is

Sub-domain Name

`http://www.nytimes.com/pages/technology/index.html` ☆ ▼

FIGURE 11.16   Subdomain name.

`W` **en.wikipedia**.org/wiki/Main_Page   ☆ ▼ C

FIGURE 11.17   Subdomain name example for Wikipedia.

"webloginportal.com," not the expected identity for Bank of America. In this case, phishers carefully named their subdomains www.bankofamerica. us to fool their victim into thinking that the correct website was selected.

Subdomains by themselves cannot be used as indicators of website legitimacy. Using the subdomain www does not mean the website is safe. To determine the legitimacy of a URL, subdomains must be considered in the context of their domain name. Consider the two examples in Figures 11.18 and 11.19. For the URL in Figure 11.18, the subdomain www3 might seem awkward and thus suspicious at first, but when analyzed in context of the domain name (jcpenney.com), it can be clearly seen that this is JC Penney's domain name. The second URL, on the other hand, employs the commonly recognized subdomain www, which could lead one to believe that the website is safe, but before this designation is made, carefully examine the domain name. Microsoft's domain name is microsoft.com not microsoft-verify.com, and thus the second URL is that of a phishing website.

11.4.6 File Path

In a URL, the file path (Figure 11.20) designates the location of the web document on the server hosting the website. The file path in a URL is very similar to that of a file path on a personal computer, such as /documents/ Fall2011/CprE131/Homework5/. To locate the file path in a URL, start at the end of the protocol http:// and read from left to right. Locate the first backslash and mark this spot (also the end of the domain name). From this marker, continue reading left to right until you encounter the last backslash / in the URL and mark this spot. The text between the two markings is the file path name (i.e., /pages/technology/).

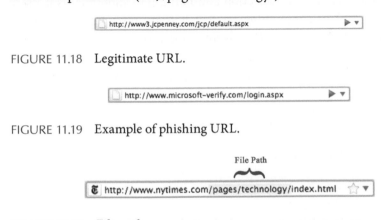

http://www3.jcpenney.com/jcp/default.aspx

FIGURE 11.18 Legitimate URL.

http://www.microsoft-verify.com/login.aspx

FIGURE 11.19 Example of phishing URL.

File Path

http://www.nytimes.com/pages/technology/index.html

FIGURE 11.20 File path.

FIGURE 11.21 URL file path deception.

Like subdomain names, file paths are chosen by the website owner, are not unique, and are used by malicious websites to trick users into a false sense of security. Also like subdomain names, file paths alone cannot be used to determine legitimacy of a website and must be considered in the context of the domain name. In Figure 11.21, the file path name—from an actual phishing email—is crafted to trick one into believing that the URL is legitimate and belongs to Wells Fargo. Notice how the file path name /demo/WellsFargo.CoM/wellsfargo.com/wellsfargo.com/ includes the actual domain name for Wells Fargo (i.e., wellsfargo.com) several times. The objective of the attacker is to fool the victim into thinking that the file path, which can be named anything the attacker wants, is actually the domain name. While the file path in Figure 11.21 is not likely to be but yet could conceivably be that of Wells Fargo, when analyzed alongside the domain name of indigitalworks.net, it can be clearly seen that this URL naming convention is a façade; thus, the URL is that of a phishing website.

11.4.7 File

The last component of the URL is the name of the actual file that one requests to view when typing a URL into a web browser or by clicking on a hyperlink. In a URL, the filename follows the file path. In Figure 11.22, the file name is index.html. There are many different naming conventions and different types of file names used on the web. For the purposes of

Filename

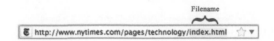

http://www.nytimes.com/pages/technology/index.html

FIGURE 11.22   URL filename.

detecting a phishing website, the filename offers little forensic value for determining the legitimacy of a URL.

11.5 APPLICATION OF KNOWLEDGE

Now that you have learned how to decipher a URL and consider each of its components with respect to a possible phishing attack, let us put that knowledge to the test with a few examples of common phishing URL tricks. For each of the five hyperlinks that follow, list each of the respective components of the URL, determine whether the URL is malicious, and explain how you came to this decision.

1. http://www.facebook.com.us.face32info.cc/login/facebook.com/index.html

2. https://socialiving.info/index.html

3. http://espn.go.com/

4. http://www.infomagnet.net/www.ebay.com/login/ebay/home.html

5. https://www.amazonan.com/electronics/ipod/

Example 1: http://www.facebook.com.us.face32info.cc/login/facebook.com/index.html

Protocol: http

Subdomain name: www.facebook.com.us

Domain name: face32info.cc

File path: /login/facebook.com/

Filename: index.html

Conclusion: Malicious. The domain name is not that of Facebook (i.e., facebook.com), and both the subdomain and file path were constructed to make the victim believe that this is the case.

Example 2: https://socialiving.info/index.html

Protocol: https

Subdomain name: none

Domain name: socialiving.info

File path: none

Filename: index.html

Conclusion: Malicious. Despite the use of HTTPS, one must consider the domain name to determine the legitimacy of the URL. In this case, the malicious URL does not use trickery for either the subdomain or the file path. Instead, the URL attempts to deceive the victim by registering a domain name similar to that of Living Social (livingsocial.com)—a popular deal-of-the-day company.

Example 3: http://espn.go.com/

Protocol: http

Subdomain name: espn

Domain name: go.com

File path: none

Filename: none

Conclusion: Legitimate. Even though one would expect the domain name for ESPN to be espn.com, go.com is a domain name owned by the Walt Disney Internet Group, the parent company for ESPN. Similarly, Disney's URL is http://disney.go.com. In each of these cases, the subdomain names are used to further distinguish different websites under the go.com domain name.

Example 4: http://www.infomagnet.net/www.ebay.com/login/ebay/home .html

Protocol: http

Subdomain name: www

Domain name: infomagnet.net

File path: /www.ebay.com/login/ebay/

Filename: home.html

Conclusion: Malicious. In this case, the file path is obviously attempting to trick the victim into believing the domain name is that of ebay.com when in fact it is infomagnet.net.

Example 5: https://www.amazonan.com/electronics/ipod/

Protocol: https

Subdomain name: www

Domain name: amazonan.com

File path: /electronics/ipod/

Filename: none

Conclusion: Malicious. Example 5 provides an example of typo-squatting. When coupled with the use of HTTPS, the hope of the attacker is that the malicious domain name is similar enough to Amazon's actual domain name (amazon.com) that the victim will be fooled.

As has been demonstrated, there are many ways in which an attacker can attempt to fool a victim through the construction of a URL. This is why it is important to break a URL down into each of its components and analyze each of its pieces in the context of the domain name and the medium in which it is presented.

11.5.1 Tools of the Trade

In addition to being able to read URLs, link-scanning applications such as SiteAdvisor, LinkScanner, and Web of Trust (WOT) can also be used (explained in more detail in Appendix C). Coupling this technology with the ability to read a URL provides a defense-in-depth technique for vetting malicious URLs. Figure 11.8 provided an example of a phishing email using hyperlink misdirection to fool the victim into clicking on a hyperlink claiming to belong to YouTube. Without the skill of being able to read the URL for what it is, determining the legitimacy of the hyperlink, and ultimately the email, can be difficult. To assist in making such a decision,

WOT provides a clear visual indicator (red is bad, and green is good) for each hyperlink in the email—making it obvious that the provided example is a malicious email (Figure 11.23). In contrast, WOT also makes it quite observable when hyperlinks are legitimate (Figure 11.24).

It should be noted that, while link-scanning technology provides a convenient and effective means of determining the legitimacy of a URL, one should not rely solely on such technology to vet all phishing attempts. It is unlikely that every computer one uses will have such a program installed, and like antivirus software, link scanners are also prone to false positives and false negatives. When used in conjunction with careful reading of a URL, link scanners can provide a strong defense-in-depth duo to mitigate phishing and malware distribution attacks.

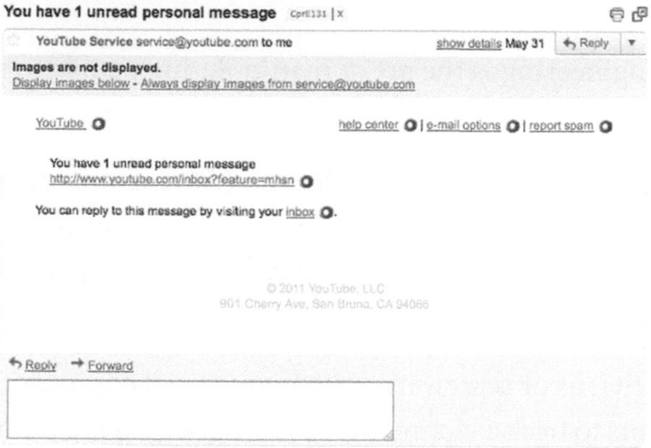

FIGURE 11.23   Phishing email and WOT link scanner.

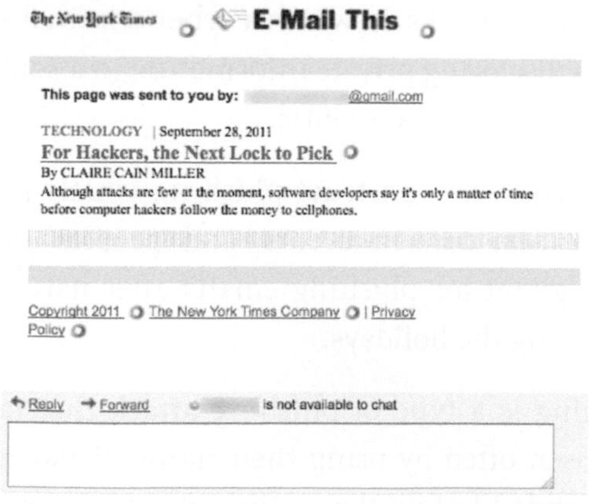

FIGURE 11.24   Legitimate email and WOT link scanner.

11.6 SUMMARY

As Bruce Schneier has said, "Only amateurs target systems; professionals target people." There is a great deal of truth in this statement since it is often much easier for a hacker to use social engineering tricks to dupe a victim into divulging sensitive information or installing malware onto a computer than it is for the hacker to compromise the victim's security mechanisms (i.e., a firewall). One of the best defenses—and sometimes the only defense—against social engineering attacks is user education. Social engineers are very tricky, and the tactics they use purposefully exploit known human vulnerabilities. Understanding the purpose of these attacks, how they are actually carried out, and how they can be defeated are important first steps toward strengthening your defense-in-depth approach to practical computer security.

- Social engineering is the art of manipulating people to reveal information or perform actions that are not in their best interest.

- Many malware distribution schemes (instant messages, fake antivirus, emails, and even phone calls) incorporate social engineering tactics to bypass security mechanisms (i.e., firewalls) and to increase the success ratio.

- Fake antivirus or scareware epitomizes social engineering at work—it attempts to trick a victim into installing or paying for malware that did not previously exist on the victim's computer.

- Perhaps the most common type of social engineering in the digital world is phishing attacks, in which a cyber criminal attempts to trick a victim into disclosing private information to a source the victim is tricked into believing is authentic.

- Cyber criminals who construct phishing emails prey on catastrophes, hard times, current events, and peoples' goodwill to help others. Be vigilant for phishing emails after natural disasters and especially during the holidays.

- Spear phishing is a type of phishing attack that targets a specific individual user, often by using their name. Personalizing phishing emails is intended to fool the victim into thinking the sender must know them and thus the email must be legitimate.

- Telltale signs of a phishing email include poor grammar and punctuation, security alerts, time-sensitive actions, and hyperlinks.

- Apart from recognizing a phishing attempt, being able to dissect and discern the components of a URL is a key skill to prevent identity theft.

- The presence of HTTPS in a URL does not indicate that a website is secure.

- The domain name of a website is its unique identifier on the Internet and cannot be forged.

- Typo-squatting, or the registering of domain names very similar to legitimate and popular domain names, is a technique used by cyber criminals to trick users into visiting a phishing website.

- Subdomain names, which are not unique to a URL or domain name, are used to fool a victim into thinking that a subdomain name is actually the website's domain name.

- Similar to subdomain trickery, misleading file path names are also used to fool phishing victims.

- In addition to being able to read a URL, link scanners can be used to identify malicious hyperlinks.

BIBLIOGRAPHY

Abagnale, F.W., and Redding, S. 1980. *Catch Me If You Can: The Amazing True Story of the Youngest and Most Daring Con Man in the History of Fun and Profit.* New York: Random House Digital.

BBB. 2010. BBB advises donors on how to vet Chile earthquake charity appeals. Better Business Bureau. http://wynco.bbb.org/article/bbb-advises-donors-on-how-to-vet-chile-earthquake-charity-appeals-17967 (accessed May 7, 2012).

Fallon, T.J. 2000. *The Internet Today.* Indianapolis, IN: Prentice Hall.

Gibson, D. 2011. *Microsoft Windows Security Essentials.* New York: Wiley.

Greene, B. 2010. The "with tears in my eyes" email. CNN. http://articles.cnn.com/2010-03-28/opinion/greene.email.scam_1_e-mail-first-byline-subject-line/2?_s=PM:OPINION (accessed May 7, 2012).

Hadnagy, C. 2010. *Social Engineering: The Art of Human Hacking.* New York: Wiley.

Knapton, K. 2009. *Cyber Safety: Maintaining Morality in a Digital World.* Springville, UT: Cedar Fort.

Kulkarni, M. 2010. Spammers unrelenting with the Haiti earthquake scam campaign. Symantec. http://www.symantec.com/connect/blogs/spammers-unrelenting-haiti-earthquake-scam-campaign (accessed May 7, 2012).

Liebowitz, M. 2011. Tips to avoid Japanese earthquake phishing scams. MSNBC. http://www.msnbc.msn.com/id/42036358/ns/technology_and_science-security/t/tips-avoid-japanese-earthquake-phishing-scams/#.T6fQ3L8sFi4 (accessed May 7, 2012).

malwaresecurityscan-com_03. © 2009 by Kevin Jarrett, under a Creative Commons Attribution 2.0 Generic (CC BY 2.0) license: http://creativecommons.org/licenses/by/2.0/.

Mitnick, K.D., and Simon, W.L. 2003. *The Art of Deception: Controlling the Human Element of Security*. New York: Wiley.

Mitnick, K.D., and Simon, W.L. 2005. *The Art of Intrusion: The Real Stories Behind the Exploits of Hackers, Intruders and Deceivers*. New York: Wiley.

Morley, D., and Parker, C.S. 2010. *Understanding Computers: Today and Tomorrow, Introductory*. Independence, KY: Cengage Learning.

Oates, J. 2011. Microsoft warns of support scams. The Register. http://www.theregister.co.uk/2011/06/16/tech_support_scam_calls/ (accessed May 7, 2012).

Savage, M. 2005. FBI Investigating Hurricane Katrina online scams. *SC Magazine*. http://www.scmagazine.com/fbi-investigating-hurricane-katrina-online-scams/article/32511/ (accessed May 7, 2012).

Schneier, B. 2000. Semantic attacks: the third wave of network attacks. Schneier on Security. http://www.schneier.com/crypto-gram-0010.html (accessed May 7, 2012).

Schwartz, M. J. 2011. Phishing attackers use subdomain registration services. Information Week. http://www.informationweek.com/news/security/attacks /229402436 (accessed May 7, 2012).

Singel, R. 2010. Google launches encrypted search. Wired. http://www.wired.com/threatlevel/2010/05/google-https-search/ (accessed May 7, 2012).

Walmart. 2012. Walmart gift card text message scams. Walmart. http://www.walmart-stores.com/PrivacySecurity/10840.aspx?p=9620 (accessed May 7, 2012).

CHAPTER 12

Staying Safe Online:
The Human Threat

12.1 INTRODUCTION

The Internet is a wonderful resource, and many consider it to be a life-changing technology. As with every new technology, there are opportunities both to do good and to do harm. This chapter explores some of the human threats that may arise when people interact using the Internet. Some of the discussed threats are new to the Internet, while some are no different from threats typically faced in the real world. It should be noted that some of the issues discussed in this chapter are serious and can be life threatening. If you, your friends, family, or any children you know are facing these types of problems, the authorities should be contacted immediately. The goal of this chapter is to raise awareness of cyber-human-related issues and direct you to resources where you can find more information.

The threats that exist in the digital world are in many ways similar to the threats that exist on a playground, in a lunchroom, or in a locker room. Parents allowing their children to use the Internet unsupervised should have the same conversations with their kids about online threats as they do about other common threats their children face during a normal day (i.e., stranger danger, don't do drugs, sexual education, etc.). Although much of the context in this chapter is targeted toward adolescents, many of these same issues can be attributed to any age group. In the remainder of this chapter, several issues are examined through the perspective of fictitious security characters Alice, Bob, and Carol. Several more characters are introduced to play supporting roles in the provided scenarios to help explain the issues: Anonymous Annie, Creepy Charlie, Bullying Barney, Dumped Duane, Nosey Nancy, Imposter Ivan, Shy Sally, Hiring Hank, Posting Paul, Sharing Sam, and Victim Vince.

12.2 THE DIFFERENCES BETWEEN CYBERSPACE AND THE PHYSICAL WORLD

To set the context for this chapter, ask yourself the following question: How is the Internet different from the "real world"? We would argue that many of the human threats that lurk on the Internet are not necessarily new, but rather people generally perceive these threats in a different way. For example, start with the way people often describe the Internet: People use terms like *cyberspace* and *virtual world*. Each of these terms, including the term Internet itself, implies a place different from that of the real world. Also, the Internet enables and encourages people to assume multiple personas and create alter egos. All these factors can lead people to believe that the two worlds (real and virtual) are separate, and actions in one have no or little effect on the other. Exploring a few differences in the way the virtual world operates relative to the real world will shed more light on this issue.

As previously mentioned, one of the major differences between the real world and the cyber world is that your identity or identities do not have to be related to your real identity. The Internet creates numerous opportunities for users to create profiles, avatars (graphical representations of users or alter egos), and online identities. This gives the user a feeling of anonymity and the associated ability to act in ways he or she would never act in the real world. Anonymity can be both good and bad. Consider the example of Anonymous Annie, who creates a profile so she can discuss some personal issues online. Annie is using the anonymity of the Internet to talk about private issues that she might not discuss if her identity is known. Imposter Ivan, on the other hand, has created an online profile to pretend to be someone he is not, perhaps a doctor, for the sole purpose of conning people out of their personal and private information. If Alice and Ivan meet in a chat room, Ivan could use his fake persona to convince Alice to reveal information about herself. Depending on the context and motivation, anonymity can be both a strength and a weakness of the Internet experience.

Another aspect of perceived anonymity is that people can act in ways they would not in real life. As discussed further in the chapter, people sometimes say things to others while using the Internet that they would never say to them in person. They will talk to people they do not know and tell them information they would never tell a stranger on the bus, for example. It can be said that the Internet makes the weak strong, the shy outgoing, and everyone beautiful.

A characteristic that makes the Internet a different place from the real world is the speed and ease with which information can be widely shared. In the real world, except for television, radio, and mass publication, it is difficult to spread information among a large group of people, and it is even more difficult if that information is nonverbal (pictures, text, etc.). To distribute information among a geographically dispersed group of friends, one would have to rely on making physical copies and using physical distribution systems (post office, etc.). On the Internet, however, it is much easier to create and distribute copies of pictures or text to hundreds or thousands of people. Furthermore, the speed of dissemination on the Internet makes such sharing almost instantaneous. These Internet qualities of course make it harder to keep information contained within a small group of people.

There is also a tendency among many to think that if something is read on the Internet, it is probably true. Part of this belief stems from the innate trust people tend to place in computers and the Internet; they perceive them as objects, and objects, in their view, do not deceive. Before the Internet, only a select few entities (books, newspapers, magazines) had the power to create and distribute the printed word. Today, anyone can produce professional-appearing written material and disseminate it around the world. Also, in the past, when people wanted to spread false rumors, they often would have to rely on the spoken word as their only means of expression. While these actions are no less hurtful, often such rumors would not spread widely, and people could make a judgment through knowing their source. The modern Internet, however, allows people to make false statements that can spread through distributed social circles around the world in the matter of seconds. Since such statements are written in professional-looking printed form, people may have a tendency to believe them without question. We must strive to remember the obvious fact that not everything read and seen on the Internet is true.

12.3 CONSIDER THE CONTEXT: WATCH WHAT YOU SAY AND HOW IT IS COMMUNICATED

By examining human communication over time and focusing on the differences between oral and written communication, one can see how valuable context and emotion are to the meaning of a message. In the distant past, written communication tended to be used for keeping historical records, storytelling, or private communications between people with established relationships. Oral communication, on the other hand, was the primary method individuals used to interact with one another. With the advent of the telephone, this distinction still held true. One of the primary differences between written and oral communication is that oral communication provides individuals with the means to express emotion through tone, volume, inflection, and so on. Written communication, on the other hand, does not provide an equally effective method for expressing such emotions. This is why authors of fiction must typically describe the emotional state of a character instead of allowing a reader to discover or infer it from textual dialogue.

When using the Internet as a method of communication, it is important to understand that emotion can be difficult to convey via simple text messages. A single message might be interpreted differently by each person reading it, and without proper context, it is possible that a given reader will be unable to interpret the message correctly. Take, for example, the simple question, "Why did you leave the party early?" It is difficult to tell if the writer posing the question is upset, concerned, annoyed, or simply curious. People sometimes try to add emotional content to statements by using capital letters or extra characters. So the same statement written as "WHY did you leave the party EARLY?" could imply that the questioner was either upset or perhaps conveying a completely different emotion, that a friend missed a really good time at the party. Without the proper context, readers of the message are left to interpret it in any way they see fit, which may or may not lead to the correct interpretation. Not only is it difficult to express emotion and the level of emotion in written text, it is equally, if not more, difficult to extract the true meaning from written messages. Furthermore, certain aspects of spoken dialogue, like sarcasm, are difficult enough to interpret orally and are almost impossible to fully understand in written form. To aid in conveying of expression and emotion through typed text, many use emoticons—keystroke representations of faces, such as :) for happy. Even with emoticons to assist in the framing of the emotion, without context, written messages can still be difficult to fully understand. A prime example is the use of Twitter by professional athletes, who often have to apologize for Twitter statements because, if considered in a certain (perhaps unintended) context, such messages can be considered highly insensitive and offensive.

Another issue with the written word on the Internet is that people tend to write statements that they would not make directly to someone's face or would be likely to share so vigorously with a large group of people. Many of us are guilty of such actions, and more often than not, we end up regretting what we wrote and regret not taking more time to cool down and collect our thoughts before sending such a message. When President Abraham Lincoln was upset with an individual, he was famous for drafting letters (referred to as "hot letters") but never actually sending them to the intended recipients. When one is emotionally upset and writing on the Internet, one should take the following lesson from President Lincoln: First, wait until you calm down before sending an emotionally charged message. When you are upset, the saying "count to 10 before speaking" translates to "sleep on it before sending" when using the Internet. Some user agents (UAs) like Gmail enable a user to cancel the sending of email a short time after the "send" button has been pressed. A second admonition to help guide you when sending messages is to ask yourself, "Would I let my grandmother read that message?" Messages in digital form can be spread quickly via email and social networking, and they often find their way to unintended recipients. Finally, Newton's second law—every action has an equal but opposite reaction—does not necessarily have to translate into emotional Internet exchanges. In other words, not every comment, text, or post requires an equal or greater reaction in the opposite direction. Remember that it is difficult to understand the full meaning and emotional content or grasp the full context of a text message. By reacting in a hostile manner, an innocent situation can quickly escalate into an unintended negative exchange that may be deeply regretted afterward.

As an example, let us say Nosey Nancy sent a message, "Why did you leave the party early?" to Shy Sally. Staying true to her character, the intention of Nosey Nancy's message was simple curiosity. Shy Sally could interpret the message as it was intended and not get upset, or she might think that Nancy was upset with her. If Shy Sally misinterprets the message, she might reply with an angry message like, "WHY DO YOU WANT TO KNOW? IT DOES NOT CONCERN YOU!" This message could in turn cause Nancy to send an even nastier message, and one can envision the problems this could cause and how quickly an innocent situation could escalate into hard feelings. The bottom line is that one should always be careful when creating or responding to a message. Another rule of thumb is that one should send no more than three messages when trying to resolve an issue or dispute. After three messages, it is best that the two involved parties talk in person.

In addition to being concerned with how you say something, you should also be concerned with what you say. When posting messages or sending emails you should always ask the question, "Would I say this to the person if the person was standing in front of me?" In many cases, messages like email, texts, or social networking posts can be just as hurtful and damaging as in-person encounters. You should be aware that there are both legal and disciplinary consequences for what you do and say online as a student, employee, or citizen. In addition to school and corporate policies forbidding such action, most states have laws that make cyber bullying (i.e., cyber harassment) or cyber stalking illegal in any context. Contributing to a victim's ability to seek out legal or disciplinary actions against an attacker is the fact that digital correspondence is easy to record, preserve, and use as evidence.

To summarize, you should always think before sending or posting messages online, and you should ask yourself these three questions:

- Would I show this message to my grandmother?

- Would I say the same thing to this person if the person was standing in front of me?

- How would I feel if I were the person who received this message?

12.4 WHAT YOU DO ON THE INTERNET LASTS FOREVER

One of the great characteristics about the Internet is there is no single place where all its information is stored. Rather, the information comprising the Internet is spread across millions of computers distributed around the planet, making it a truly global network. The problem with such a global network is that, once something becomes part of the Internet, not only can it be shared globally and stored on many different computers, but its nature is such that it may remain stored in the Internet forever. Furthermore, search engines have become incredibly adept at scouring the Internet and making huge volumes of information easily findable with a simple search. A picture or a message you send today could be available for years to come, stored on multiple computers, and might be returned each time there is a search for your name. This may resemble a situation like your mother pulling out your naked baby pictures when you are 18 and showing them to your friends. Those pictures last forever.

As many have experienced, there are dozens of ways to share information using the Internet. One may think that if they post content on one Internet-based platform like Facebook that it will remain in that platform. As discussed in Chapter 10, such information is only relatively private, and once posted in one online environment, it can spread outside that domain and be redistributed in many different contexts. Take the example of Posting Paul. While in college, Posting Paul was notorious for posting pictures of himself and things he did when he was drunk. While it seemed funny at the time, when Posting Paul graduated from college, he sought to establish a new and more professional reputation. Now, if we fast-forward several years to a time when Paul is interviewing for a professional job, Hiring Hank may do a simple search for information about Paul and find embarrassing posts from Paul's past. Although Paul has worked hard to establish a new reputation, the pictures he posted in college are still part of his digital footprint on the Internet.

12.5 NOTHING IS PRIVATE, NOW OR IN THE FUTURE

Throughout this book, we have talked about privacy and how to keep information private. The issues of privacy have also been discussed as they related to social networking. At the risk of being too repetitive, we would like to discuss privacy one more time, but this time as it relates to staying safe online. The most important concept you should understand is that any time you share information online (even if it is only with one person), you should consider that information no longer private. Any text or picture you share on the Internet can be copied and shared with others without your knowledge. For example, Sharing Sam could post a message or picture meant only for Nosey Nancy. Once he does this, it is easy for Nancy to repost or email the same message to as many people as she desires, both now and at any time in the future. If Nosey Nancy shares the message, it can then continue to be reposted or sent to other people, like, for example, Creepy Charlie. Sharing Sam, naïve to believe that his digital correspondences are truly secrets, has no idea his message has been shared with so many people and may be mortified if he learned that it was so shared. If this is not bad enough, messages could be altered or comments added to the original message, making the situation even worse for Sharing Sam.

In many different contexts, there have been numerous documented cases of messages meant to be private being reposted or released to the public, causing incalculable damage. A more comical example is that of a Facebook birthday invitation that was accidentally made public, prompting more than 1500 guests to show up to what was intended to be a private party.

Another issue to consider is that one's view of privacy can change over the course of his or her life and may even drastically change over a short time window. Most of us have done things in the past that only exist as memories and for which many of us are thankful that such occurrences are not documented for all to see and read about. At one time, a certain action might have been considered "cool," but years later one might not reflect on the same action with a similar attitude. When it comes to digital content, remember that once information is shared or posted on the Internet, that same information is likely to follow you around for the rest of your life. This includes blog entries, IM chat logs, emails, pictures, videos, and many other forms of digital information.

You may be telling yourself that you do not care what others think, and therefore it is OK to post messages about the things you do or post pictures showing you in a bad light (drinking, doing something illegal, etc.) that you think are funny. Ask yourself how you are going to answer questions about such content when you are involved in pursuits in which character matters, like finding a job. Would you bring the same pictures or messages to a job interview now or 10 years from now? As discussed in Chapter 10, studies have shown that employers are often required by corporate policy to perform online searches about job candidates, and many have rejected candidates because of the information they found through such searches. Again, the most important thing to take away from this section is that nothing shared is private, and you should ask yourself if you would want a stranger, your grandmother, or your boss to see this now or in the future.

12.6 CAN YOU REALLY TELL WHO YOU ARE TALKING WITH?

Many Internet users feel that there is no way they can be identified on the Internet unless they so desire. A computer, by providing the capability for creating multiple identities, may give Internet users a feeling of anonymity. Throughout the book, we have talked about how attackers can pretend to be anyone they want. Attackers, different from more normal Internet users, may possess a skill set and a good understanding regarding how to cover their digital tracks. Internet users may think they are anonymous, but are they really? Let us look at the cases of Imposter Ivan and Anonymous Annie.

Ivan has created multiple Internet identities that he uses to send email selling various "health" products. He also uses the same fake accounts to steal identities using phishing emails. The question of anonymity in this context should revolve around trying to tell if Ivan's fake identities are real, which is different from trying to identify the real person sending the email messages (i.e., Ivan). There may indeed be ways to identify Ivan, but such methods often involve law enforcement and are outside the scope of this book. For the average Internet user, it is much more important simply to know that Imposter Ivan is not who he claims to be.

While we addressed the issue of phishing in Chapter 11, it is worth repeating that someone like Ivan is only as anonymous as we allow him to be. This form of anonymity protects the attacker from identification and places the burden on the user to tell if the person is real. As discussed many times throughout this book, everything on the Internet from websites to emails can be faked, and it is up to you, the user, to play an active role in protecting yourself. Again, cyber criminals are cunning and will go to great lengths to lie to you—often telling you what you want to hear, appealing to your emotions, or scaring you into performing an action. As a rule of thumb, never do something online you would not do in the real world.

The other side of anonymity involves Anonymous Annie, who seeks to obtain information about her medical problems but does not want people to know her true identity. In this context, her anonymity depends on her own actions. If Annie searches the Internet for information, it is unlikely she will be identified unless she reveals information about herself. Appendix C discusses both NoScript and private browsing, features that will keep Annie's browser from providing information about her to a website and likewise prevent the next person who uses Annie's computer from learning her actions. The more information Annie reveals about herself to a computer or website, the more she erodes her anonymity. Now, after a drastic turn of events, let us assume that Annie wants to threaten someone using her computer. She might think she is anonymous, but in reality, without special knowledge of computers and networking, it is highly likely that Annie has left digital tracks that law enforcement can follow to specifically identify her as the culprit. A point that should be made is that you can often stay anonymous on the Internet if no one cares enough to find out who you are.

12.7 CAMERAS AND PHOTO SHARING

As has been discussed throughout the book, technology has enabled people to communicate in ways we never dreamed of decades ago. One aspect of this technology growth is in the area of pictures and videos. Almost every computing device produced today (cell phones, computers, smart phones, tablets, etc.) has the ability to take pictures, stream video, and record movies. While this is technically not a practical security problem, it clearly represents a privacy issue. To expedite the ease of sharing, there are phones having a single button that will flash when a picture is taken, and if this button is pressed, the picture will be posted to a social networking site. There are two general types of privacy issues we should discuss with respect to cameras.

The first type of camera-related privacy involves Sharing Sam, who is always taking pictures of everything he is doing and sharing them with friends. Sam needs to be aware that pictures he posts are not easily deleted or perhaps are even impossible to delete, and they will certainly not be private. As discussed previously in this chapter, Sam may cause himself problems depending on just what he decides to share. Again, ask yourself the question, "Would I want my grandma to see me in that picture?"

The second type of camera-related security issue involves Posting Paul, who has a camera/video phone. Paul likes to take pictures of everything he sees no matter how embarrassing or hurtful it might be to others. This situation is difficult to deal with and can have legal implications. Paul could be charged with a crime depending on just what he records and how he obtained it. If you find yourself a victim of people like Paul, you should contact law enforcement.

Now, let us look at a few examples of problems that might be caused by Sam and Paul. Sam and his friends are out one night having fun and decide to do something illegal. Sam records the whole episode and posts it to YouTube. A few days later, the police are knocking at Sam's and his friends' doors. In this situation, Sam has incriminated himself by not understanding the real-world effects of his digital actions.

Sharing Sam has a girlfriend (Shy Sally), and one afternoon he is texting Sally and asks her to send him a sexy picture of herself. Sally takes a revealing picture and sends it to Sam; this is a type of "sexting." At this point, we need to consider a couple of scenarios regarding the ages of Sam and Sally. If one or both are minors, then this is a *very serious* crime. There have been cases when minors have been charged with child pornography. Sam can be charged with possession, and if he forwards the picture, he can be charged with distribution. To reiterate, picture sexting when a minor is involved is a very serious issue. In addition, if Sam forwards the picture to his friends, they can also be charged with possession and distribution, depending on what they do with the picture.

Even if Sam and Sally are not minors, there are still many serious issues that can arise if the picture is shared. The shared picture could be hurtful to Sally (no matter what her age), and because Sally now has no control over the shared picture, Sharing Sam can give a copy to whomever he pleases, including Creepy Charlie. Before Sally decides to take such pictures, she should think back to the question, "What would Grandma think?"

The issue of Posting Paul taking pictures of everything is much more difficult to handle. If Paul is in a public place taking pictures of things in plain sight, then he can post anything he wants without legal recriminations. For most people, this is not a problem since only if you are doing something you do not want others to see would you be concerned about Paul's actions. On the other hand, if Paul decided to hide a camera and take pictures of nonpublic places, legal action could be taken against Paul if he is discovered. Of course, once Paul posts pictures from the hidden camera, whether Paul is caught or not, it will be difficult to remove the pictures completely from the Internet. With the help of law enforcement, most posting sites (Google, Facebook, Twitter, etc.) will remove illegal content. However, these sites will often not remove content if it is simply embarrassing to one or more of the parties represented. Even removal will not help if someone has copied the picture.

12.8 I AM A GOOD PERSON, THAT WOULD NEVER HAPPEN TO ME

Most of the issues presented in this chapter have involved actions that may not be intended as malicious. There are a number of things caused by someone who intends to do harm. Throughout the book, we have addressed the issues of phishing, malware, and other acts against Internet users by people intent on causing harm. For the most part, these are attacks of opportunity. The attacker usually does not personally know his or her target and is only looking for the most gullible people. This is often referred to as "picking the low-hanging fruit." This section focuses on attacks against a targeted individual that can be categorized as either character-based or asset-based attacks. A character-based attack involves targeting a person with the goal of harm (emotionally, reputation, etc.). An asset-based attack targets the physical assets of a person (money, identity, possessions, etc.).

To counter the predominant focus of this book on asset-based attacks, this section discusses character-based attacks. Such an attack is aimed at a specific person and is often referred to as "cyber bullying" or "cyber stalking." Cyber bullying is a very real problem and, while it has some similarity to face-to-face bullying, the Internet has made bullying much easier to perform and harder to combat. Cyber bullying and, similarly, cyber stalking do not occur as isolated incidents and in reality happen in every town across America on a regular basis. As previously discussed, the Internet allows people to feel anonymous and to take on different personas. Before the Internet, bullies were typically characterized as strong, popular, or overaggressive persons. Now, behind the cloak of a keyboard and computer screen, virtually anyone can be a bully; likewise, anyone can be a victim. Before the Internet, a bully had to establish face-to-face contact with the victim, and only the people physically watching knew what happened to the victim. Today, the bully need not physically talk to the victim, and with online posting, everyone can "watch" the bullying. Before the Internet, a bully had limited access to the victim (in school, at the workplace, etc.). Today, the bully has unlimited access to the victim via email, chat, social networking, cell phone, texting, and so on.

Let us consider an example. Bullying Barney is a quiet kid who keeps to himself and for some reason does not like Victim Vince. Barney starts by posting rude and mean comments about Vince on several social networking sites. Other kids at school pick up on this and start to make their own comments about Vince. It does not take long for Vince to feel like a victim. Conversely, because of both his own actions and reactions of others, Barney is starting to feel important and powerful, which encourages him to say even nastier things. Barney continues to make false accusations about Vince and even goes so far as to create fake photos of Vince and post them online. It should be clear to anyone reading this that Barney has caused harm to Vince, but since this all occurs in cyberspace, it is often difficult for outsiders to notice. Unfortunately, such cases are often not brought to anyone's attention until significant damage has been done, or unfortunately, it is too late.

First it should be stated that nearly every state has laws that make cyber bullying illegal. Anyone who is the victim of cyber bullying should seek help from parents, law enforcement, school officials, police officers, counselors, or others. It is beyond the scope of the book to provide materials to help educate students about cyber bullying. Several websites provide excellent learning materials for students and adults (NetSmartz, Stop Cyberbullying, and NSTeens). They also provide information and videos to help educate students about other aspects of cyber safety (sexting, predators, etc.):

1. NetSmartz: http://www.netsmartz.org/Parents

2. Stop Cyberbullying: http://www.stopcyberbullying.org/index2.html

3. NSTeens: http://www.nsteens.org/

Cyber stalking is the online equivalent of physical stalking. Take the example of Dumped Duane, who was dating Alice. Duane and Alice were so deeply "in love" that they shared everything about their lives, including their passwords. One day, Alice told Duane that she did not want to see him anymore, which really upset Duane. In anger, Duane started to track Alice's every online movement. He would log in to her email account, read her emails, and follow her on social networking sites. When Alice started dating Bob, Duane became very jealous and upset. He logged in to her email account and started sending emails to Bob pretending to be Alice. He also used her Facebook account and posted harmful status information, all in an effort to cause Bob to dump Alice. What Duane did was illegal, and when Alice found out, she contacted local authorities, who were then able to trace the activity back to Duane. Much of this online stalking activity could have been prevented if Alice had never told Duane her password or at least had changed her password when they broke up.

This section outlined a couple of examples of character-based attacks. It is important for the reader to know that the same rules apply to cyberspace as to the physical world. If you or someone you know thinks they are becoming a victim, it is best to contact a trusted source or proper authorities immediately. Also, every child using the Internet should be made aware of these issues and should be taught what to do and what not to do if such situations arise. The next section provides a few more tips and technologies that can help.

12.9 IS THERE ANYTHING I CAN DO TO MAKE THE INTERNET A SAFER PLACE FOR MY CHILD?

For most children, the Internet is going to be an integral part of their childhood. While there are obvious benefits to allowing children to explore the Internet, there are also are many threats that parents should know about to provide a safe home-computing environment and safely educate their children. If you have younger kids using the Internet, there are several software programs that will help prevent kids from viewing websites with questionable content. It is also advisable to place the computer your child uses to access the Internet in a public area in the house. Creating an environment where kids feel safe talking to parents about what they encounter on the Internet enables parents to detect problems early and can provide educational moments. Remember, when children fall victim to online crimes, it is typically not their fault. Although older children might possess enough technical savvy to defeat filtering software, it is still effective to talk with them about both the good and the bad aspects of the Internet. One great way to start a conversation is to ask kids for help with something on the Internet (even if you know how to do it). Most kids love to show off what they know, and this can provide a great opportunity to discuss safety issues.

As kids get older and start to use social networking, it is often advised that a parent become his or her child's friend on social networking sites. In fact, it is often suggested that parents should not allow their children to be on such sites unless they become friends with their parents. Granted, kids can still choose to post information that their parents cannot see, but this will provide a way to somewhat keep in touch with the online interactions of a child. It also tends to keep both kids and parents from posting information that may be regretted.

The bottom line is that, while there are some technologies that might help provide kids with a measure of safety on the Internet, it really comes down to education and being respectful, cautious, and aware while on the Internet—the same practices parents teach their children about in the physical world.

BIBLIOGRAPHY

Baringer, W.E. 1971. *Lincoln's Rise to Power*. Boston, MA: Little, Brown & Co.

Daigle, K. 2012. Google, Facebook remove content on India's order. CBS News. http://www.cbsnews.com/8301-505250_162-57371786/google-facebook-remove-content-on-indias-order/ (accessed May 8, 2012).

Hoffman, J. 2011. States struggle with minors' sexting. *New York Times*. http://www.nytimes.com/2011/03/27/us/27sextinglaw.html (accessed May 8, 2012).

Humphries, M. 2011. HTC sticks a Facebook Button on ChaCha and Salsa smart-phones. Geek.com. http://www.geek.com/articles/mobile/htc-sticks-a-face-book-button-on-chacha-and-salsa-smartphones-20110215/ (accessed May 8, 2012).

Lewin, T. 2010. Rethinking sex offender laws for youth texting. *New York Times*. http://www.nytimes.com/2010/03/21/us/21sexting.html?pagewanted=all (accessed May 8, 2012).

National Conference of State Legislatures. 2012. State cyberstalking and cyberha-rassment laws. http://www.ncsl.org/issues-research/telecom/cyberstalking-and-cyberharassment-laws.aspx (accessed May 8, 2012).

Sengupta, S. 2012. Censoring of tweets sets off #outrage. *New York Times*. www.nytimes.com/2012/01/28/technology/when-twitter-blocks-tweets-its-out-rage.html?pagewanted=all (accessed May 8, 2012).

Stanglin, D. 2011. Girl's miscue on Facebook invitation draws 1,500 to her birthday party. *USA Today*. http://content.usatoday.com/communities/ondeadline/post/2011/06/girls-miscue-on-facebook-invitation-draws-1500-to-her-birthday-party-/1#.T6k12r8sFi4 (accessed May 8, 2012).

Case Studies

13.1 INTRODUCTION

Security concepts and principles are often best understood when presented in the context of real-life situations. In this chapter, to illustrate practical security best practices, many of the key topics discussed throughout the book are applied and presented as case studies related to situations you might typically encounter in your everyday use of computer security. Although these case studies are based on actual events, the fictitious characters of Alice and Bob have been cast into the star roles.

13.2 UNABLE TO REMOVE MALWARE: HELP!

Alice is using her computer and notices an unfamiliar application on the task bar that keeps displaying pop-up messages indicating that her computer is infected with 81 variants of malware. While the program appears to be antivirus software, Alice is well aware that it must be a rogue program and clearly not the antivirus software she installed on her computer. She suspects that it must be scareware (i.e., fake antivirus). To rid her computer of this malware, Alice updates her antivirus software to include the most recent virus signatures and performs a complete system scan of her hard drive for malware. At the conclusion of this scan, the antivirus software did not indicate the presence of new malware, but the rogue application on the task bar still continues to display unwanted messages.

The process of removing malware can be a very challenging endeavor, even for the security elite. For this reason, it is important to be proactive about one's security and actively practice the defense-in-depth strategy discussed in Chapter 6. Following this path will reduce the risk of contracting malware and help prevent one from needing to be reactive and experience the onerous task of attempting to remove malware from a computer. The purpose of this case study is not to provide a "how-to" guide on removing malware from a computer because this process is simply too complicated. The purpose of this case study is rather to discuss what are generally accepted as the four predominant options that might be chosen if one is faced with Alice's situation. The option that works best for you will greatly depend on your comfort level in performing the discussed tasks and the time, effort, and money you are willing to invest to rid your computer of malware.

For Alice, the most common method to remove malware from her computer is to rely on her chosen antivirus software. However, as previously described, situations can arise in which antivirus software, even if it has the most current virus signatures, is unable to detect and remove all malware on a computer. In this situation, the first option for Alice is simply to deactivate or uninstall her current antivirus software and try another antivirus program in the hope that the alternative option can detect the malware. This process can be repeated until the malware is removed. There are many free versions of antivirus software that Alice can choose from, including AVG Free Antivirus, avast! Free Antivirus, Microsoft Security Essentials, Sophos Free Antivirus, Malwarebytes Free Anti-malware, Avira Free Antivirus, and others. The madness behind this method lies in the hope that, although Alice's antivirus software did not contain the correct signature for the malware infecting her computer, another security software vendor might have the needed signature. It should be noted that installing two antivirus software programs simultaneously does not necessarily double the protection, but instead often the two programs conflict or decrease overall computer performance. This is why it is best for Alice to deactivate or uninstall her current antivirus program before installing another.

If Alice is unable or not willing to make the effort to remove the malware from her computer, she has a second option to employ a commercial technology service, perhaps a local computer store, to perform the malware removal on her behalf and at a cost. Although these services may have experienced and highly skilled technicians, there are no absolute guarantees that such services can remove the malware from Alice's computer. Furthermore, Alice should be aware that the computer technician will have full access to all of her files and data, a serious privacy concern.

A third option is for Alice to attempt to restore her computing environment from a previously known good state by means of a system image backup or system restore (Chapter 6). This option requires that Alice perform a regular backup of her computer. While in certain circumstances this method can be effective when dealing with a malware infection, the major risk when performing this task is dealing with potentially corrupt or "dirty" backups. For instance, if Alice restores her computer to a previous state, let us say 1 week earlier, but the malware infection occurred 2 weeks earlier, Alice has not solved the problem. Even if Alice restores to a previously known good state, but the malware-infested document is also contained in the backup, by reopening or installing the malware-infested document Alice can infect her computer again. Remember that a malware-infested document is not directly harmful unless it is opened or executed. If Alice is concerned about a dirty backup, she can always scan the backup drive with her antivirus software, or if Alice is quite certain which file caused the malware infection, Alice can also manually delete that file from the backup drive.

The fourth option for Alice to rid her computer of malware is simply to erase the computer's hard drive and reload the computer's operating system, drivers, and applications. Although this is the most intrusive of the four options, it also represents the most dependable way to ensure that the malware has been removed from Alice's computer. This is yet another situation in which it is crucial to create backups of one's most-valued data. During this process of reformatting the hard drive, both the legitimate software as well as the malicious software will be completely erased from Alice's hard drive. Before one decides on this option, it must be recognized that the process of rebuilding a computer in this fashion can be quite time consuming and will often require use of an operating system installation CD, a valid product key, and reinstallation of both application software and hardware driver software.

As one can gather from discussing the options described, removing malware from a computer is often neither a straightforward nor a desirable task. Furthermore, it is important to note that the removal of malware does not necessarily prevent future occurrences of the same or new malware. If one resorts to the same computing habits that resulted in contracting malware in the first place, one runs the risk of continually being in the predicament of either using a malware-infested computer or having to remove malware constantly. Despite all the advances in technology and computer security, in general there exists no quick, reliable, and straightforward way to remove malware. As a result, it is much more practical to be proactive about security by installing software patches when they become available, routinely updating antivirus signatures, backing up data, and exhibiting the computer security best practices highlighted in this book.

13.3 SECURELY HANDLING SUSPICIOUS EMAIL ATTACHMENTS

As has been presented many times throughout the book, attackers often use emails to target their victims. Whether through a cunning message attempting to induce the user to reply to the email, to click on a hyperlink, or to open an attachment, such attacks have been and continue to be devastatingly effective. When opening an email, there are best practices that should be followed to prevent the loss of personal information, a malware infection, or both. In the situation under discussion, Bob receives a suspicious email (Figure 13.1), supposedly from the Internal Revenue Service (IRS), that contains an attachment asking Bob to disclose a great deal of information. What should Bob do?

Before taking any action, even that of opening the email, Bob should first ask himself whether he knows the sender of the email or is expecting an email message from that sender. If the answer is no, and if the email appears at all suspicious, Bob should simply delete the email without opening it. In this case, an unsolicited email from the IRS stating in capital letters "TAX EXEMPTION NOTIFICATION" should raise red flags for Bob and prompt the action of deleting the email. If, on the other hand, the sender email address or subject content appear to be familiar, before opening the email Bob should ask himself the following questions: (1) Am I expecting this email? (2) Could this email be malicious? By asking himself these questions, Bob will be in a critical frame of mind before taking any further action with respect to the email. Even if the email has been sent to Bob by a family member, a friend, a coworker, or an acquaintance, Bob should not let his guard down. Many of the most successful computer worms and viruses have been permitted to spread due to the trust that people place in emails and attachments apparently received from people they may know and trust.

Phishing emails (Figure 13.1) often contain telltale signs that they are malicious in nature, and Bob could potentially use these clues to determine the correct course of action when dealing with suspicious emails. Despite the highly suspicious claim in the email shown in Figure 13.1, at first glance it appears legitimate. Although phishing emails are often brief

Subject:TAX EXEMPTION NOTIFICATION
Date:Thu, 11 Aug 2011 15:08:17 -0700
From:
Reply-To:
To:

Internal Revenue Service
United States Department of the Treasury

Sir/Madam,
Our records indicate that you are a Non-resident. As a result you are exempted from United States of America Tax reporting and withholdings on interest paid to you on your account and other financial benefits. To protect your exemption from tax on your account and other financial benefits, you need to recertify your exemption status and enable us confirm your records with us.

Therefore, you are to authenticate the following by completing form W-4100B2 and return to us as soon as possible through fax numbers no +

When completing form W-4100B2, please follow the steps below:

1. We need you to provide your permanent address if different from the current mailing address.

2. You must indicate as a Non-US resident, the country you are residing, to support your non-resident status and if your bank or other financial institutions you are dealing with has a US address for mailing purposes.

3. If any joint account holder is now a US resident or citizen, or in any way subject to US tax reporting laws: please check the box in this section.

4. Please complete 1 through 19 and have all account holder/s (if more than one account holder) sign and date the form separately and fax to the above-mentioned fax numbers.

Please complete Form W-4100B2 (attached) and return to us with one week from the receipt of this letter by faxing it, to enable us confirm your records immediately. If your records are not confirmed on time, you will lose your Non-resident status tax exempt benefits and your account or any other financial benefits will be subject to US tax reporting and back up withholding*
*If back up withholding applies, we are required to withhold 30% of the interest/benefits paid to you.

We appreciate your cooperation in helping us protect your exempt status and also confirm our records.
Sincerely,
Isabella Charlotte,
IRS Public Relations

FORM W-8BEN.doc
50K View Download

FIGURE 13.1 Phishing email with attachment.

in content and may contain odd text formatting, misspelled words, and poor grammar, the authors of this suspected phishing email have invested a higher level of effort to make the email appear legitimate than most scammers, even including an IRS image as an email header. In this case, Bob must consider the context of the email to make an educated decision as to how to proceed.

Bob, born and raised in Iowa, is quite confident that he is not a "Non-resident" as the email claims. Furthermore, Bob is well aware that the IRS or any corporation or bank will never solicit his personal information via email. Finally, Bob may ask himself the question, "Could this email be malicious?" By considering the context of the message under a critical lens, Bob can be extremely confident that the email message is indeed malicious and that he should not engage in any further interaction with it, like clicking on potential hyperlinks or opening attachments.

For the remainder of the case study, let us pretend that Bob was unable to determine if the email was legitimate. To further investigate its content, Bob notices that the email in Figure 13.1 contains a word-processing attachment labeled "FORM W-8BEN.doc." Although it may be tempting for Bob to open this document and discover its contents, if he is not expecting such a document from the sending email address he should treat the attachment as malicious. Because he knows that he could possibly contract a malware infection by simply opening the email attachment (Chapter 5), Bob should first contact the email sender by phone to verify the authenticity of the attachment before performing an action. If the email was sent from someone unknown, Bob should not trust any phone numbers provided in the email and seek out the proper phone number by other means. One call to the actual IRS, or any corporation or bank for that matter, describing the nature and content of the email will reveal to Bob if he has received a phishing email. Unless the content of the email is expected or can be verified, Bob's safest course of action is to simply not open the email attachment.

In case Bob is in a pickle because he believes he needs to open the email attachment and does not have time to verify the origin of an email, there is a less-secure process that Bob can follow. Bob can download the file to his desktop computing environment and perform an antivirus scan on the suspect document. Remember that the act of downloading a file itself will not result in a malware infection since a malware infection occurs only when the file is opened and the computer executes its malicious lines of code. To assist Bob in this process, many antivirus programs allow for scanning of a single file. Thus, before opening the document, Bob can scan the suspicious email attachment for known malware. It would also be to Bob's advantage in this situation to have his operating system and applications (especially the application that is to open the document) properly updated and patched. If the file is indeed infected with malware undetectable by the antivirus software and if Bob's computer has installed the proper patches for the vulnerabilities the malware is attempting to exploit, Bob has effectively thwarted the immediate threat of contracting malware.

From this case study, the importance of the defense-in-depth security strategy can be seen. If Bob did not know attackers' methods for using emails to target victims and how to handle such emails, how to effectively use antivirus software to his advantage, and the importance of keeping a properly updated and patched computing environment, Bob's name could be added to the long list of those victimized by phishing emails.

13.4 RECOVERING FROM A PHISHING ATTACK

One morning, in a rush to get out of the house and to work on time, Bob opens and quickly reads the email shown in Figure 13.2. He wants to quickly resolve this security alert before he leaves for work, so he proceeds to "Click here to resolve the problem" and is taken to a website that is an exact replica of his bank's website. Bob attempts to log in to his bank account multiple times but is unsuccessful in achieving access. Still in a hurry, and increasingly frustrated, Bob closes his laptop, throws it in his bag, and decides to deal with the issue at a later time. On his subway ride to work, Bob realizes that he fell for a phishing scam hook, line, and sinker. What should Bob do now?

This case study illustrates just one example of how phishing scams can play out. Sometimes, the victim realizes the mistake immediately and at other times the victim may be completely fooled. In Bob's situation, his first course of action should be to change the password to his bank account immediately. If Bob also uses the same username and password for other online accounts, he should change those passwords as well. As a second step, Bob should alert his bank at once and discuss his options with the bank's fraud division on how to proceed given his specific circumstance.

FIGURE 13.2   Classic phishing email.

Finally, Bob should consult the Federal Trade Commission's (FTC's) Fighting Back against Identity Theft website (http://www.ftc.gov/bcp/edu/microsites/idtheft/index.html). This website provides a wealth of information, helping Bob to "learn more about identity theft," what to do "if your information may have been stolen, but may or may not have been used by an identity thief," and how to proceed "if your information has been stolen and used by an identity thief."

In addition to dealing with problems like Bob encountered, the FTC website provides information for a much broader range of identity theft issues. Remember, identity theft is not always the result of a victim's error, as was the case with Bob. Hackers are increasingly breaching computer systems and flooding underground markets with information used for identity theft. Being aware that such attacks happen regularly with real consequences and knowing how to proceed if one suspects that his or her identity has been stolen are important steps in helping to securely navigate in the digital age.

13.5 EMAIL ACCOUNT HACKED? NOW WHAT?

Alice receives a phone call from her friend Carole informing her that she has received the suspicious email (shown in Figure 13.3) from Alice's email account. Both Alice and Carole suspect that Alice's email account has been compromised and used by a spammer. On further examination of her email account, Alice notices that the same email was sent not only to Carole, but also to all her contacts as well as many other email addresses that she does not recognize. How did this happen, and what should Alice do?

There are a number of indications that an online account such as a social networking or email account may have been compromised (i.e., the username and password has been discovered by an unauthorized source). Often, the most telling sign that an attacker has gained access to an account is through the discovery of an abundance of unauthorized wall posts or outgoing messages from an account—just as Alice noticed. In other

show details Aug 27   ↰ Reply ▾

I know what are to do to improve your health!.. http://www.os-bc   lybhot=21la7

↰ Reply   ↰ Reply to all   → Forward

FIGURE 13.3   Suspicious spam/phishing email.

situations, determining whether a hacker or an ex-boyfriend (Dumped Duane, for example) has accessed Alice's account is not as obvious. If Alice is at all suspicious that an online account has been compromised, her first action should be to change her password immediately using a trusted and secure computer—one void of malware (i.e., a key-logger). It may well be that the secrecy of Alice's password was compromised through a key-logger on her primary computer, and changing a password on that computer and continuing to use it does little to thwart the attacker. At this point, Alice should also change passwords to any other accounts that share the compromised password or that she may have accessed while using the potentially infected computer. Again, this illustrates why one should not reuse the same password across multiple websites: If one account becomes compromised, then all accounts with the same login credentials could also be compromised. Once Alice has successfully changed her password using the secure computer, her second task is to pinpoint the method through which her password may have been stolen. Chapter 3 describes many of the threats faced by passwords and best preventive practices for dealing with such problems. If key-logging malware is the suspected culprit, it is important that Alice retrieves the most current signatures for her antivirus software and performs a complete system scan.

If her account has been compromised and the attacker has changed Alice's password, effectively locking her out of her own account, additional measures are needed. Since this is not an uncommon occurrence, many websites have procedures in place to deal with this very issue. Figure 13.4 illustrates the instructions given to a Hotmail user who "think[s] someone else is using my Windows Live ID." These instructions can often be found by clicking the "Forgot your password?" option, usually found in close proximity to the screen area used for username and password entry. In

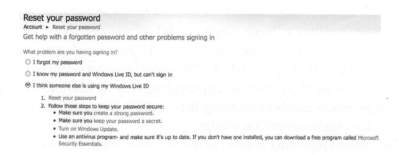

FIGURE 13.4 Password recovery options.

this scenario, some websites require the user to answer a security question or contact customer service to reset a password, while others may send a new password to an account's backup email address. Although procedures may differ, Alice can be rest assured that there are most likely procedures in place to deal with this specific issue.

13.6 SMART PHONES AND MALWARE

Bob recently purchased a smart phone. While driving home from work one day, he hears on the radio that smart phones, like personal computers, are vulnerable to malware and phishing attacks. Bob is curious: Do malware and phishing attacks really exist for smart phones? If so, how can he go about protecting the integrity of his phone and the confidentiality of his personal information?

Cell phones and smart phones are more than just phones; they are actually computers with phone-calling capabilities. When examined closely, many cell phones can be found to have a CPU (central processing unit), memory, permanent storage, an operating system, input/output ports, a monitor, a keyboard, wireless Internet cards, and so on, so it should come as no surprise that smart phones (and tablet computers) suffer from many of the same security threats as desktop and laptop computers. As with traditional computers, the two most significant threats for cell phone users are malware and phishing. For the sake of brevity, this case study focuses primarily on cell phone use, but the same threats and security best practices also apply to tablet computers.

While the volume and diversity of malware seeking to compromise cell phones is nowhere near that focusing on traditional computers, malware for cell phones is indeed a real threat of increasing significance. The primary means for malware to adversely affect cell phones is through the downloading of Trojan horses—seemingly legitimate cell phone applications (i.e., apps) containing embedded malware. While the victim may think he or she is installing a "Super Ringtone Maker" app, the person may also be installing malware. Consequences of smart phone malware infection range broadly all the way from theft of personal information stored on the phone (phone number, contacts, key-logging, etc.) to sending text messages to premium numbers, resulting in incurring financial consequences without the phone owner's knowledge.

The decision regarding whether to install an application on a cell phone is ultimately in the hands of the cell phone user. To avoid downloading a malicious app, stick to familiar applications with positive reputations and only download apps from well-known app marketplaces (i.e., Android Marketplace, Apple App Store). Although a more reputable source, even well-known app stores have been known to distribute malware-infested applications. If you are not familiar with an application, carefully research it before downloading it on your phone. Also, beware of malvertising ads that attempt to trick cell phone users into installing malicious applications. As a security best practice, it is best not to install unsolicited applications on your cell phone. Last, like computers, cell phones are also susceptible to drive-by downloads in which the simple act of viewing a malicious webpage is enough to install malware on a cell phone.

As is the case with desktop or laptop computers, it is good security practice to install antivirus software on your cell phone, especially if you frequently download apps. Antivirus software for cell phones has been available for some time, and many software vendors offering antivirus software for personal computers, such as AVG, Symantec, and McAfee, also make antivirus software for cell phones—sometimes even offering free antivirus apps. The same limitations discussed in Chapter 6 for personal computer antivirus protection apply to cell phone antivirus software as well; namely, antivirus software cannot detect a specific type of malware if it does not have the corresponding signature.

Regardless of the cell phone service provider, cell phone model, or cell phone OS (operating system), cell phone users are as susceptible to phishing attacks in the same way as laptop-toting computer users. If a cell phone can open an email or text message or display a website, its user is susceptible to phishing attacks. To an attacker, it does not matter whether a victim errantly enters a username and password on a smart phone or on a desktop computer; the end result is the same. Also, as discussed in Chapter 11, cell phone users may also be susceptible to SMiShing attacks, similar to phishing attacks usually carried out via email, but done in the cell phone case via text messages. While surfing the web or texting on your cell phone, the same best practices discussed throughout this book, especially in Chapter 11, apply. Do not submit information to a website after clicking on a hyperlink in an email message and do not reply to emails or text messages soliciting your personal or private information.

As cell phones and smart phones grow in popularity, so will the attacks targeting these devices. Appendix A (Reading List) provides websites that can help you stay current on the latest cell phone security trends.

13.7 HEY! YOU! GET OFF MY WIRELESS NETWORK

If Bob is at all suspicious that his neighbor or someone else within the vicinity of his wireless router is piggybacking on his wireless network, there are a number of steps Bob can take to ensure that this action ceases. The majority of content appropriate to this specific case study is found in Chapter 9, Wireless Internet Security.

First and foremost, if Bob has not already enabled the wireless security features on his wireless router, he should do so. Enabling the security features on a wireless router requires that each user wanting to access the network must first provide authentication credentials to the router by supplying a preestablished password. If Bob suspects that the unauthorized piggybacker knows his router's password, Bob should immediately reset the password to a strong new password and subsequently keep that password a secret. To prevent unauthorized users from attempting to guess the wireless network password, Bob should change his router's SSID (Service Set Identifier; i.e., network name) and then disable it from being broadcast. This action would make Bob's wireless network virtually invisible to all but the most determined of perpetrators.

In addition to the security measures discussed, most wireless networks provide the capability for the owner and network administrator—in this case Bob—to view a list of computers currently accessing his wireless network. To access this feature, Bob must first be connected to his wireless network and then log in to the wireless router's administrative controls. Directions for performing this task typically come included with the wireless router or are available from its manufacturer's website. Each wireless router is slightly different; thus, the controls and formatting shown in the following illustration may vary among particular devices. As shown in Figure 13.5, Bob's wireless router presents a list of computers currently connected to his wireless router. These computers are not listed by their owner's names but instead by each individual computer's wireless network card's MAC (Media Access Control) address, a unique address given to each networking hardware device (Chapter 9). Bob, knowing that his

Wireless Devices (Wireless intruders also show up here)

#	IP Address	MAC Address	Device Name
1	192.168.1.5	1C:65:9D:98:4E:61	BOBS-COMPUTER
2	192.168.1.4	1C:65:9D:98:4D:88	ALICE-LAPTOP
3	192.168.1.6	1C:65:9D:98:50:C6	EVES-LAPTOP

FIGURE 13.5 Wireless router client list.

own computer's MAC address is 1C:65:9D:98:4E:61 and that Alice's MAC address is 1C:65:9D:98:4D:88, has confirmed his suspicion that another computer (MAC address 1C:65:9D:98:50:C6) is connected to his wireless network. As discussed in Chapter 9, Bob can further secure his network by enabling the MAC address-filtering feature on his wireless router.

13.8 BAD BREAKUP? SEVER YOUR DIGITAL TIES

Although it is not a good idea to share one's passwords with anyone, people in relationships sometimes share their passwords with significant others. In this case study, Alice and Bob's relationship comes to a dramatic end, and Alice is worried about how much information Bob knows about her online accounts and passwords. As a rule of thumb, it is good security practice for Alice (and Bob) to change their passwords after the end of a relationship. Jealous or revengeful lovers have been known to go to great lengths to make their ex's lives miserable after breakups. This may include spying on one's emails or social networking accounts, sending messages from an ex's online accounts, or even changing an ex's password to lock the ex out of his or her account. In one specific example, an ex-boyfriend even went so far so as to decline a job offer—one his girlfriend never knew she received—on behalf of his girlfriend. Even if Alice does not think Bob knows her passwords, there is a possibility that Alice's online account information may have been saved by the web browser on Bob's computer or that Bob knows enough information about Alice to effectively guess her passwords or answers to her security questions. For these reasons and more, it is best for Alice to change her passwords and security questions after the end of her relationship with Bob (also see Chapter 12).

After a breakup, if either Alice or Bob is tempted to engage in any type of harassment behavior using text messaging, emails, or social networks, he or she should be advised that such activities are considered criminal, and there are laws specifically addressing such issues. Just because communications may take place in the virtual world does not mean they are not punishable in the physical world. If either Alice or Bob feels they are being harassed, he or she should contact the local law enforcement agency immediately.

13.9 "DISPLAY IMAGES BELOW"? THE MEANING BEHIND THE QUESTION

Email clients often prevent the automatic display of pictures embedded in an email to protect users' privacy (Figure 13.6). Spammers will often send emails out to hordes of email addresses—not knowing if the email

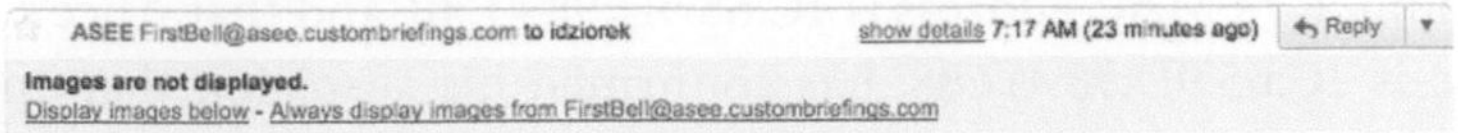

> ASEE FirstBell@asee.custombriefings.com to idziorek   show details 7:17 AM (23 minutes ago)   ↩ Reply ▾
>
> **Images are not displayed.**
> Display images below - Always display images from FirstBell@asee.custombriefings.com

FIGURE 13.6   Email client preventing the displaying of email images.

addresses are valid or if each of the individual email accounts is active. Because the action of opening an email does not indicate back to a spammer that an email account is valid or that a user has actively opened an email—the type of situation a spammer is looking for—the spammer must use some other method to determine whether their emails have been viewed. To accomplish this, spammers will sometimes embed a picture in an email. For Alice to be able to view the pictures in her email client, Alice must first download the pictures from the sender's server by clicking on "Display images below" in Figure 13.6. This action of requesting pictures to be displayed in the email indicates to a spammer that Alice did indeed open the spam email. By blocking emails from automatically requesting images, email clients protect their users' privacy. In this case, Alice can "opt out" of the most private state by choosing to display pictures from presumably trustworthy senders.

Legitimate companies may also track email views through requested images in emails to help the company compile statistics relating to the effectiveness of their ads, coupons, or newsletters. Furthermore, the inclusion of an image in an email does not necessarily mean that the email view is being tracked. Many emails simply contain images for the sake of presenting a more visually appealing and informative message. As a result, not all emails containing pictures are malicious in nature, and the fact that one chooses to display images below is not always a hazardous action. For this reason, there may be an option to "Always display images from" a particular email sender. This allows the user to place trust in an email sender (i.e., a university, work, etc.) and not be burdened by frequently having to manually display images for each email received from the trusted source. This is yet another example of how many technological features on the Internet can be used for both good and bad.

13.10 PHISHING EMAIL FORENSICS

As discussed in Chapter 4 (Email), attackers can spoof the sender address of emails, enabling the attacker to craft emails appearing to originate from a trusted entity (i.e., a bank). Alice receives the email shown in Figure 13.7 and is highly suspicious of its contents. The first clue for Alice should be that

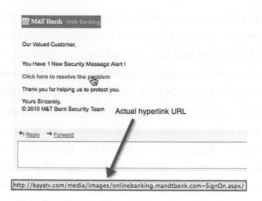

FIGURE 13.7   Phishing email.

legitimate businesses customarily do not send emails asking for account information. Furthermore, Alice may get similar messages from banks or corporations with whom she does not do business—a dead giveaway that the email is a scam. However, there is a chance that Alice will receive a message claiming to be from a bank or organization with which she does business. On the surface, the email message Alice has received does not appear overly suspicious and even contains her bank's real logo, suggesting authenticity. The text, while short, contains no obvious spelling, grammatical, or formatting errors. Despite this, Alice suspects that the email is a phishing attack and wants to confirm her suspicions. One approach for Alice is to call her bank and talk to it directly about the email's contents. Most banks have specialists who deal with these types of phishing schemes and would be interested in knowing of such emails and happy to provide Alice with the proper guidance—basically, delete the email without interacting with it. In addition, Alice can play the role of a digital detective by performing digital forensics to confirm her own suspicions.

Another way Alice can tell whether the email is authentic is to look at the real domain name address of the web link provided (Chapter 11). In this case, the URL (Uniform Resource Locator) is http://kayatv.com/media/images/onlinebanking.mandtbank.com=SignOn.aspx/, with a domain name of kayatv.com, not that of Alice's bank. Note how cleverly the file path in the URL is crafted (media/images/onlinebanking.mandtbank.com) to make it look very close to the real URL for Alice's bank (https://onlinebanking.mandtbank.com). Alice should realize from this misleading hyperlink that the email is not authentic, so she should not click on the hyperlink and should immediately delete the email.

As discussed in Chapter 4, while Alice's email client (the User Agent) will usually display only a small part of the actual email header, the email itself does contain the full header, and this information can be used to discover the true sender of the email. Remember that the email system—each individual Message Transfer Agent (MTA)—appends information to the email message (i.e., headers) to indicate from where it was received and to where the email is to be sent next. To interpret the original MTA header attached to the email, Alice must first inspect the entire contents, not just the displayed message of the email. Each email client reveals the entire content of an email slightly differently. In Alice's case, to reveal the headers of a specific email, she selects the "Show Original" option from her email's option menu as shown in Figure 13.8. Revealing the original email message provides a very cryptic text-based version of the email message—much different from what Alice is accustomed to seeing when viewing an email (Figure 13.9). The top of the email in Figure 13.9 contains the header information for the email, including the sender MTA header.

As seen in Figure 13.9, the email headers show the full path the email took from sender (phisher) to receiver (Alice). The first part of the email is the header from the last MTA (the receiver MTA). The next MTA header entry comes from the MTA that forwarded the email from the original sender. Note that this domain name is not mtb.com as the From field in the email suggests. Instead of the correct domain name of her bank (i.e., mtb.com), the actual domain of the email author is shown to be kimsurfi.com; thus, Alice has confirmed her suspicions that this email is not authentic and is indeed a phishing email.

Now, let us follow this example a little further and discover what would happen if Alice fell for the phishing message. If Alice clicks on the link, as requested by the email, her email client may ask her if she really wants

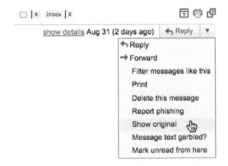

FIGURE 13.8 Reveal email header information.

```
Return-Path: <anonymous@ks355778.kimsufi.com>
Received: from despam-3.iastate.edu (despam-3.iastate.edu [129.186.140.8])
        by vulcan.ece.iastate.edu (8.13.8/8.13.8) with ESMTP id p8CGCJc1014663    Header 1
        for <                        >; Mon, 12 Sep 2011 11:12:20 -0500
Received: from ks355778.kimsufi.com (ks355778.kimsufi.com [91.121.138.6])
        by despam-3.iastate.edu (8.14.4/8.12.4) with ESMTP id p8CGCI77029380 ,     Header 2
        for <                      >; Mon, 12 Sep 2011 11:12:18 -0500
Received: (qmail 24593 invoked by uid 1016); 12 Sep 2011 15:38:35 -0000
Date: 12 Sep 2011 15:38:35 -0000                                      MTA used by Phisher
Message-ID: <20110912153835.24592.qmail@ks355778.kimsufi.com>
To:                                 ◀──────────────────────────────  Alice's email address
Subject: M&T Bank : You Have (1) Important Message2
From: M&T Web Banking <webbanking@mtb.com> ◀───────────── Fake return address
Reply-To:
MIME-Version: 1.0
Content-Type: text/html
Content-Transfer-Encoding: 8bit
X-PMX-Version: 5.6.1.2065439, Antispam-Engine: 2.7.2.376379, Antispam-Data: 2011.9.12.160015
X-Perlmx-Spam: Gauge=XXXXXIIIIIII, Probability=57%, Report='
 REPLY_TO_EMPTY 1.699, PHISH_PHRASE_X2 1.5, URI_HOSTNAME_CONTAINS_EQUALS 1, CTYPE_JUST_HTML 0.848
```

FIGURE 13.9   Email headers.

to perform this action since it may result in traveling to a malicious web-page. Many email clients attempt in this way to warn their users before performing a potentially malicious action. If Alice chooses to ignore that warning, she may encounter still another similar warning from her web browser. In this case, the action of actually clicking on the hyperlink in Figure 13.8 (by one of the authors: please do not try this at home) resulted in the display shown in Figure 13.10 on the author's web browser screen. This message was generated by the web browser after first checking to see whether the website was a forgery before allowing the user to view it. This is an example of proactive security in which the user is required to opt out of the most secure state if for some reason he or she wants to ignore the warning and travel to the potentially malicious website. While both email clients and web browsers seek to prevent their users from traveling to phishing websites, there are no guarantees that all bad websites will be reported and blocked in a similar manner.

FIGURE 13.10   Web forgery message.

If Alice does not receive any type of warning or chooses to ignore the warnings she receives, by clicking on the hyperlink Alice would probably be directed to a website with an appearance virtually identical to that of her bank's real website. The fake website and real website messages are shown in Figures 13.11 and 13.12, respectively. As you can see, the phishing website is almost a carbon copy of the original, and it is very difficult to distinguish between the two. Of course, if Alice were to try to log in to her bank account on the fake website using her user ID and password, that information could be captured by the fake website and sent directly to the attacker, and her real bank account could thereby be compromised.

13.11 IT'S ON THE INTERNET, SO IT MUST BE TRUE

The Internet contains a wealth of knowledge that is easily accessible with just a few mouse clicks or keystrokes. This ease of access does not imply that, just because something is available via the Internet it is open for anyone to use as they please. People often have a tendency to perceive their actions on computers and particularly on the Internet differently from those for similar situations in the physical world; however, when it comes to usage of information posted on the Internet, there are not many differences between acceptable actions in the real world and those in cyberspace.

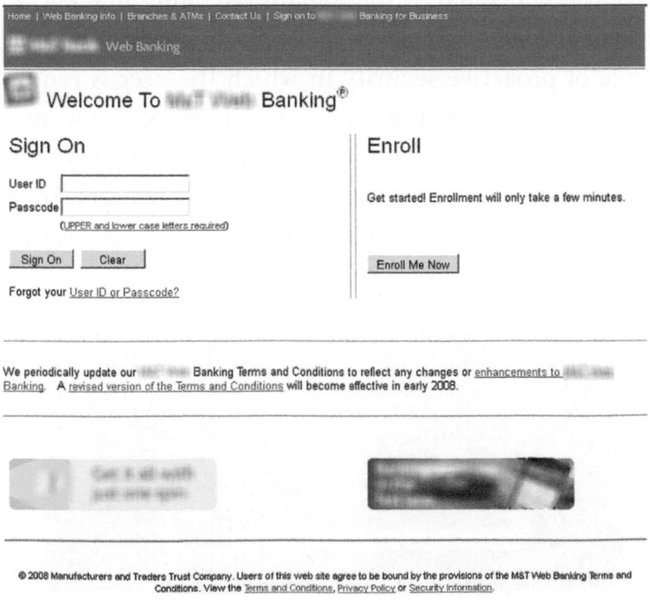

FIGURE 13.11   Fake banking website.

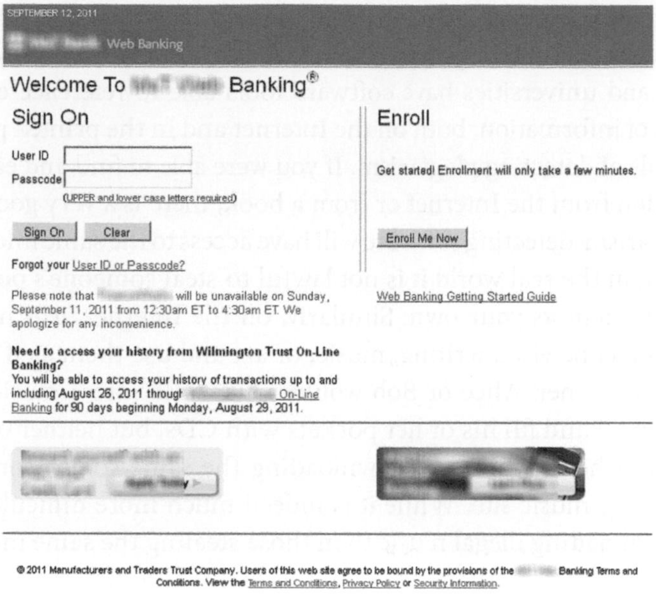

FIGURE 13.12   Real banking website.

Students like Alice and Bob should also be well aware that just because content is posted on the Internet this does not mean that it is either truthful or complete. Anyone can post information on the Internet, and with the possible exception of libelous information, the author can represent it in any way he or she chooses, even if it is clearly misleading or incorrect. Furthermore, much of the content on the web does not go through any type of formal vetting or editing process, and thus belief in and proper usage of such information should be only at the user's discretion. The simple fact that something is viewable on the Internet does not deem it as coming from a trustworthy, accurate, or respectable source.

Even if Bob may find information on the Internet that he believes to be truthful, that information is not Bob's to use in any way he sees fit. For example, if Alice posts a paper describing her research in cell biology, Bob cannot rightfully copy this work and submit it as his own research—that would be plagiarism. To properly use the information, Bob can reference Alice's work using a proper citation, but if proper reference to the original work is lacking, Bob will run the risk of being brought up on charges of academic dishonesty. Similarly, if Bob is writing a physics lab report and is required to explain the principles of electrical current, it is not acceptable for Bob to copy and paste information from Wikipedia's website and try to pass it off as his own. Once again, Bob must properly paraphrase or quote the work and provide a proper citation. Students beware: Many schools, colleges, and universities have software tools able to reference enormous amounts of information, both on the Internet and in the printed press, and are capable of detecting plagiarism. If you were able to find and easily copy information from the Internet or from a book, there is a very good chance that plagiarism-detecting software will have access to the same information.

Finally, in the real world it is not lawful to steal someone's possessions and claim them as your own. Similarly, on the Internet, it is not lawful to steal someone else's writing, music, or art and use them as if you were the rightful owner. Alice or Bob would never walk into a music store in the local mall and fill his or her pockets with CDs, but neither one might bat an eye when it comes to downloading the same songs from a peer-to-peer (P2P) music site. While it is indeed much more difficult to catch those downloading illegal music than those stealing the same music from a store, this does not mean the action is right, and just because pirated content is posted on the web does not make it legally usable.

13.12 BUYING AND SELLING ONLINE

Many different types of online marketplaces exist on the Internet, and users can buy and sell items from them, often from the comfort of their homes. While community-based marketplaces are certainly not new, the ease and low cost of entry to engaging in online marketplaces encourage common and widespread interaction with them. Two types of marketplaces are typically used to sell items online. The first is an online marketplace (i.e., eBay, Amazon Marketplace), which allows people to pseudoanonymously buy and sell items. Money is exchanged through a trusted third party (i.e., PayPal or credit card), and the seller typically mails the item directly to the buyer. The second type of online marketplace uses a method similar to placing an ad in the newspaper (i.e., Craigslist). This type of marketplace typically employs a website to facilitate communication between buyers and sellers. Differently from websites like eBay, the exchange of merchandise and money is managed directly between the buyer and seller and often done in person. As with most things in life, with the good comes the bad. When selling her personal belongings online, Alice should observe the same security best practices as if she were putting an ad in the Sunday paper.

When selling items online, the main security issues for Alice involve the exchange of money for merchandise and the revelation of personal or private information. As specified on eBay's Security Center website (http://pages.ebay.com/securitycenter/index.html), the predominant threats when shopping include phishing and fraud. Just like phishing emails that claim to be from your bank, there are many types of phishing emails targeting the credentials of online buyers and sellers. It is safe to assume that when money is exchanged on the Internet, phishing emails are sure to follow. Furthermore, when selling an item online, Alice should never send the merchandise to a buyer before the item is paid for and the buyer's check clears the bank. In addition, Alice should never reveal her bank account number, Social Security number, or any similar private information to complete a transaction. PayPal and other trusted third-party services enable Alice to sell items securely and without revealing any sensitive information during an exchange of funds with the buyer.

For websites like Craigslist, it is asserted that 99% of scams can be avoided by dealing only with people who Alice can meet in person (please see Craigslist's safety website: http://www.craigslist.org/about/scams). While Alice can post her items for sale under the cloak of anonymity, if Alice is to indeed sell her item to a local buyer, at some point in time Alice must reveal her name or a pseudonym and, potentially, her phone number or email address; this is no different from placing an ad in the paper. When meeting a buyer for the first time, it is suggested that Alice meet in a public place and avoid inviting strangers to her home. If Alice observes the same precautions when selling items online as she would when placing an ad in the Sunday paper, she can significantly decrease her chances of becoming a victim. To find more information, please visit eBay's Security Center and Craigslist's safety website, as previously referenced, as they contain a wealth of knowledge about specific threats and security best practices.

BIBLIOGRAPHY

Constantin, L. 2012. Android malware writers exploit Instagram craze to distribute SMS Trojan horse. *PCWorld*. http://www.pcworld.com/businesscenter/article/254078/android_malware_writers_exploit_instagram_craze_to_distribute_sms_trojan_horse.html (accessed May 8, 2012).

Craigslist. 2012. Scams. http://www.craigslist.org/about/scams (accessed May 17, 2012).

eBay. 2012. Stay safe on eBay. http://pages.ebay.com/securitycenter/index.html (accessed May 17, 2012).

Federal Trade Commission. 2012. Identity theft. Federal Trade Commission. http://www.ftc.gov/bcp/edu/microsites/idtheft/index.html (accessed May 8, 2012).

Kessler, T. 2011. How to manage malware in OS X backups. CNET. http://reviews.
cnet.com/8301-13727_7-20064035-263.html (accessed May 8, 2012).

Kirk, J. 2012. For the first time, hacked websites deliver android malware. CIO.
http://www.cio.com/article/705549/For_the_First_Time_Hacked_Websites
_Deliver_Android_Malware (accessed May 8, 2012).

Rubenking, N.J. 2012. The best free antivirus of 2012. *PC Magazine*. http://www.
pcmag.com/article2/0,2817,2388652,00.asp (accessed May 8, 2012).

Tapellni, D.L. 2012. Malware on mobile devices jumps 155 percent since last year.
Consumer Reports. http://news.consumerreports.org/electronics/2012/02/
malware-on-mobile-devices-jumps-155-percent-since-last-year.html
(accessed May 8, 2012).

Tynan, D. 2011. Mobile malware epidemic looms. *PCWorld*. http://www.pcworld.
com/article/244346/mobile_malware_epidemic_looms.html (accessed May
8, 2012).

CHAPTER 14

Moving Forward with Security and Book Summary

14.1 INTRODUCTION

Even though you have nearly completed this book, your journey into the world of practical computer security is not over; in fact, it has only begun. The objective of this book was not to be the end-all of computer security literacy texts, but instead a resource to help you go forth and perform computer security best practices with confidence, to discuss computer security topics, to understand your role in the security equation, and, most important, to enable you to continue to learn about computer security. After completing this book, there are a number of remaining educational and security tasks one should perform to continue gaining knowledge of computer security and to keep the defense-in-depth strategy current.

14.2 AFTER THE COMPLETION OF THE BOOK

1. **Explore:** Now that you possess the knowledge of computer, Internet, and security terminology, explore your computer, operating system, applications, web browsers, and networking devices to better understand what security options are available to you and how you can use them to protect yourself. Research, read, and inquire about features

or settings about which you may be unsure. Instead of being a passive user of technology, be an active user and continually push yourself to learn about technology and security's role in technology.

2. **Share:** Share the knowledge gained reading this book with those around you. Not only will you increase your understanding and retention, but also you will be helping your family and friends to better protect themselves online. This represents our principal goal in creating this book: to share security knowledge in an accessible way so that others can go forth and protect themselves from dangers lurking on the Internet.

3. **Read:** Although attackers' objectives will most likely be unchanged (i.e., malware distribution and theft of confidential information), if history is any indicator, the manner in which these attacks are carried out most certainly will. Not only will reading about computer security topics keep you abreast of the most current security issues, but also it will reinforce what you have learned in this book, broaden your knowledge base, and support more in-depth learning about subjects that interested you the most. Appendix A (Reading List) provides a list of websites and a broad selection of books to help you continue to read and learn further with respect to the topic of computer security.

4. **Reflect:** As you go forth and continue to interact with information technology, reflect on what you have learned. After you have had time to internalize and apply knowledge you have learned, in addition to exploring your computing environment with a more critical eye, reread this book or at least specific chapters to hone your skills with respect to concepts or subtleties that may have been missed during the initial read.

5. **Discuss:** Identify one or more individuals in your life with whom you can start an ongoing dialogue about security. By continually sharing and learning, you will increae your own understanding of security as well as how others perceive security. Once you feel comfortable discussing security, branch out and engage a wider circle of friends. One of the general problems nagging online users is that few people engage in conversations dealing with online dangers and computer security best practices. Security threats will not lessen in intensity or effectiveness if we simply ignore them. Education is the key, and we must all play a role in educating each other.

14.3 DEFENSE-IN-DEPTH TASKS

Well-managed computer security hygiene requires that one perform daily, weekly, and monthly security exercises to keep their defense-in-depth strategy current. This section provides a summary and quick reference for such tasks that should continue to be performed after completion of this book.

On a daily basis:

1. Perform either a file backup of new documents or a system backup. Failures and malware infections often occur at the most inconvenient of times and can result in complete loss of availability for the information stored on your hard drive. A daily routine backup schedule prevents many different scenarios and is a necessity for maintaining good computing hygiene.

2. Update virus signatures. Antivirus vendors distribute virus signatures on a daily basis. Remember that to detect the most current malware, your antivirus software needs the most current virus signatures. Without a daily update, new malware strains have the potential to infect your computer and operate unrestrained.

On a weekly basis:

1. Ensure that all software is up to date and patched. In the past, malware has often been highly successful because people were remiss in updating their software—both applications and operating system—and installing patches in a timely manner. To prevent malware infections and drive-by downloads, it is imperative that you check your operating system, web browser, and frequently used applications (office suite, PDF viewer, etc.) at least once a week to ensure that they are up to date and properly patched. An alternative is to automatically schedule operating systems or applications to check for patches on a weekly basis.

2. Perform a quick scan or full scan with antivirus software. As part of your weekly computing routine, schedule time to perform a quick scan or complete system scan with your antivirus software to verify that your computer is void of malware. Before performing the scan, equip your antivirus software with the most recent virus signatures.

3. Stay current with the latest security news. At minimum, read a few articles a week from the list of suggested security websites (Appendix A). Alternatively, reading the RSS (Really Simple Syndication, RDF Site Summary) feeds for the provided websites provides a quick and consolidated method to quickly review the day's or week's popular security topics. Much can be learned, and being aware of the most current attack threats, security strategies, and data breaches can help prevent disasters.

On a monthly basis:

1. Verify that your firewall is enabled. Firewalls require little maintenance other than ensuring that they are enabled. A highly likely indicator of malware is a disabled firewall, and checking for proper activation on a monthly basis serves the dual role of checking the integrity of your computer environment and keeping your defense-in-depth security strategy intact.

14.4 CHAPTER SUMMARIES

Now that you have completed the book, this section reviews the main points of each individual chapter.

Chapter 1: Introduction

With respect to practical computer security, you, the user, often play the most important role in protecting your own security by the decisions you do or do not make. As we as individuals continue to rely more heavily on personal computers to complete everyday tasks, personally taking an active role in the security of our own computer environments will continue to grow in importance. Cyber criminals and malware, the two most likely sources of attacks, are thieves of opportunity and typically do not target specific individuals but rather target the "lowest-hanging fruit on the tree." To protect the confidentiality, integrity, and availability of your data and computing environments, it is necessary to understand both human and computer vulnerabilities, how attackers exploit such vulnerabilities, and how to invest in your own security.

Chapter 2: Computers and the Internet

Computers, through the execution of an operating system and application software, allow users to interface with hardware devices. While the actions of opening and executing (i.e., running) software applications are typically perceived to be performed only by human users, this is not always true, and some applications possess the capability of executing software programs or code without user knowledge. While most such actions may be useful and convenient, they may also allow surreptitious malware to execute and perform actions on one's computer but without the user's permission. In other words, malware can either become you or spy on you.

When one connects a computer to the Internet, he or she is truly connecting to a global network. While this may allow a user in northern Minnesota to conveniently buy sheepskin boots from Australia, it also allows a teenage hacker sitting on his family couch in southeast England to attack a nuclear power plant in Brazil. The ubiquity and ease of access to the Internet continues to be used for both good and bad.

Chapter 3: Passwords

The goal of password security is to create strong (i.e., hard-to-guess) and unique passwords and then keep these passwords a secret against the many threats seeking to observe private information. More often than not, the greatest threat to the confidentiality of a password is not an attacker attempting a brute-force attack but rather the user himself or herself accidentally disclosing a password to the attacker through a key-logger or phishing website. In such scenarios, it does not matter how strong the password may be because the victim provides the password directly to the attacker in clear text. When creating a password or passphrase, the goal is to create a strong password but one that can be easily remembered. If you are unable to remember passwords effectively, there are a number of password management techniques and tools to aid you in this process. Furthermore, it is important not to reuse passwords across different accounts. There are many ways that a password can be compromised, and the loss of a single password shared by multiple accounts could enable an attacker to access all of them using the same credentials. Because passwords can be lost and used without one's knowledge, it is good security practice to change them often—more so for more valuable accounts—to prevent unauthorized access.

Chapter 4: Email

Because email has become a predominant form of both business and personal communication, it is often targeted by attackers. In many ways, the email infrastructure on the Internet is analogous to the ordinary postal system. Like a snail mail letter, an attacker, pretending to be a trusted entity, can send an email with a spoofed sender address and misleading content to potential victims. Enabled by the ease of digital communication, an attacker, at little or no cost, can send out hordes of emails to many potential victims in a short period of time. For the attacker to be successful, he or she may only need a small percentage of success.

There are two predominant forms of email attacks. The first type is the phishing email that attempts to trick the victim into divulging sensitive information. Phishing emails are crafted to appear to come from a trusted entity and to entice the user either to click on a hyperlink leading the victim to a phony website or to respond to the email and reveal private information. The second type of email-based attack attempts to trick the user to install malware on the user's computer through either drive-by downloads or emails enticing users to open malware-laden attachments. Because of such threats, one must proceed with caution when opening an email from someone unknown or from someone you do know but from whom the message is unexpected. Some of the most successful email attacks have resulted from compromised email accounts, with victims receiving malicious email from people they thought they knew and could trust.

Chapter 5: Malware

It should come as no surprise that virtually every action one performs on a computer could result in a malware infection. This is why education is such a critical component of practical computer security. Consider drive-by downloads, for example. Many people are unaware that simply clicking a hyperlink in an email, or in a malicious ad on a legitimate website, can result in a malware infection spread by code embedded in a webpage surreptitiously executing on a user's computer. Without knowledge of the many ways malware can spread, it is difficult to know how one can prevent against such attacks.

The objectives of modern-day malware are quite different from those of more dated malware. Today's malware producers are motivated by profit, and they craft their malicious code in such a way that it remains hidden on one's computer to maximize its damage. The task of malware is typically to observe information about the victim (i.e., password, credit card numbers, etc.), to present the victim with malicious or deceiving ads, or to use the victim's computer to attack other computers (i.e., botnet). Furthermore, malware creators often use their malware to create backdoors on their victims' computers so that the malware creator can access or download new malware to the victim's computer at a later time.

Chapter 6: Malware Defense

There is no single security mechanism that users can buy or use to protect them and their computers against all threats. Instead, practical computer security consists of a system of layers, representing a defense in depth. This way, if a given security mechanism fails, there are others potentially in place to prevent an attack. The essential components of a defense-in-depth strategy are data backup, firewalls, software patches, antivirus software, and user education. Each of these components has its own respective strengths and inherent limitations, and each must be maintained on a regular basis to minimize the risk of an attack. Central to this defensive scheme is user education, the overall goal of this book.

Chapter 7: Securely Surfing the Web

The web browser is the predominant tool used by people in interacting with content, services, and applications hosted on the Internet. Accordingly, attackers often target web browsers and actions their users perform on the web. Chief among attack techniques are misleading users by way of hyperlinks. Attackers also exploit the conveniences web browsers afford in automatically opening documents or executing code on behalf of the users. While these automatic behaviors can enhance one's web browsing experience, a single errant click of the mouse can accidentally open and execute a malicious PDF document, subjecting a user to a potential malware infection.

In addition to security threats, web browsers can be in conflict with privacy. Often, for purposes of convenience, web browsers retain a great deal of information about its users' browsing actions. However, if untrusted users gain access to the computer or such actions are performed on a public computer, this saved information poses a risk to privacy and security (i.e., saved passwords, session cookies). To protect one's privacy, it is essential to understand exactly what information web browsers store on the user's behalf, how such information can be accessed, and how one can delete such information or prevent a web browser from remembering it in the first place.

Chapter 8: Online Shopping

Online shopping is a billion-dollar industry, and it should come as no surprise that cyber criminals have followed the money trail. Because online shopping is a voluntary activity, the decisions shoppers make or do not make often determine whether they fall victim to a scam. Applying the same level of shopper skepticism as that exhibited in the physical world to the cyber world can prevent many online shopping scams. Also, when dealing with the online exchange of money, users are afforded the maximum protection under U.S. federal law and regulated payment procedures when they purchase items with a credit card rather than a debit card. When shopping online, stick to reputable websites by navigating to the website yourself, ensure that the website uses encryption-protected HTTPS, and provide only the necessary amount of information needed to make a purchase.

Chapter 9: Wireless Internet Security

When using an unsecure public wireless network, the information you send over such a network is vulnerable to eavesdropping. To mitigate attackers from viewing your sensitive data, send sensitive information only over an HTTPS (Hypertext Transfer Protocol Secure), not HTTP (Hypertext Transfer Protocol) connection, or use a VPN (virtual private network) (Appendix C: Web Technologies). Each of these options encrypts your confidential data so that even if an attacker is eavesdropping on your wireless traffic, the attacker will be unable to read or decrypt your communications.

Most of us are not running a charity service for those who lack their own Wi-Fi connection. Providing a wireless Internet signal in one's residence costs money, and allowing piggybackers to share network bandwidth decreases the quality of service you receive from your paid-for service. Furthermore, allowing piggybackers to connect to your wireless network presents a definite security issue and one that should be avoided to prevent the loss of confidential information.

Chapter 10: Social Networking

The pervasiveness of social networking has grown to represent billions of users from multiple demographics and in all corners of the world. Despite the obvious benefits of social networking, there exist security and privacy trade-offs. Central among these trade-offs is the loss of privacy when sharing information online. Even information labeled as "private" on social networking sites is only relatively so, and there is nothing to prevent a "friend" from removing shared content from a social networking platform and distributing it to whomever he or she pleases. When posting information on a social networking site, strongly consider how that information will affect you both now and in the future. Many corporations have rejected job candidates based on information discovered online. Furthermore, attackers can and have used information posted on social networking sites to mount attacks that range from spear-phishing emails to physical break-ins.

Due to the vast number of users, social networking sites have become a key target for those distributing malware and performing phishing attacks. Beware when interacting with content generated by friends that not everything posted on a social networking site may be what it seems to be, and often attackers use compelling messages coupled with hyperlinks and videos to trick their victims.

Chapter 11: Social Engineering: Phishing for Suckers

Social engineers are the scam artists of the Internet, adept at tricking users into performing actions not in their best interests. To accomplish their deeds, social engineers exploit human vulnerabilities either by enticing users to install malware on their own computers or by convincing users to errantly disclose their confidential information. Because these attacks often involve nontechnical components, user education is often the key defense. An important skill one can use to defeat social engineers is to recognize their attacks prior to falling victim to them. This often involves considering the context of an attacker's ploy and developing a firm understanding of how social engineers carry out their attacks. Perhaps the best-known form of social engineering is phishing, in which attackers target users, generally through emails, to reveal confidential information like bank login credentials. In addition to being able to identify phishing ruses, one should also be able to read, decipher, and analyze URLs (Uniform Resource Locators) as a key defense against phishing attacks.

Chapter 12: Staying Safe Online: The Human Threat

Actions that take place in the cyber world have real-world consequences. Cyber bullying and cyber stalking have both emerged as serious threats to children and adults alike. With nearly constant access to potential victims through cell phones, social networking, and the Internet, the actions of present-day bullies are not confined to face-to-face encounters. Furthermore, when dealing with people online, one should realize that not everyone is who they claim to be, written messages can easily be taken out of context, nothing is private, anything posted on the Internet can last forever, and one is often held responsible for the content they post online and for content others post about them.

Chapter 13: Case Studies

Practical computer security is an applied field of study. Because this is the case, the real test of the knowledge that you gained while reading this book cannot be measured with a standard test but rather when you put the book down and begin to interact with technology. Chapter 13 presents a number of case studies in the context of security describing situations you will very likely face as a user of technology. These case studies provide examples that can be used to share and discuss what you have learned with those around you.

Glossary

Adware: Advertising software that displays commercial ads to a computer user

Antivirus software: Security software used to prevent, detect, and remove malware from a computer system

Application: General term for a software program

Attack code: A software implementation of an exploit used to take advantage of a vulnerability

Attacker: General term to describe someone wishing to cause harm

Authentication: The process of confirming the validity of one's identity

Authorization: Approval or permission for someone or something (software) to perform an action

Availability: The quality of a system, program, or data, ensuring that it is accessible to those who need it when they need it

Backup: A duplicate copy of data on a secondary storage device

BIOS (Basic Input/Output System): Computer program that prepares a computer for operation by initializing hardware devices and loading (i.e., booting) the operating system

Bookmark: A quick-reference record of a webpage or website address

Boot sector virus: A computer virus that resides in the boot sector of a disk (or removable media) and is executed when the disk is accessed

Botnet: A network of computers infected with malware that enables a malware creator to control, access, and synchronize infected computers to carry out computer attacks

Brute-force attack: An exhaustive guessing algorithm that attempts all possible solutions

Cache: Local storage of data obviating the need for subsequent requests of stored data

Certificate: An electronic document binding an identity to a public cryptographic key

Cipher: Cryptographic algorithm used for both the encryption and the decryption of data

Ciphertext: Encrypted output of a cipher

Client: Generic user of a computer system; also referred to as a user

Cloud: A high-level abstraction for the Internet and its interworkings

Cloud computing: Offering and delivery of computing capacity and storage as a free or metered service

Confidentiality: The quality of data that ensures it is only accessible to those who are authorized

Cookie: A persistent or temporary data file stored in a web browser that is used by a website to store, track, and retrieve information about a user's actions

Cracker: Malicious hacker

Cryptanalysis: The process of deciphering meaning from an encrypted message

Cyber: Prefix or adjective pertaining to something that is Internet related

Cyber bullying: The act of using the Internet to harass a victim

Cyber criminal: A scam artist of the cyber world, often using malware or phishing attacks to steal money or confidential information

Cyber stalking: The act of using the Internet to stalk or harass a victim

Decryption: The process of using a cipher to transform ciphertext into plaintext

Defense in depth: Multilayered approach to security relying on multiple complementary and overlapping mechanisms to protect against attacks

Denial of Service (DoS) attack: An attack resulting in the partial or complete loss of availability for a given system

DHCP (Dynamic Host Configuration Protocol): Automatically assigns IP addresses to client machines on a network

Dictionary attack: A guessing attack that uses a specially crafted list often composed of dictionary words, popular passwords, and common passphrases

DNS (Domain Name Service): Computing system that translates domain names into IP addresses and vice versa

Domain name: Unique identity and location of an entity on the Internet

Drive-by download: The downloading of malicious software onto a computer without the knowledge or consent of the user

Eavesdropping: Listening to digital conversations with an objective of learning private information

Encryption: The process of using a cipher to transform plaintext into ciphertext

Exploit: A malicious attack that takes advantage of a security vulnerability

Fake antivirus: A malicious computer program or website pop-up that falsely claims the user's computer is infected with malware and attempts to scare the user into downloading and paying for a fake antivirus program to solve the phony malware problem

File infector virus: A computer virus residing inside a computer document or program

File path: The specific location of a computer file in a file system

Firewall: Networking security mechanism that prevents unwanted and unauthorized network connections

Full scan: Antivirus scan that analyzes every file on a hard drive

Hacker: A person gaining unauthorized access to computer networks, systems, or data

Hacktivist: Politically motivated hacker

Hash function: A cryptographic algorithm that computes a unique random output for each given input; often used to encrypt passwords

Hash value: The output of a hash function, used for irreversible encryption of a password

HTTP (Hypertext Transfer Protocol): Web protocol used to request and retrieve web content

HTTPS (Hypertext Transfer Protocol Secure): Secure web protocol enabling computers to request and send encrypted web content

Hyperlink: A link to another document or webpage, typically retrieved by clicking on a highlighted or underlined word

Identity theft: The fraudulent use of private identity information for the purpose of information theft or financial gain

Information security: The process of protecting information from threats

Integrity: The quality of a system or information that ensures that it has not been changed accidentally or maliciously and is complete and truthful

Internet: A public and international system of interconnected computer networks

IP (Internet Protocol) address: A unique numerical address assigned to each device participating on a computer network

ISP (Internet service provider): A company providing access to the Internet

Key-logger: Hardware device or software program that covertly records a series of keyboard strokes

Login credentials: Username and password

Macro virus: A computer virus written in a macro language and embedded within a document

Malicious adware: Purposefully deceitful adware that attempts to trick a user into clicking on an ad or purchasing a fraudulent product

Malicious insider: A malicious employee using his or her legitimate privileges to compromise the security of a corporation's computer systems

Malvertising: *See* Malicious adware

Malware: Malicious software; a general term used to describe all malicious software, including viruses, Trojan horses, and worms

Message Transfer Agent (MTA): Software application that transfers emails from one email server to another

Mitigate: Lessen or decrease the risk of a threat

NAT (Network Address Translation): A service that translates the private IP of a computer on a private network to a suitable public IP address to be used on the Internet and vice versa

Network mask: Determines the subnet of an IP address

Next hop: The router that data will be routed to next

On-access scan: An automatic antivirus scan invoked when a document or application is about to be accessed or executed

On-demand scan: An antivirus scan of part or all of a computer system, invoked or scheduled by a user

Operating system: A set of software programs that control a computer's various components and provide an interface between hardware devices and applications chosen by a user

Packet: A block of data routed through a network

Passphrase: A sequence of combined words, similar to a password

Password: A secret word or phrase used to gain access to a computer system or network

Password cracking: The automated process of guessing password hashes in a password file

Password fatigue: The act of being overwhelmed by password management, sometimes leading a user to resort to more convenient and less-secure practices

Password file: A file that contains a system's collections of usernames and passwords

Peer-to-peer (P2P) network: Ad hoc file-sharing network in which individual users share digital content

Penetration tester: A security professional who performs ethical and sanctioned hacking actions that attempt to gain access to a computer, network, or corporation

Phishing: The act of using emails or other means to masquerade as a trustworthy source to trick a user into divulging personal and private information

Piggybacker: A person using a wireless network without permission or knowledge of the wireless network owner

Plaintext: A text message in ordinary language readable by humans

Plug-in: Software program that is installed within an existing application to expand its functionality

Polymorphic malware: Malware that changes its virus signature each time it propagates

Pop-up: An advertisement or message displayed in a small window

Privacy: The degree of control an individual possesses with respect to access of his or her personal information by others

Promiscuous mode: A computer setting that allows a computer connected to a wireless network to capture and read all network traffic

Protocol: A defined set of specifications allowing computers to communicate

Public computer: *See* Untrusted computer

Quick scan: An abbreviated antivirus scan that scans the files and folders where malware is most likely to reside

Ransomware: Malicious software that holds part of a computer's hard drive hostage and then demands a ransom fee for the user to regain access

Risk: The likelihood of a successful attack

Risk assessment: The process of identifying risks and determining their impact

Route table: A table found in a router or computer that maintains a record of the possible routes for which network data can travel

Router: A networking device connecting computers together by forwarding information

Scareware: *See* Fake antivirus

Script kiddie: An amateur computer hacker using well-known techniques to compromise computer systems, often without regard for potential consequences or true knowledge of his or her actions

Secret password: A password only known by the password owner

Secure wireless network: A wireless Internet network that requires a password for access and encrypts wireless communications

Security question: A form of authentication allowing a user to recover or reset a password

Server: A computer system hosting services and responding to requests from clients

Session hijacking: The observation and exploitation of a session cookie that enables an attacker to gain unauthorized access to a victim's account

Sexting: The sending of sexually explicit messages or photos

Shoulder surfing: The act of looking over a person's shoulder to observe private or confidential information

Sniffing: *See* Eavesdropping

SMiShing: Phishing attack carried out using text messages

SMTP (Simple Mail Transfer Protocol): A common protocol used by many email providers to control email transfers

Social engineering: The art of manipulating people to reveal information or perform actions not in their best interest

Social networking: A general term used to describe the communal sharing of information on websites like Facebook or Twitter

Software patch: A software update released by a software vendor to fix one or more software vulnerabilities

Spam: Unsolicited electronic messages, usually in the form of email

Spear phishing: A personalized phishing attack targeting a specific person

Spoofing: Impersonation of a legitimate person or entity

Spyware: Malicious software that observes user's information (passwords, etc.) and actions and then sends that information to a cyber criminal

SSID (Service Set Identifier): Username or identifier of a wireless network

Strong password: A virtually unguessable password

Subdomain: A smaller partition of a larger network

Threat: Likelihood of a computer system attack

Threat assessment: Identifying threats that a person or computer system might encounter

Threat source: A potential violation of security; a source of danger

Top-level domain: The root or highest category for the Internet DNS

Trojan horse: A malware program using the façade of a legitimate program to mask its malicious function

Uniform Resource Locator (URL): The address defining the location of a file or webpage on an Internet server

Unsecure wireless network: A wireless network that neither requires a password nor encrypts wireless traffic

Untrusted computer: Any computer on which one has not personally maintained a defense-in-depth strategy and therefore cannot verify its integrity with high assurance; includes computers at a public library, coffee shop, electronics store, and the like

URL shortener: Internet service mapping URLs to significantly shorter URLs

USB (Universal Serial Bus) flash drive: An external storage device that plugs into a USB port

User Agent (UA): An email application that enables a user to interact with MTAs to send and receive emails

Username: Name used to identify a user on a computer system, often unique to the given system

Virus: A self-replicating malicious software program requiring both a host, like a file or external storage device, and human action for propagation between computers

Virus signature: A pattern of computer code used to uniquely identify a malicious program

Vishing: Phishing attack carried out using a phone service

Vulnerability: A security weakness in the design, configuration, or implementation of software that enables an attack to occur

War driving: Process of identifying unsecure wireless networks

Web browser: Client computer application to facilitate web document display and interaction

Website: A publicly accessible collection of web pages on the World Wide Web

Whale phishing: Phishing attacks targeted toward high-level company executives like chief executive officers (CEOs) or chief financial officers (CFOs)

Wireless network: A network accessed by multiple users in the physical vicinity of a wireless transmitter or router; often available in public spaces like restaurants, coffee shops, or private residences

Wi-Fi: Protocol that enables the wireless transmission of data between networking devices

World Wide Web (WWW): A subset of the Internet consisting of a vast assembly of interlinked hypertext documents

Worm: An autonomous and malicious software program propagating among computer networks

Zero-day vulnerability: A vulnerability that is exploited before a patch is available

Appendix A: Reading List

SECURITY IS AN EVER-CHANGING field in which news occurs on a daily, if not hourly, basis. While the core objectives of cyber criminals are not likely to change (i.e., malware distribution and the stealing of private and financial information), the way these attacks are manifested in practice changes just about as quickly as technology changes. To remain current with respect to the ways malware is spread, how phishing schemes are devised, and much more, it is necessary to read about security, particularly in terms of current events. The following is a list of websites that provide timely and easily accessible accounts of recent security-related events. Each website provides a slightly different angle on security, and collectively they address a diverse set of potential reader backgrounds and interests.

A.1 SECURITY WEBSITES

Networkworld: Security Research Center

http://www.networkworld.com/topics/security.html

Computerworld: Security Topic Center

http://www.computerworld.com/s/topic/17/Security

CNET Security

http://www.cnet.com/internet-security/

CIO: Security

http://www.cio.com/topic/3089/Security

Schneier on Security

http://www.schneier.com/

NYTimes/technology

http://www.nytimes.com/pages/technology/index.html

Threat Level: Privacy, Crime, and Security Online

http://www.wired.com/threatlevel/

The Register

http://www.theregister.co.uk/security/

The objective of this book is to provide an introduction to practical computer security knowledge and literacy. To gain additional understanding in particular areas or to read a bit deeper into the principles of security and general security issues or to expand in greater detail on the topics covered in this text, the books indicated next would serve as excellent sources.

A.2 SECURITY BOOKS

General Security

Schneier, B. 2009. *Schneier on Security*. New York: Wiley.
Schneier, B. 2011. *Secrets and Lies: Digital Security in a Networked World*. New York: Wiley.
Schneier, B. 2012. *Liars and Outliers*. New York: Wiley.
Viega, J. 2009. *The Myths of Security: What the Computer Security Industry Doesn't Want You to Know*. Sebastopol, CA: O'Reilly Media.

Cryptography

Singh, S. 2000. *The Code Book: The Science of Secrecy from Ancient Egypt to Quantum Cryptography*. New York: Random House Digital.

Hacking and Social Engineering

Hadnagy, C. 2010. *Social Engineering: The Art of Human Hacking*. New York: Wiley.
Mitnick, K., and Simon, W.L. 2005. *The Art of Intrusion: The Real Stories Behind the Exploits of Hackers, Intruders, and Deceivers*. New York: Wiley.

Mitnick, K., and Simon, W.L. 2011. *The Art of Deception: Controlling the Human Element of Security*. New York: Wiley.

Mitnick, K., and Simon, W.L. 2011. *Ghost in the Wires: My Adventures as the World's Most Wanted Hacker*. Boston: Hachette Digital.

Poulsen, K. 2011. *Kingpin: How One Hacker Took Over the Billion-Dollar Cybercrime Underground*. New York: Random House Digital.

Fiction

Russinovich, M. 2011. *Zero Day: A Novel*. New York: Macmillan.

Technical Computer Security Texts

Bishop, M. 2003. *Computer Security: Art and Science*. Boston: Addison-Wesley Professional.

Cheswick, W.R., Bellovin, S.M., and Rubin, A.D. 2003. *Firewalls and Internet Security: Repelling the Wily Hacker*. Boston: Addison-Wesley Professional.

Erickson, J. 2008. *Hacking: The Art of Exploitation*, 2nd edition. San Francisco: No Starch Press.

Jacobson, D.W. 2008. *Introduction to Network Security*. Boca Raton, FL: Chapman & Hall/CRC.

Appendix B: Basics of Cryptography

B.1 INTRODUCTION

Cryptography is one of the most heavily relied-on security mechanisms to preserve confidentiality of information at rest (i.e., data stored on a computer hard drive) and in transit (i.e., data traveling over the Internet). Without cryptography, the Internet would be a drastically different place than we have come to know and depend on in our daily lives. The average user of information technology, whether or not aware of it, relies on cryptography virtually every day of his or her life (i.e., via HTTPS [Hypertext Transfer Protocol Secure], secure wireless networks, password hashes). This appendix describes cryptography's underpinnings and explores classic cryptographic algorithms, principles, and terminology and also provides rudimentary knowledge regarding when and how cryptography is protecting a user's communication of data.

B.2 BASIC TERMINOLOGY

This section defines a number of common terms used to describe cryptography and subsequently referenced not only in this appendix but also throughout the book.

- **Confidentiality:** Ensuring that information is only accessible to authorized people.

- **Cryptography:** The practice and study of hiding information so that it can be viewed and accessed only by authorized users.

- **Plaintext:** Information exchanged before any cryptography has been applied.

- **Ciphertext:** Plaintext that has been converted through cryptography into a format unreadable to anyone except authorized users.

- **Cipher:** The algorithm used to convert plaintext to ciphertext.

- **Key:** The secret information required to convert plaintext into ciphertext and subsequently to convert ciphertext back to plaintext.

- **Encryption:** The process of using a cipher and a key to convert plaintext into ciphertext.

- **Decryption:** The process of converting ciphertext into plaintext using a cipher and a key.

- **Cryptanalysis:** The process of converting ciphertext to plaintext without knowledge of the key.

B.3 HISTORY OF CRYPTOGRAPHY

Cryptography has been used to preserve the confidentiality of information for thousands of years. The first documented case of written encryption occurred around 1900 BC when Egyptians substituted symbols in hieroglyphic messages. In 1500 BC, the Mesopotamians used cryptography to safeguard the secrecy of a pottery glaze recipe—not too different from the modern-day equivalent of encrypting a hard drive containing intellectual property. A better-documented case of historic cryptography was that of a system used by Julius Caesar around AD 56. Caesar used a simple system in which letters of the alphabet were substituted (A = X, B = Y, and so on) to communicate with his generals. This cryptographic cipher is now referred to as a substitution cipher and more specifically the Caesar shift cipher. Cryptography also played a central role in the 1586 Babington plot, in which Mary Queen of Scots sought to assassinate Queen Elizabeth in an attempt to take over the throne of England.

There have been many other examples of encryption based on various types of substitutions and rearranging of letters, but it was not until World War I and World War II that significant advancements were made in the area of cryptography and technology—necessity is the mother of invention. Many historians believe that the effectiveness or lack thereof of cryptography played a central role in outcomes of both world wars. During

World War II, the Germans (Enigma), Japanese (Purple), British (TypeX), and the Americans (SIGABA) all had devices (i.e., cipher machines) that could encrypt and decrypt messages. These devices resembled typewriters into which a user could type a message in plaintext and the machine would print it out in ciphertext. During World War II, American, British, and Polish intelligence services cracked both the German and the Japanese ciphers, leading to the discovery of many secret messages and contributing heavily to battle victories. To this day, it is largely believed that neither the American nor the British ciphers were cracked during the war. The success of the Allies was in part due to the invention of a computer (Colossus) used to crack the German Enigma machine. History, especially that of World War II, is riddled with many fascinating tales of cryptographic innovation, espionage, heroism, villainy, and even romance. Simon Singh's book *The Code Book* (referenced in the reading list in Appendix A) provides excellent reading for anyone wanting to learn more about the history of cryptography and the principles and implementation of modern-day cryptography. The next several sections examine different cryptographic systems and discuss a methodology for cryptanalysis.

B.4 SYMMETRIC KEY CRYPTOGRAPHY: CLASSICAL CIPHERS

Symmetric key cryptography is a method by which everyone needing to encrypt and decrypt information knows the same secret key. For example, if Alice and Bob are to send each other encrypted messages using symmetric key encryption, they must therefore agree on a shared secret key beforehand. As shown in Figures B.1 and B.2, the processes of encryption and decryption are virtually the same when using a symmetric cipher. When a secret key is applied to the cipher with the plaintext data as input, it is converted to ciphertext. The ciphertext can then be converted back into plaintext by using the ciphertext as input to the cipher and applying the same key used for encryption to the cipher. Shift, substitution,

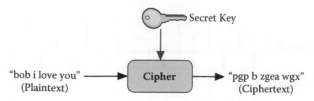

FIGURE B.1 Process of encryption.

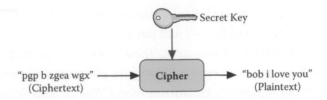

FIGURE B.2   Process of decryption.

and permutation ciphers are three classical examples of symmetric key ciphers, and their underpinnings are discussed next.

B.4.1 Shift Cipher

As mentioned, the cryptographic key for a shift cipher is the shifting of one or more alphabetic characters in the alphabet. As seen in Figure B.3, the key for an example shift cipher is the shifting of the normal alphabet to the right one character.

To encrypt a message with a shift cipher, each letter of the plaintext message is mapped to the corresponding character in the key as shown in Figure B.4. For the plaintext message "hello bob," the shift cipher produces the output of "gdkkn ana." To decrypt the ciphertext, as seen in Figure B.5, the reverse mapping of the key is used to obtain the plaintext message. Notice that the same key is used in both processes of encryption and decryption. If Alice and Bob were to use such a cipher, they would first need to negotiate a key (i.e., number of shifts to the left or right) before exchanging messages. Alice and Bob could create a Caesar shift cipher

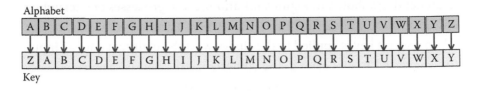

FIGURE B.3   Shift cipher example.

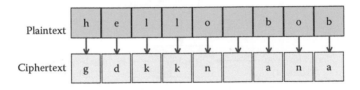

FIGURE B.4   Shift cipher encryption.

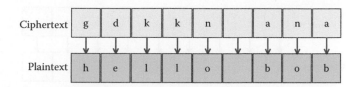

FIGURE B.5   Shift cipher decryption.

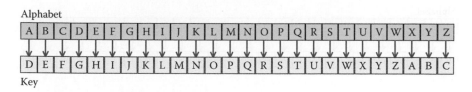

FIGURE B.6   Caesar shift cipher.

(Figure B.6) by shifting the alphabet three times to the right. In AD 46, this cipher represented the state of the art in cryptography for the Roman army.

B.4.2 Substitution Cipher

In a substitution cipher, each character in the original alphabet is mapped to a random character pairing, forming the key. It follows that a substitution cipher key is used to provide the mapping between the original alphabet and the ciphertext. As seen in Figure B.7, each letter in the plaintext alphabet is paired with a different letter in the alphabet, and the mapping pattern is the key. Like a shift cipher, to encrypt a message each character in the plaintext is changed to the character specified by the key. To decrypt the message, the same process is applied in reverse by taking the ciphertext letter and using the key to determine the plaintext letter. It is worth noting that if Alice uses the key in Figure B.7 to encrypt a message (Figure B.8) and Bob uses a different key shown in Figure B.9 to decrypt Alice's message, then, as seen in Figure B.10, the resulting message will be meaningless. When using symmetric key ciphers, it is essential that the same key and the same cipher be used to both encrypt and decrypt a message.

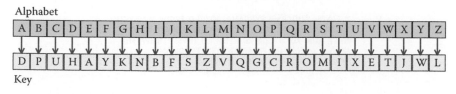

FIGURE B.7   Substitution cipher 1.

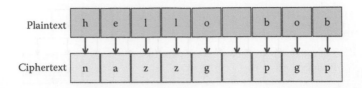

FIGURE B.8 Substitution cipher encryption.

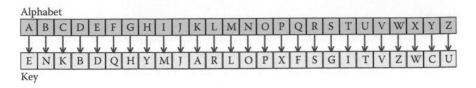

FIGURE B.9 Substitution cipher 2.

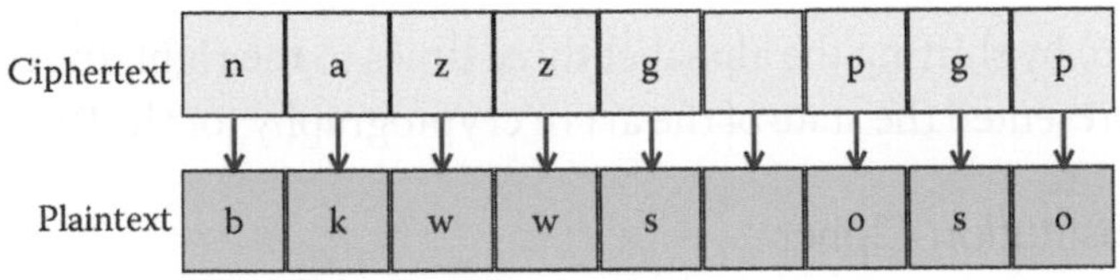

FIGURE B.10 Substitution cipher decryption.

To try your own hand at cryptanalysis—the process of obtaining meaning from ciphertext—consider the message in Figure B.11 that is encrypted using a substitution cipher. The remainder of the section demonstrates how cryptanalysis can be used to decipher such a message when the key is unknown. The answer to this crypto challenge can be found at the conclusion of the appendix (Section B.8). Note that the punctuation from the plaintext was omitted, and the substitution cipher thus consists of alphabetic characters only.

Because substitution ciphers typically maintain the structure of the original message, they can be fairly easily cracked using one of several procedures. If English is the plaintext language, one can break the ciphertext

```
Y ROYDV FZJHGRMB SYBGAMA AOZGKQ FZGDR WA KYEM
Y ROYDV YR AWNA AZJMROYDL WUZGR OGJWD DWRGBM
ROWR ROM ZDKN EZBJ ZE KYEM TM OWSM FBMWRMQ
AZ EWB YA HGBMKN QMARBGFRYSM TM OWSM
FBMWRMQ KYEM YD ZGB ZTD YJWLM
```

FIGURE B.11 Substitution cipher crypto challenge.

by using what is known about characteristics of the English language. The most common method used for this purpose is called frequency analysis. Figure B.12 shows the frequency or number of times each letter in the English language is expected to be found in a "typical" message. Given a long enough ciphertext message, it is possible to guess which letters in the ciphertext correspond to letters in plaintext just by counting the number of times a particular letter appears. Figure B.13 provides a frequency analysis for the crypto-challenge message in Figure B.12. Given Figures B.12 and B.13, it would be logical to guess that "e," the most frequently used letter in the English language, maps to "m," the letter that appears most often in the frequency analysis of the cipher text.

A more advanced version of frequency analysis is to examine the number of times that pairs of letters or groups of three letters appear in the ciphertext. Such two- and three-letter combinations are called *bigrams* and *trigrams*, respectively. Figure B.14 shows the most common 15 bigrams and trigrams in the English language. As stated in Figure B.14, the most common three-letter combination is "the." When examining a long ciphertext message, by identifying the most commonly used three-letter combination, one can reasonably assume that it corresponds to "the." This is, of course, only a guess, and a person performing cryptanalysis may need to try multiple guesses before achieving success. The advantage of a substitution cipher is the ease of encryption and decryption. However,

Letter	Frequency	Letter	Frequency	Letter	Frequency
a	8.2%	j	0.2%	s	6.3%
b	1.5%	k	0.8%	t	9.1%
c	2.8%	l	4.0%	u	2.8%
d	4.3%	m	2.4%	v	1.0%
e	12.7%	n	6.7%	w	2.4%
f	2.2%	o	7.5%	x	0.2%
g	2.0%	p	1.9%	y	2.0%
h	6.1%	q	0.1%	z	0.1%
i	7.0%	r	6.0%	sp	6.4%

FIGURE B.12 Letter frequency in the English language.

M	R	Y	W	Z	A	B	G	D	O	E	K	F	J	Q	S	N	T	H	L	V	U	C	I	P	X
20	15	14	12	11	10	10	10	9	9	6	6	5	5	4	4	3	3	2	2	2	1	0	0	0	0

FIGURE B.13 Frequency analysis of crypto challenge ciphertext.

Rank	Bigram		Rank	Trigram
1	th		1	the
2	he		2	and
3	in		3	ing
4	er		4	her
5	an		5	hat
6	re		6	his
7	nd		7	tha
8	on		8	ere
9	en		9	for
10	at		10	ent
11	ou		11	ion
12	ed		12	ter
13	ha		13	was
14	to		14	you
15	or		15	ith

FIGURE B.14   Most frequent 15 bigrams and trigrams in the English language.

this efficiency can also be a downfall since it can be seen that a substitution cipher is fairly easy to crack.

B.4.3 Permutation Cipher

The key for a permutation cipher is a bit different from that of the shift cipher or substitution cipher. In a permutation cipher (Figure B.15), the letters of the plaintext message are simply rearranged into a different order, and the key represents the permutation order. Jumble puzzles, often seen in a newspaper's game section, are a simple example of a permutation cipher. In practice, permutation ciphers typically function using character groups of fixed size called *blocks* (i.e., 56 characters). The cipher will perform a permutation on each block of the message. Ciphers that work on one message block at a time are called *block ciphers*. The next section briefly describes two block ciphers in use today.

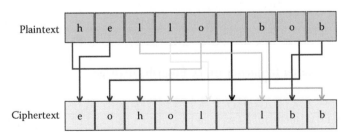

FIGURE B.15   Permutation cipher.

B.5 MODERN SYMMETRIC KEY CIPHERS

In 1976, the Data Encryption Standard (DES), a symmetric key encryption algorithm, was adopted as the federal standard. DES uses a 56-bit (7-character) key and uses a block size of 64 bits (8 characters). DES is ideally suited for the encryption of computer data since it works with individual bits of information and not just letters of the alphabet. At one time, DES was considered to be uncrackable, but as computers have become faster, this is no longer the case. DES was in widespread use until around 2002, when the Advanced Encryption Standard (AES) was adopted. AES uses larger key sizes (128, 192, or 256 bits) with a block size of 128 bits. AES is considered at this time to be practically immune to cryptanalysis and is presently used in most computer and network systems requiring encryption.

One of the main security issues with symmetric ciphers is the strength of the key used to encrypt the messages against cryptanalysis. In many respects, the strength of a cryptographic key is very similar to the strength of a password against a brute-force attack, as discussed in Chapter 3, Passwords. Differently from passwords, which are based on alphabetical characters, cryptographic keys operate on bits, namely, 1s and 0s (8 bits = 1 byte = 1 character). While the probability of guessing a single character in a password is 1/93 (93 possible characters from which to choose), the probability of guessing a single bit in a cryptographic key is only 1/2 (either a 1 or a 0). While this might lead one to believe that passwords are composed of characters more resilient to guessing than cryptographic keys, this is not the case. Consider an eight-character password. The probability of randomly guessing the password is $(1/93)^8 = 1/5.6E15$. Now, consider an eight-character cryptographic key. The probability of randomly guessing the key would be $(1/2)^{64} = 1/1.8E19$. Although the probability of guessing a single bit is much higher than that of a character, the significantly longer key length makes a cryptographic key much harder to guess. Each additional bit added to a cryptographic key actually doubles the number of keys an attacker must guess. As a result, the difference between a 128-bit key and a 256-bit key is not twice as much work for the attacker but actually 2^{128} more work for the attacker. Needless to say, the longer the key length, the more resilient is the implementation of DES or AES against cryptanalysis or brute-force guessing of the encryption/decryption key.

B.6 PUBLIC KEY CRYPTOGRAPHY

In the case of symmetric key encryption, Alice and Bob had to establish a secret shared key before they were able to encrypt and decrypt communications, seeming to require that Alice and Bob must meet in person. What if Alice and Bob are on opposite sides of the globe, without a shared key, and need to exchange confidential data? Even though cryptography had been used, practiced, and studied for thousands of years, this problem eluded cryptographers until 1976, when Whitfield Diffie and Martin Hellman introduced the Diffie-Hellman key exchange. Asymmetric key encryption, often called public key encryption, uses two mathematically related keys (one public key and one private key) instead of a single shared key. As shown in Figure B.16, Alice's key is split into two parts: a public key (A_{public}) and a private key ($A_{private}$). In fact, everyone who uses public key cryptography has a matched public and private key. As the name suggests, the public key is known to everyone and is often used for the task of encrypting a message. The matching private key, on the other hand, is only known by its owner, in this case Alice. The private key is used to decrypt a message encrypted by Alice's public key. The principle and beauty behind this cryptographic algorithm is that anyone can encrypt and send a message to Alice using her public key. However, if Alice's key is kept private, Alice is the only person that is able to decrypt the message.

Figure B.17 demonstrates the functionality of asymmetric cryptography. In this example, Bob wants to confess his love to Alice with a love letter but is intent on keeping his message a secret from his jealous ex-girlfriend Eavesdropper Eve. To encrypt the message, Bob obtains Alice's public key, available on Alice's public website for everyone to use. Bob encrypts the message "Alice I love you" with Alice's public key and sends the message to Alice halfway across the globe. Even if Eve intercepts the message, without Alice's private key she will be unable to decrypt the message. When Alice receives the message from Bob, Alice simply decrypts

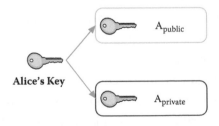

FIGURE B.16   Public and private key pair.

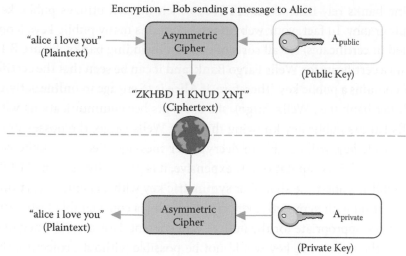

FIGURE B.17   Public key cryptography.

the message using her own private key. Likewise, Alice can send a return reply to Bob by encrypting a message with Bob's public key, posted on this Facebook profile. Again, because the message was encrypted with Bob's public key, only Bob is able to decrypt the message with his private key.

Public key cryptography has fundamentally changed the way people communicate. Bob, Alice, or anyone for that matter is able to create a personal matched public and private key pair. In the example provided, Alice and Bob are not required to establish a preshared secret before engaging in secret conversations. Alice can further rest assured that it is virtually impossible for anyone to decrypt messages intended for her without her private key. Much like a symmetric key, public key cryptography algorithms rely heavily on the secrecy of the private key.

B.7 PRACTICAL APPLICATIONS

The most common use of public key cryptography that you are likely to come across in your everyday use of computers is in HTTPS. Although the provided example of public key cryptography uses people as examples, banks, online retailers, and other entities also use public key cryptography to encrypt information between themselves and their customers. Consider online banking: Do you remember establishing a shared secret key (i.e., symmetric key cryptography) with your bank before engaging in online banking actions? The answer to this question should be "no" because online banks rely instead on HTTPS, which in turn utilizes public key cryptography. In fact, your web browser contains many public keys (contained in certificates) for all sorts of entities, including banks. Figure B.18 shows a certificate for Wells Fargo Bank, and it can be seen that the certificate contains a public key. Therefore, if Alice is to engage in online activity with her bank (i.e., Wells Fargo), she encrypts her communications with Wells Fargo's public key knowing that only Wells Fargo, the possessor of the private key, will be able to decrypt her message. Because public key cryptography is computationally expensive, it is primarily used in HTTPS to establish a one-time shared or symmetric key with a client. Encrypting information with symmetric key cryptography is considerably faster and thus more appropriate for the bulk of web content. However, the negotiation of the symmetric key would not be possible without protecting the

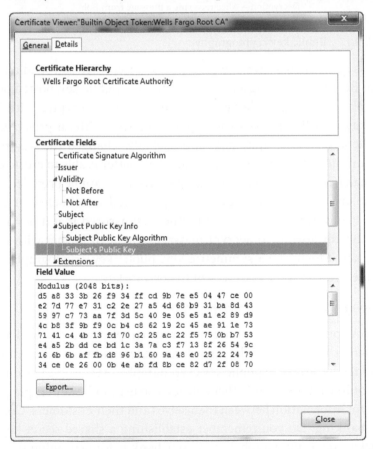

FIGURE B.18   Wells Fargo certificate.

initial communications with public key cryptography. Several different algorithms, including Diffie-Hellman and RSA (Ron **R**ivest, Adi **S**hamir, Leonard **A**dleman), are commonly used for asymmetric encryption, but it is beyond the scope of this book to discuss these algorithms in more detail.

Another area in which cryptography is often encountered is in wireless networking. As discussed in Chapter 9, a wireless network can be insecure since anyone within its range can surreptitiously monitor the communication. The three different encryption algorithms used to protect users of wireless networks are called Wired Equivalent Privacy (WEP), Wi-Fi Protected Access (WPA), and Wi-Fi Protected Access 2 (WPA2). Each of these algorithms is dependent on a preshared key, usually in the form of a password. Thus, the effectiveness of cryptography in this context is dependent on both the strength and the secrecy of the preshared key. Because of these two factors, WPA2 is considered to be the most resilient to cryptanalysis, followed by WPA and then WEP.

B.8 CRYPTO CHALLENGE SOLUTION

The answer (i.e., plaintext) for the crypto challenge is a quotation from the physicist Stephen Hawking:

> I think computer viruses should count as life. I think it says something about human nature that the only form of life we have created so far is purely destructive. We have created life in our own image.

BIBLIOGRAPHY

Bauer, F.L. 2007. *Decrypted Secrets: Methods and Maxims of Cryptology*. New York: Springer.

Bruen, A.A., and Forcinito, M.A. 2011. *Cryptography, Information Theory, and Error-Correction: A Handbook for the 21st Century*. New York: Wiley.

Calabrese, T. 2004. *Information Security Intelligence: Cryptographic Principles and Applications*. Independence, KY: Cengage Learning.

Copeland, B.J. 2006. *Colossus: The Secrets of Bletchley Park's Codebreaking Computers*. New York: Oxford University Press.

Hinsley, F.H. 2001. *Codebreakers: The Inside Story of Bletchley Park*. New York: Oxford University Press.

Hoffstein, J., Pipher, J.C., and Silverman, J.H. 2008. *An Introduction to Mathematical Cryptography*. New York: Springer.

Kahn, D. 1996. *The Codebreakers: The Story of Secret Writing*. New York: Simon and Schuster.

Katz, N. 2005. *Everything Cryptograms Book: Fun and Imaginative Puzzles for the Avid Decoder.* Avon, MA: Adams Media.

Oriyano, S.P., and Gregg, M. 2010. *Hacker Techniques, Tools, and Incident Handling.* Sudbury, MA: Jones & Bartlett.

Pincock, S. 2006. *Codebreaker: The History of Codes and Ciphers, from the Ancient Pharaohs to Quantum Cryptography.* New York: Bloomsbury.

Puzzle Baron's Cryptograms. 2012. Frequency of letters. http://www.cryptograms. org/letter-frequencies.php (accessed May 9, 2012).

Schneier, B. 1996. *Applied Cryptography: Protocols, Algorithms, and Source Code in C.* New York: Wiley.

Schneier, B. 2011. *Secrets and Lies: Digital Security in a Networked World.* New York: Wiley.

Sebag-Montefiore, H. 2011. *Enigma.* London: Orion.

Stamp, M., and Low, R.M. 2007. *Applied Cryptanalysis: Breaking Ciphers in the Real World.* New York: Wiley.

Van Tilborg, H.C.A., and Jajodia, S. 2011. *Encyclopedia of Cryptography and Security.* New York: Springer.

Whitman, M.E., and Mattord, H.J. 2011. *Principles of Information Security.* Independence, KY: Cengage Learning.

Appendix C: Web Surfing Security Technologies

C.1 INTRODUCTION

The objective of this appendix is to introduce and discuss a handful of web and Internet security technologies that can be used to further mitigate the threats discussed in this book. Given the correct context, each of these technologies can, in its own way, increase one's defense in depth when surfing the web and using the Internet. Although this is not nearly a complete list of all additional security technologies above and beyond those discussed in Chapter 6, they do represent some of the most effective and widely used security technologies that one could utilize as part of an everyday computing routine.

C.2 PRIVATE BROWSING

To enhance a user's experience while surfing the web, and often in coordination with many websites, web browsers track user behavior by storing a plethora of information about one's web surfing actions (Chapter 7). This may include pages one has visited, what was clicked on those pages, how often a particular webpage or website has been visited, what was typed (i.e., form history), cached photos, and items purchased, to name a few examples. While this may be convenient in some cases, the storing of such information can be at odds with one's personal privacy and security. In response, and to defeat a web browser's capability for storing every move one makes on the web, many web browsers (i.e., Firefox, IE (Internet Explorer), Safari, Chrome) are now equipped with a separate viewing mode known as "private browsing." When Firefox is put into private browsing mode (Figure C.1), the web browser will not remember any "browser history, search history, download history, web form history, cookies, or temporary Internet files."

FIGURE C.1   Enabling private browsing mode.

Private browsing is advantageous to use on a computer if a user desires that subsequent users not be able to discover his or her actions, such as on a shared computer at home or in a public place. For example, when using a shared computer at home, one might not want a browser to remember search history for the topic "engagement ring" or plans for a surprise birthday party. Private browsing is also useful if one wishes to browse the web without allowing websites to track his or her session history using cookies—temporary files websites use to store user information on one's computer (Chapter 7).

Beware that, while private browsing will enable one to surf the web anonymously with respect to a user or website that may have future access to the same computer, this does not mean that one's actions on the web are anonymous from the network administrator's viewpoint. If you are in a work environment, putting your web browser into private browsing mode will not prevent those monitoring the corporate network from learning which websites you have visited and the content uploaded and downloaded from such sites. What private browsing will do is prevent the next person or website accessing your computer from learning those actions.

C.3 NOSCRIPT

As has been discussed in many parts throughout the book, drive-by downloads present a serious threat to web browsers and the integrity of a computer. The simple act of requesting a webpage can result in the downloading and execution of malicious code embedded within the requested webpage, resulting in a malware infection. Recalling the discussion on malware from Chapter 5, remember that malicious code is not a danger until it has been executed—malicious web code falls under the same rules. When a webpage is requested, the default behavior of a web browser is to execute all code retrieved to properly render the webpage's contents for the user. Often, this includes the execution of scripts, videos, and other code elements that can possess malicious lines of code inserted by an attacker. To block the execution of all scripts, both malicious and legitimate, there exist web browser add-ons that enable a user to determine which websites can be trusted and which cannot. Two popular and free examples are NoScript (*https://addons.mozilla.org/en-US/firefox/addon/noscript/*) for the Firefox web browser and NotScripts (https://chrome.google.com/webstore/category/home) for the Chrome web browser.

As shown in Figure C.2, on requesting the webpage at the URL www.iastate.edu/, the NoScript add-on prevents five scripts from being automatically executed by the web browser. In this case, the user is able to view most of the website, but some of the website functionality has been potentially restricted by the blocking of these scripts. In a different context, such as a request for a malicious website, the five blocked scripts would represent the prevention of a potential drive-by download or other malicious actions. Thus, the malicious code has been downloaded to the computer but was not permitted to execute.

The downside to NoScript and other similar security add-ons is that they require the user to play an involved role in determining which websites are to be trusted and thus able to execute code automatically and which websites are not to be trusted. By default, NoScript automatically assumes that a website is potentially malicious and forces the user to grant

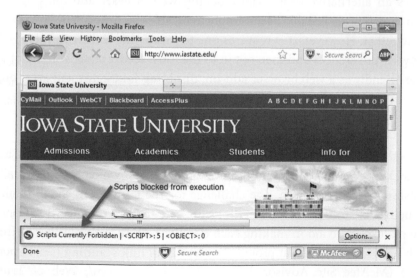

FIGURE C.2   NoScript add-on example.

FIGURE C.3   NoScript permission options.

the browser access to execute scripts for a particular website. This means that a user must opt out of the most secure state, a sound security practice (Chapter 10). To do this, as shown in Figure C.3, NoScript provides a number of user options in granting such privileges (either temporarily or permanently) to a webpage or domain name. For instance, if the user clicked on "Allow all this page" the particular website would be permitted to execute all scripts, and the user would not have to grant permission to the same website in the future. Although the process of declaring trust for a website may initially seem a bit involved, the overall security benefit of not automatically executing potentially malicious code as the result of an errant click of a mouse can outweigh the initial inconveniences.

As an alternative to a script-blocking web browser add-on, popular web browsers also enable users simply to disable the running of JavaScript all together. However, this requires one to locate this feature in their web browser preferences and then opt in to the most secure state. While not as user friendly as a web browser add-on, disabling JavaScript will go a long way in preventing drive-by downloads.

C.4 LINK SCANNING

Hyperlinks create an omnipresent threat due to the fact that the simple act of clicking on a hyperlink can result in a drive-by download of malware, a phishing website, or both. The challenge for the user lies in the difficulty in being able to tell which hyperlinks are safe to click on and which ones are malicious. To aid in making such decisions, there are a number of free web browser add-ons that provide the service of link scanning (i.e., hyperlink) (McAfee Site Advisor, http://www.siteadvisor.com/; Web of Trust [WOT], http://www.mywot.com/; AVG Secure Search link scanner, http://

linkscanner.avg.com/). Generally, the objective of link scanners is to continuously visit, scan, or track URLs (Uniform Resource Locator) and website domains comprising the web for malicious content, pop-ups, phishing tactics, bad linking practices, poor reputations, and so on. The results are compiled and then queried by a link-scanning add-on each time a web browser displays a hyperlink. As a result, when a hyperlink appears in a web browser, as in the case of returned search engine results, a visual indicator is placed next to the hyperlink to indicate the security rating of the link and the domain name to which it belongs. Typically, hyperlinks with a green mark next to the name are safe (or low risk), yellow or orange indicates a minor risk, and red represents a URL or web domain that is a significant risk. It should be noted that each of the presented link scanners works a little bit differently, and that each has its own rating system and visual indicators. A generic description of the function of link scanners was provided for the sake of brevity. To find out more information about how each of these link scanners specifically work, please visit the provided URLs.

Figure C.4 shows Google search results obtained without the assistance of a link scanner. From this display, it is difficult to tell which websites

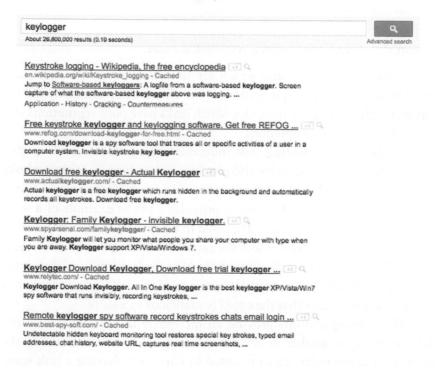

FIGURE C.4   Search results without a link scanner.

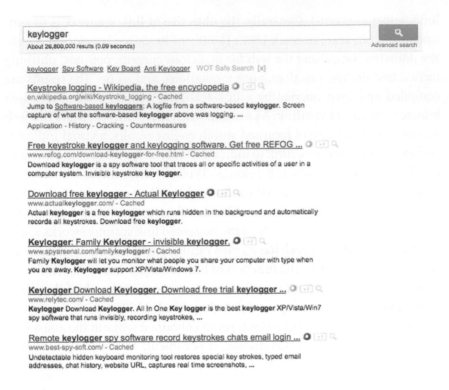

FIGURE C.5   Search results with a WOT link scanner.

are potentially malicious and which are not. With the WOT link scanner enabled in Figure C.5, it becomes quite clear, as designated by the red circle adjacent to some of the links, which links have poor reputations and which have excellent reputations.

In addition to providing risk indicators adjacent to search engine results, the WOT link scanner also provides risk indicators for hyperlinks that appear in web-based applications like Facebook, Twitter, and various web-based email clients. Figure C.6 provides a prime example of a well-constructed phishing email, as discussed in Chapter 11. Without the assistance of a link scanner or without the capability to confidently dissect and read a URL, it becomes difficult to determine the legitimacy of the email. However, in Figure C.7, with the assistance of the WOT link scanner, it becomes quite evident that the email is malicious in nature.

Link scanning add-ons provide an incredibly useful and free utility for preventing a number of attacks. Although not included among the defense-in-depth techniques presented in Chapter 6, having a link scanner installed in one's web browser should really be a requirement since

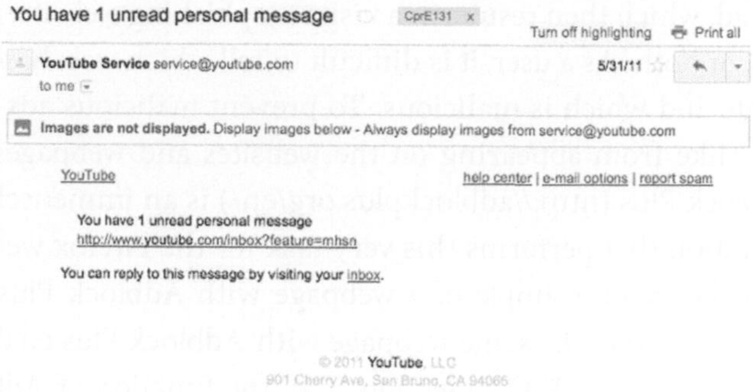

FIGURE C.6   Phishing email without WOT enabled.

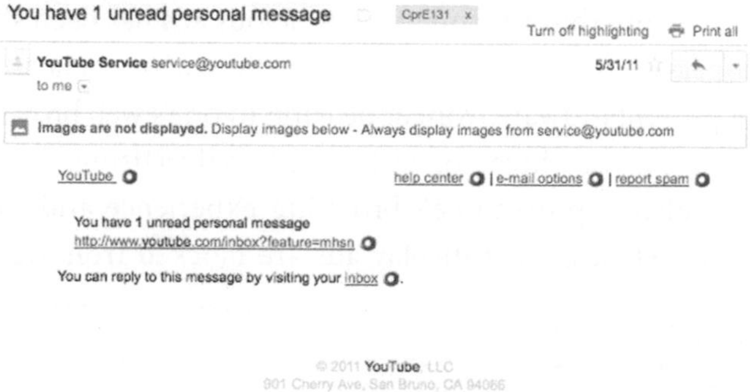

FIGURE C.7   Phishing email with WOT enabled.

it provides an immensely valuable defense-in-depth layer. Like antivirus software, link scanners are not 100% accurate and are challenged by new threats. The results presented from link scanners should be used as a quick visual indicator but should not be trusted blindly, and a user should not forsake other methods for discovering malicious hyperlinks or phishing emails as presented in Chapter 11.

C.5 ADBLOCK PLUS

Not all advertisements that appear on a webpage are honest in their intentions. As discussed in Chapter 5, malware distributers and scammers alike have found it profitable to purchase ads to be displayed on legitimate websites. Banking on the implicit trust that a user may feel when on a respected website, malvertising seeks to trick unsuspecting users into clicking on a malicious ad, which then results in a visit to a phishing website, a drive-by download, or both. As a user, it is difficult to tell which web-based adware is legitimate and which is malicious. To prevent malicious ads and legitimate ads alike from appearing on the websites and webpages that one visits, Adblock Plus (http://adblockplus.org/en/) is an immensely popular and free add-on that performs this very task for the Firefox web browser. Figure C.8 shows an example of a webpage with Adblock Plus disabled, and Figure C.9 shows the same webpage with Adblock Plus enabled.

When coupled with WOT (Section C.4), the function of Adblock Plus can further be seen when it is used to examine the results returned from a search engine. In Figure C.10, the search for "key-logger" returns a number of ads that WOT deems risky and one ad that is considered extremely risky. With Adblock Plus enabled (Figure C.11), the malicious ads are prevented from appearing, and thus the threat of malicious ads has been stymied.

From the perspective of the user, Adblock Plus is a beneficial web browser add-on that prevents adware from appearing in one's web browser—effectively eliminating the threat of web-based malvertising. Furthermore, Adblock Plus also improves one's browsing experience and web surfing speed because webpages that display ads are blocked from downloading

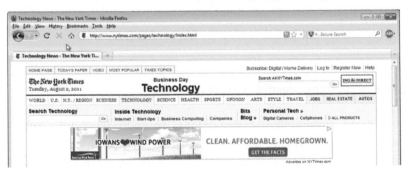

FIGURE C.8 Webpage without Adblock Plus.

FIGURE C.9 Webpage with Adblock Plus enabled.

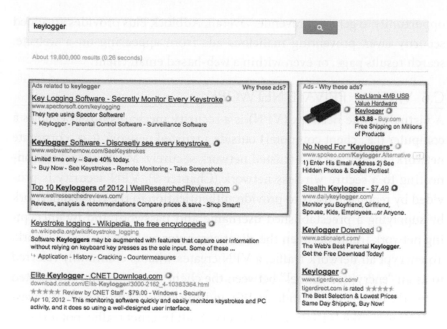

FIGURE C.10 Adblock Plus disabled and WOT search results.

FIGURE C.11 Search results with Adblock Plus enabled and WOT link scanner.

content needed to display the ads. The only downside to Adblock Plus is that while blocking malicious ads—a minority of all ads displayed—it also blocks all legitimate ads. Many websites rely on the funding they receive from online advertisers to pay for their operating costs, and Adblock Plus prevents such websites from displaying ads and thus eliminates their opportunity to generate revenue. Overall, Adblock Plus provides an added security layer, preventing malicious ads from appearing on a website, search results page, or even within a web-based email client.

C.6 VIRTUAL PRIVATE NETWORK

A virtual private network (VPN) is a security mechanism that enables a computer (i.e., client computer) outside a trusted network (e.g., corporate network) to connect to a trusted network securely. Much like when connecting to a secure wireless network (Chapter 9), VPN security is provided by requiring users to provide authentication to the trusted network by supplying a preestablished username and password and by encrypting network traffic between the client computer and the trusted network. To encrypt all network traffic, a VPN creates what is commonly referred to as an "encrypted tunnel" between the client computer and the trusted network, preserving confidentiality and mitigating any threat of eavesdropping. Unlike HTTPS, a VPN encrypts all Internet traffic, not just web traffic. A VPN is most similar to that of wireless security; however, instead of encrypting wireless Internet traffic between a client computer and a wireless router, a VPN encrypts Internet traffic between a client computer and a trusted network (i.e., encrypted tunnel) regardless of the underlying network infrastructure.

Often used in the corporate world, a VPN allows employees working from home or on the road to securely connect their computers to a corporate network just as if their computer actually resided in their regular office. The virtual network this creates enables the client computer to benefit from corporate network security mechanisms (i.e., firewalls and intrusion detection systems) as well as access to network services (i.e., file servers) available only to those connected to the corporate network. Figure C.12 provides a diagram showing the level of encryption provided by a VPN and demonstrates the function of a VPN through an explanation of how a web request from a client computer connected to a VPN would be routed through the VPN to the Internet and back to the client computer. It should be noted that there are many different kinds of VPNs providing many different types of security services. The following illustration and explanation of a VPN is used to give you a general idea of the concept of a VPN and how a VPN can be used as a defense-in-depth layer:

1. By means of a desktop application, Alice connects her computer to a trusted network through a VPN, thus creating an encrypted tunnel of network traffic between Alice's computer and the trusted network.

2. When Alice makes a request to view CNN's homepage, the request is routed through the Internet via the encrypted tunnel to the trusted network.

3. From the trusted network, the request for CNN's homepage is then routed to the Internet as if it originated from the trusted network and eventually is routed to CNN's server.

4. The response generated by CNN's web server is then routed back to the trusted network.

5. The trusted network then routes the response back through the encrypted tunnel to Alice's computer.

This example illustrates how a request for a website located outside the trusted network (i.e., on the Internet) is handled by Alice's computer connected to a VPN. Alice's computer does not directly communicate with CNN's web server but instead uses the corporate network as an intermediary hop to do so. If Alice's computer requests a service located in the trusted network, the request would then be transported through the

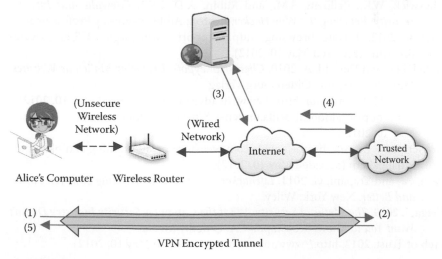

FIGURE C.12   VPN diagram.

encrypted VPN tunnel to the service in the corporate network, and the response would be routed back to Alice's computer via the VPN tunnel.

In addition to allowing secure remote network access, VPNs can be used in another context to provide secure communications. In the case of accessing an unsecure wireless network, as discussed in Chapter 9, a VPN provides a secure means to encrypt all network traffic to and from the client computer. Even if an attacker were sniffing wireless Internet traffic, the security provided by a VPN mitigates the threat of eavesdropping. As a result, VPNs provide a sound security solution for performing sensitive online activities when connected to an unsecure wireless network in a coffee shop or hotel lounge. It should be noted that a VPN does not prevent against spyware such as key-logging malware that may reside on the client computer.

Many corporations offer free VPN access for their employees, and some even require that remote users connect to a VPN to conduct business. If you do not have access to a VPN and would like to use such a security mechanism, there are a number of service providers that offer personal VPN access for around $10 a month. If you are in frequent need of secure Internet access on unsecure wireless networks, having access to a VPN is a must-have security mechanism since it prevents against all types of eavesdropping threats discussed in Chapter 9, including session hijacking.

BIBLIOGRAPHY

Adblock Plus. 2012. http://adblockplus.org/en/ (accessed May 10, 2012).

AVG. 2012. LinkScanner. http://linkscanner.avg.com (accessed May 10, 2012).

Cheswick, W.R., Bellovin, S.M., and Rubin, A.D. 2003. *Firewalls and Internet Security: Repelling the Wily Hacker.* Boston: Addison-Wesley Professional.

Firefox. 2012. Private browsing. http://support.mozilla.org/en-US/kb/Private-Browsing (accessed May 10, 2012).

Gobel, J.G., and Dewald, A. 2010. *Client-Honeypots: Exploring Malicious Websites.* Munich, Germany: Oldenbourg Verlag.

McAfee. 2012. SiteAdvisor. http://www.siteadvisor.com (accessed May 10, 2012).

NoScript. https://addons.mozilla.org/en-US/firefox/addon/noscript/ (accessed May 10, 2012).

NotScripts. https://chrome.google.com/webstore/detail/odjhifogjcknibkahlpidmdajjpkkcfn (accessed May 10, 2012).

Pash, A., and Trapani, G. 2011. *Lifehacker: The Guide to Working Smarter, Faster, and Better.* New York: Wiley.

Viega, J. 2009. *The Myths of Security: What the Computer Security Industry Doesn't Want You to Know.* Sebastopol, CA: O'Reilly Media.

Web of Trust. 2012. http://www.mywot.com/ (accessed May 10, 2012).

Printed and bound by CPI Group (UK) Ltd, Croydon, CR0 4YY

22/10/2024

01777642-0008